Pioneer Tales

Clark Ruppe Legacy Book 2

Also by R.S. Kellogg

Non-Fiction
Colonial Tales (Clark Ruppe Legacy Book 1)
Pioneer Tales (Clark Ruppe Legacy Book 2)
Georgetown and Vernal (Clark Ruppe Legacy Book 3)

Books Coauthored
The Autobiography of Brenda Clark Sederberg
As It Happened: The Autobiography of Warren C. Sederberg

Books Edited
Line Upon Line: The Autobiography of Alan C Clark
Remembering: The Autobiography of Janet Ruppe Clark
My Wonderful Life: The Biography of Shirley Sederberg by Maria Sederberg

Fiction
Norrit and Hale Series (The Patron Saints of Grandparents)
Breadcove Bay Series
Everyday Goddess Stories
Mermaid Magic Tales
Agratica Stories
And other works . . .

Clark Ruppe Legacy Book 2

Pioneer Tales

Of the Alan and Janet Clark Family

by R.S. Kellogg

RKI

Copyright Information

Pioneer Tales
Clark Ruppe Legacy, Book 2
Copyright © 2022 by R.S. Kellogg
Published by Rebecca Kellogg International
Cover and Layout copyright © 2022 by Rebecca Kellogg International
Cover designs by R.S. Kellogg/Rebecca Kellogg International
Cover art "Mormon Tabernacle – Photo," copyright © weris7554/Depositphotos

This book is licensed for your personal enjoyment only. All rights reserved. This book, or parts thereof, may not be reproduced in any form without permission.

ISBN (Hardback): 978-1-956123-84-5
ISBN (Ebook): 978-1-956123-85-2

—To Alan, Janet, and Brenda's friends and family

The heart of this book has been inspired by the following quote from Charles Redd, a leading Utah citizen of his day and a grandson of Janet's ancestors John and Caroline Butler:

"I would like somehow to get into the hearts and souls of young people the lessons of history, particularly those of Western America. The American pioneer has much to teach us, with . . . his spirit of adventurousness and his willingness to accept challenge. . . . Perhaps more important to youth today is how acceptance of challenge and risk taking strengthens character and contributes to individual growth. . . . Learning of the successful settlement of this country, we may gain courage to face squarely the challenges and problems of present-day frontiers."

—Charles Redd (BYU)

Acknowledgements

This book is made better by the support of many individuals. In particular, I would like to thank the following:

First and foremost, Thomas Sederberg. Thank you for being so supportive and encouraging of this work and for instilling in me a great love for family history.

LeAnne Bunn, resident historian of the Alan and Janet Clark family, was extraordinarily helpful and generous with both providing source material and helping to verify or debunk particular stories and family history claims. It's helpful to have an analytical skeptic to look over facts and available information.

Figure 1: The author with Aunt Gladys Clark Farmer Fetzer and the Alice Randall Clark tribute book. Photo by Tom Sederberg.

A. Charles Clark, author of an excellent book on Timothy Baldwin Clark, is a solid family historian who helped with locating source material, served as a great source of information for research questions, and gave the manuscript a cursory read to fact check the lines on which he has expertise (namely Ezra Clark and ancestors).

Ray (Rachel) Farmer provided encouragement and lent knowledge of available family history resources to the project.

Gladys Clark provided information and the loan of a key book on the life of Alice Randall Clark, which helped bring that branch of the family into focus.

My cousins Sandra and Deborah both provided support and encouragement as I dove deep into the stories. Thank you both for sharing my enthusiasm for better understanding these ancestors.

Maxwell Kellogg served as an initial sounding board in helping to winnow down the stories and choose which ones made it into the final volume.

Matthew and Camilla Sederberg were the first readers, and caught some typos and areas that needed further explanation.

Mike Kellogg provided help on the home front on several occasions when I was working on this book.

I would like to thank the following writers and keepers of family history whose works have contributed key elements to this volume. Some of these individuals have passed on, but their work served to make this book much better by the stories, context, and information they made available to draw on in making sense of our big family tree.

Great thanks to Debra Call, Mary Stevenson Clark, Edward Stevenson, Annie Clark Tanner, Obert C. Tanner, Laura Blanche Clark Cook Silver, Bryant Randall Clark, Walter Edward Clark, A. Charles Clark, Antone Clark, Clark and Ruth Knowlton, Alfred Randall, Emily Randall Richards, Lucy

Randall Kofoed, Annie Christensen Miller, Phillis Christensen, Celeste Bunn, William G. Hartley, Charles Redd, Reva Simmons Ruppe, Janet Ruppe Clark, Brenda Clark Sederberg, Gary Lamar Olsen, Benjamin Franklin Simmons, Jr., Elizabeth F. Huff, Margaret Tueller, and Zina Goulding Johnson for their writing and their efforts in preserving family histories and making these available for future generations.

Deep appreciation to these and all other individuals whose works are quoted herein or who served as resources and guides along the way.

May these stories continue forward to bless future generations.

In the event that errors of fact are found in this book, please contact the author with appropriate sources, so that corrections may be made in subsequent editions. Please note that in some cases, where facts are disputed among different sources, interpretations have been made based on the author's best understanding after comparing the competing information available, often navigated with the consulting advice of knowledgeable family historians.

December 2022
R.S. Kellogg

Foreword

This book is the work of extensive research, and it has evolved in stages.

It started when my dad suggested I write a book about my mother's history. I found that instead, my interest was drawn to the many family history questions I had about my mother's ancestors' history.

The Clark/Ruppe genealogy is well documented, with names, dates, and locations filled out on my genealogy chart seven generations back on all my family lines.

My father's ancestry is unfortunately largely devoid of known stories—once we get back past the Scandinavian immigrant generations of the second half of the 1800s in my father's family, few stories are known.

My mother's lineage, by contrast, is filled with stories and episodes, participation in major events in the American West, and larger-than-life personalities I had captured glimpses of and snippets about in the abundance of extended family reunions and historical site tours I experienced with my parents throughout my growing up years.

I probably had the luxury of enjoying more of this than my siblings, at least during our early years—for starters, I was the eldest, so I got a head start and got to meet many great-grandparents while they were still active and participating in family events and hosting visitors, and I also benefited from being a story lover from a young age, with curiosity and great patience for sitting with people who were much older than me and asking them to tell me about their lives and favorite memories.

It felt fascinating to listen to my parents' parents' parents telling stories of growing up and of the grandparents they themselves had known. Almost it felt as if in listening I touched strings that extended back through time—a web of spoken and silent stories that had given rise to shaping my larger family group as it was today.

Even as a very young child I was conscious of the richness and vibrancy of this web of stories, the power they held, their presence around us, and the presence of the stories of the past—many of which I had not fully heard—which still, I sensed, influenced my family.

Additionally, as a young violinist growing up in Utah, I participated in countless concerts, musicals, and pageants centered around bringing to dramatic life on stage the history of the colonization of the area, which was of course primarily centered around pioneer stories.

Over time, many questions rose up for me about the pioneer history of the state in general and my family's storylines in particular.

I'd heard snippets of stories of the pioneer journeys of some of my ancestors, as well as the fact that at least one of them had seen Brigham Young's speech during which it was said he took on the appearance of Joseph Smith and subsequently was declared the true successor in leadership of the Church.

And this made me curious: given that my ancestors on my mother's side were largely Latter-day Saints throughout the majority of the seven generations prior to me, where else had they been located during significant events in the history of the American West?

Which of them had traveled the Mormon Trail, and how had the journey gone for them?

Had they known each other and lived near each other in Nauvoo or historic towns in the Western States?

It seemed to me as if bits of the genealogy chart were lit up with the warmth of stories, rooted in my understanding of historical events, but vast stretches of the rest of the genealogy felt empty—simply white paper stamped with names and dates—mysteries void of my knowing, yet still they felt like they held possibility. Given the stories and comments I heard from older family members, I sensed there was much more to find.

Over the years as I heard stories in passing, and read brief accounts and life synopses, my list of questions accumulated.

For example:

How on earth had Ezra T. Clark and his family managed to live the United Order for decades when it seemed every other experiment in this style of community living had failed in short order? Had they, in fact, pulled it off?

Who was Ebenezer Bryce, and was there more to him than getting a canyon named after him and a church "built like an upside-down ship" attributed to him?

I'd heard mention from my mother that John Lowe Butler and Ezra T. Clark had each had more than one wife during the polygamy era of the Utah Territory (and that John Lowe Butler had in fact had *eight* wives), but I wanted to know if there were other ancestral families that had followed this practice as well. And what had all their lives been like? How did they organize their family units? How might residue from this part of the family lineage have impacted my family lines?

Well.

Once I started to research the written records remaining, I found there was a wealth of information out there to be pulled together.

My mother, her mother, and her mother were all avid family historians, as were many others within the family web of connections. Many had done extensive groundwork and research in pulling together documents and histories to preserve the family legacy of stories.

In creating this work, I have endeavored to weave together an epic legacy of many generations, dating back to the point at which each of my mothers' family lines converted to the Church of Jesus Christ of Latter-day Saints. This means that the Ruppe line (which starts with Mike Ruppe's conversion in this book) does not hold as many generations as every other line in the book, many of which converted in the 1840s.

Putting together this book was in some ways akin to constructing a quilt, with material pulled from many sources to craft the narrative. Many autobiographies and biographies of ancestors and their family members are referenced and quoted from, as well as books such as William G. Hartley's excellent book on John Lowe Butler, which places the lives and adventures of John and his family within the broader historical context. The Internet made this research easier than what my mother and grandmothers would have faced in their own searches, in that I could easily review databases such as the Pioneer Overland Trail database to see when and with which company each of my ancestors are listed as coming across the trail—and can from there also access journals and narratives from pioneers who crossed in the same companies and thus learn of the many adventures that those individual groups encountered.

The Internet was also helpful in solving obscure mysteries. For example, ancestor David Park's biographical sketch mentioned he had for a time considered leaving the mainstream Latter-day Saint faith and pursuing spiritual life with a group in Walla Walla, Washington. A careful web search revealed that the group in question would have been a Latter-day Saint splinter group that centered around the mythos of the Walla Walla Jesus. Additionally, I found period images of the compound where David would have stayed with this group, as well as images of the leader of the group and his children.

I also found the Ezra T. Clark family files archive, which was a convenient gathering of family documents that allowed me to piece together a solid answer that yes, indeed, the Clark family did live the United Order (for several decades), as well as finding accounts that gave insights into the parameters of how they set it up, pulled it off, and built a small empire of land and businesses as a family.

And I was thrilled to the writings of the extended Randall family and Clark family were enough to help reconstruct and flesh out details the lives of Margaret Harley Randall and especially Alice Randall Clark—mother and daughter, both of whom lived as polygamous wives to husbands that lived in cities different from them. Each of these women functioned during their lifetimes essentially as successful single mothers who raised children while managing farms, church work, and other interests, and because of their family structures, each subsequently had an outsized impact on the developing character of their family lineage. I consider the finding of stories on these two women and putting together the contextualizing of their lives for this book to have been a particular gift.

It is the author's hope that this legacy project is enjoyable for many readers for generations to come.

May your own genealogy chart come alive for you.

A note on usage: As of the time of this writing, preferred usage for the Church of Jesus Christ of Latter-day Saints is to refer to the religion by its full name or as "the Church," "the Church of Jesus Christ," or "the restored Church of Jesus Christ." However, in earlier eras, "Mormons" and "Mormon" have been widespread and approved terms, and may occasionally appear in writings of the ancestors. Additionally, some historic spaces such as "The Mormon Trail" are officially named with the descriptive designator "Mormon." Mindful of the history of the ancestors and the usage of their time, sometimes the term "Mormon" is used in this book, always with respect.

Additionally, in today's most common approved usage, indigenous peoples of North America are usually called "Native Americans" or "Indigenous Peoples," or by their individual tribal names. The source documents for this book most commonly called these people "Indians," and didn't always distinguish tribal groups by name. In addition, in the course of my research, I learned that some indigenous Native American people prefer the term "Indian" to be used when referring to their people. I did not arrive at a single clear-cut answer as to how best to refer to indigenous people when they play a role in ancestral stories. So names and usage vary. Often the term "Indians" is used, as that is the term that was referred to in the ancestral accounts being quoted from and summarized here.

A note on audience: This book seeks to be respectful of the Latter-day Saint roots of my mother's family lineage while also providing context for readers of all backgrounds on the complex historical and religious factors that shaped the lives of those profiled on these pages.

Introduction: The Road to Rexburg

Figure 2: Alan, Brenda, Tom, and Janet in Rexburg.
Photo used with permission.

One of the Sederberg children's favorite places to go was Rexburg, Idaho, to visit Grandma and Grandpa Clark.

In winter, the roads could be very snowy driving up from Orem, Utah. The car might go slowly, with windshield wipers beating against the falling snow.

But in summer the drive could be very scenic, past the Utah State Capitol and the Great Salt Lake, past the state border with its "Welcome to Idaho!" sign, past potato fields, our favorite rest stop with hills you could run on, past a reservoir, and finally to the freeway exit at Idaho Falls, from which we'd drive the last stretch into Rexburg.

When we arrived at 532 Linden Avenue in Rexburg, sometimes right around supper time, Grandma and Grandpa Clark would be excited to see us. Grandma might greet us in her kitchen, which was always filled with the aroma of fresh-baked bread.

Grandpa would say "Well, hi!" Then he'd make a point of hugging each person. Sometimes his hugs were very tight. When he greeted each grandchild, we had his full attention. He'd want to know how each of us were doing, and he'd probably have something interesting to show the grandkids, such as how the raspberries were doing in his garden in the summer, or a craft such as a bench or a dollhouse he may be working on in his workshop, or something he'd improved in his house. He was an old teacher and had a good sense for what would interest kids.

After eating a dinner that sometimes included Grandma's fresh bread, and perhaps colorful mashed potatoes, green beans, or raspberries if they were in season, a good visit would begin. Grandma and Grandpa would have pre-assigned sleeping quarters among the many bedrooms of their house (and the floor of the storage room in the case of many guests!), so we each had a place to stay.

Early in the morning, Grandpa would go jogging, returning home before breakfast. (Matthew wondered if Grandpa's bald head was caused by the Rexburg winds.) If Grandpa gave you a hug after he got back from jogging, it would be a cold sweaty hug.

Some of us would get up to help set the table for breakfast, and we may even get to help cook. Breakfast may include Grandma's famous blueberry muffins, which we later found out were actually a recipe from our Aunt Michelle, and we might get to eat pears that Grandma invited a grandchild to retrieve from the narrow shelves in the storage room.

The kids would enjoy playing with toys from the well-stocked game and toy room under the stairs, and we might play with the children of some neighbors or visiting cousins.

We'd make ice cream using frozen raspberries from the garden, taking turns turning the hand-crank on the ice cream maker sitting on the cement floor of the storage room. We'd play on the swing set in the backyard, create plays in the basement, watch movies, and play board and card games.

We'd be excited to see relatives who lived near Rexburg—the Ritchies, and Curtis, and maybe Gordon during some years.

We might have outings to the sand dunes, take a swimming trip to Green River, or go camping.

Sometimes a lot of our extended family would gather at the house and dinner might be such a big party that people would overflow to the ping pong table downstairs as well as the picnic tables and a children's table.

It would be a lot of work to clean up all the dishes, and I didn't always love to help.

Grandpa may have sensed this, and he'd often invite me to come visit with him in his office for a bit during the clean-up time. He might share an amazing new word he'd found that could help his Scrabble game, or cheerfully let me read some of his latest writing, and sometimes even ask my opinion on it.

In part because my grandpa valued my thoughts on words so much, I gained a lot of confidence that I could help other people with their writing. When I went to college, I applied to be an editor and was hired to help edit faculty members at BYU, starting when I was a freshman.

Grandpa loved this, and invited me to be his editor for his life story. We spent four years working on it together and I enjoyed reading his essays about his life.

We have a wealth of stories in our heritage.

Stories that explain something of why we are the way we are.

Stories that explore where family traditions come from.

Stories that show us our ancestors' hopes and dreams, how they dealt with failures, and how they achieved their successes.

This is a book of stories of Alan and Janet Clark's ancestors.

This book does not have all the stories of these people. If you'd like to find out more about Alan and Janet Clark and their families and ancestors, you can read *Line Upon Line*, by Alan C Clark, and *Remembering*, by Janet Ruppe Clark.

You can read about Janet's parents and ancestors in *Side by Side*, by Reva Simmons Ruppe, Brenda Clark Sederberg, and Janet Ruppe Clark.

You can read about Alan's parents and ancestors in the autobiography of Walter, the biography of Violet and her ancestors by Brenda Clark Sederberg, and the diary of Lela Willett Clark, who raised Alan and was his stepmother. You can also read more stories in other family history books and on FamilySearch, a website that stores many stories of your ancestors.

The book you are reading now is just a place to begin.

Have you ever wondered why the Clarks are called Clarks? Or where your ancestors lived and what they did for work? Some of those stories are here, in this book.

Are you ready to begin?

Go to the first chapter, and let's explore, together.

Figure 3: Alan with some of his grandchildren: Mark, Maria, Rebecca, Matthew, and Timothy. Photo used with permission.

Table of Contents

Acknowledgements 4

Foreword 8

Introduction: The Road to Rexburg 15

Table of Contents 19

Table of Figures 29

1. Genealogy Charts for this Book / The Story Behind Last Names 35

    The Power of Record-Keeping 37

2. Legends from the Pioneer Times 39

3. Early Latter-day Saint Origins: Conversion Stories 41

    Timothy Baldwin Clark and Polly Keeler Clark 43

        Daughter Laura Introduces Timothy and Polly to a New Religion 44

    Ezra T. Clark 47

    Elizabeth Stevens Stevenson and Mary Stevenson Clark 48

    Alfred Randall 53

    Margaret Harley Randall 54

    Karen Marie Hansen 56

    Mads Christensen and Maren Johanne Jensen 58

    Jens Christensen Lamp and Trene Bendtsen 62

    Cecil P. "Mike" Ruppe 65

    Leven Simmons Sr. and Harriet Bradford 66

    Charity Lowe & John Lowe Butler I and Caroline Farozine Skeen 67

Royal Durfey and Lydia Abell	69
Ebenezer Bryce	70
David Park and Ann Brooks	71
John Goulding, Sr.	72
Daniel Goulding and Elizabeth Merrifield Pratten	73

4. The Gathered Saints 77

Kirtland, Lake County, Ohio (Headquarters of the Church, 1831–1837)	77
Alfred Randall and Emmerette Louise Davis in Kirtland	78
Independence, Jackson County, Missouri	78
Timothy Baldwin Clark and Polly Keeler in Independenc	79
John and Caroline Butler Family Moves to Missouri	79
The Clarks in Far West, Caldwell County, Missouri	80
The W.W. Phelps / Clark Connection	81
Kirtland Safety Society	82
A Daring Rescue by Laura Clark Phelps	82
Adam-ondi-Ahman (Diahman), Daviess County, Missouri	88
John Lowe Butler and the Gallatin Election Day Battle	89
The Mormon War of 1838	91
Timothy Baldwin Clark and a Secret Meeting at Far West	91
The Saints in Nauvoo	92
John Lowe Butler, Life Guard to the Prophet	92
Joseph Smith and the Butler Family Cloak	92
Timothy Baldwin Clark across the River from Nauvoo	93
Ezra T. Clark and Mary Stevenson Clark in Nauvoo	96
Elizabeth Stevens Stevenson and Family in Nauvoo	97
Alfred Randall, Emmerette Louisa Davis, and Margaret Harley in Nauvoo	97
The Simmons Family in Hancock County	98
John Lowe Butler and the Martyrdom of Joseph Smith	99
The Martyrdom of Joseph and Hyrum—Alfred Randall's Story	100
John Lowe Butler and the Aftermath of the Martyrdom	101
Mary Stevenson Clark Reflects on the Martyrdom of Joseph Smith	102
Ezra T. Clark and Mary Stevenson Clark after the Martyrdom	102
After the Martyrdom: Transfiguration of Brigham Young Witnessed by Ancestors	103
Harriet Bradford Simmons	103

    Ezra T. Clark's Account of the Transfiguration 103

5. Mormon Trail **107**

    Abandoning Nauvoo 108

        Leven Simmons and Harriet Bradford Simmons Face the Mob 108

        Ezra T. Clark and Mary Stevenson Clark Marriage and Sealing 110

        The Alfred Randall Family's False Start 110

        David Park and Ann Brooks Park Find Abandoned Nauvoo 111

        Timothy Baldwin Clark Stays Behind 111

    The Harsh Threats of the Trail 112

    Timeline and Stories from the Mormon Trail 114

        Other Ancestral Pioneer Families: 114

    Timeline of the Pioneer Trail (Offered in present tense.) 115

    Winter Quarters 115

    Mormon Trail 116

        Leven Simmons 1847? 116

        The Alfred Randall Family 1848 116

        Ezra T. Clark 1848 117

        Mary Stevenson Clark 1848 118

        Elizabeth Stevens Stevenson 1848 120

        The Willard Richards Company Encounters Indians 120

        Ebenezer Bryce 1850 121

        Leven Simmons and Harriet Bradford Simmons 1852 123

        John Lowe Butler and Kenion Taylor Butler Help Danish Immigrants 1852 124

        Caroline Farozine Skeen Butler 1852 125

        Royal and Lydia Durfey 1852 125

        Kenion Taylor Butler and the Willie and Martin Handcart Companies 126

        Mads and Maren Christensen 1857 128

        Karen Marie Hansen 1857 128

6. Polygamy Pathways **131**

    Timeline of Polygamy 134

7. Ezra T. Clark Family Stories **149**

    A Description of Ezra T. Clark 150

    The Clark Firm 151

    The Values of Ezra T. Clark 152

Second Wife Susan Leggett Clark 154

Third Wife Nancy Areta Porter Stevenson 157

Ezra's Children Who Practiced Polygamy 158

Biblical Stories as Roots 158

The Clark Family Alphanumeric Code 159

The Ezra T. Clark Home 160

Playing Host for Children and Grandchildren 162

Mary Elizabeth Clark Robinson—A Longtime Presence in the Clark Home 163

Losing Missionary Sons 163

    Ezra James Clark 164

    John Alexander Clark—Second Lost Missionary Son 165

Ezra T. Clark's Sons as Managers 166

Growing Up Clark 167

Clark Friendships with Church Leadership 168

Ezra's Arrest and Imprisonment for Practicing Polygamy 172

"Moroni Clark" 172

Ezra and Mary's Golden Wedding Anniversary 174

Ezra's End of Life 175

Biographies of Ezra T. Clark 176

8. Edward B. Clark Family Stories 179

An Unexpected Plural Marriage 179

A Childless Marriage with an Extraordinary Promise 180

Second Wife Alice 182

Alice on the Underground 185

Stories of Alice Randall Clark 187

Alice's Values 188

Alice's Yard and Home 188

Life on Alice's Farm 190

Raising Children on a Farm as a Lone Parent 191

The Local Church 191

Soda Springs 192

Alice at Bear Lake 192

Holidays at Alice's Home 193

Alice Maintained Her Relationship with Family of Origin 194

The Value of Education 194

　　Alice as a Helper in the Community 196

　　The Influenza Epidemic 197

　　Father Figures for Alice's Children 197

　　　　Wilford Woodruff Richards 198

　　　　Wilford Woodruff Clark 200

　　　　Charles C. Rich Clark 202

　　Alice and Polygamy: A Summation 203

　　Edward Barrett Clark 204

　　Leadership in the Community 204

　　Wealthy Also Served 206

　　Losses as a Father 206

　　Edward B. Clark as a Father Figure 207

　　Driving the Cattle 208

　　Driving a Car for the First Time 209

　　Edward as a Father to Alice's Children 210

　　The Realities of Pioneer Farm Life as Impacting Children's Education 210

　　Edward's Thoughts on Polygamy 211

　　Alice's Later Years 211

　　Edward after Alice 212

　　Books on Edward and Alice 213

9. Randall Family Stories **215**

　　Alfred: An Attractive and Well-Mannered Man 216

　　Margaret Harley Randall: An Active Woman 217

　　Margaret's Home in Centerville 218

　　　　Drying Fruit 220

　　　　Food at the Margaret Randall Farm 221

　　Pioneer Life 221

　　Serving her Community 221

　　Margaret in Old Age 221

　　Alfred Randall, Wheelwright and Carpenter 222

　　The Randall Family's Joseph F. Smith Story 223

　　Polygamy in the Alfred Randall Family 223

　　A Healing Prayer in the Endowment House 224

Mildred Elizabeth Johnson 224
Pony Express and the Telegraph 224
Alfred Helps Immigrants and Supplies Cross to the Valley 225
Mountain Meadow Massacre Jury Duty 226
Alfred and the Woolen Mill 226
Alfred's End of Life 228
The Autobiography of Alfred Randall 228

10. Mads Christensen Family Stories 231
Maren's Health and Faith 232
Mads' Connection to the Primary 233
The Mads Christensen Polygamy Story 234
    Mads' Autograph Book 235
    Mads' Families Band Together 235
    The Christensen Family is Pulled Apart 235
    Mads and Hannah in Idaho 236
Learning English in America 237
Mads' Death 237

11. Butler Family Stories 239
Multiple Parents to Run the Household 239
Charity's Conversion Story, and a Narrow Escape 240
Charity and Caroline and the Emmett Expedition 240
    Charity and Caroline and the Syrup Story 241
    Grandmother Squaw and Chief Henry 242
    The Butler Family Succeeds with the Emmett Expedition 243
Disagreement over "the Practice" 243
Sarah Lancaster, Frontierswoman and Sister-Wife 245
    Sarah and the Relief Society 245
    Sarah the Bridge Builder 246

12. Simmons Family Stories 247
The Springville Farm 248
An Invitation to Spanish Fork 248
Harriet's Unique Attributes 248
A Visit from Grandmother Elizabeth Scott, and Simmons Family Changes 249
Leven's Second Marriage to Lydia 250

  Lydia's Story.. 250

 The Simmons Family with Lydia 251

  Lydia's Dugout 252

 Leven's Passing 252

 Harriet after Leven's Passing.. 252

 Lydia after Leven's Passing... 253

13. Goulding Family Stories 255

 Fanny's Conversion Story... 255

 The Gouldings in Australia 256

 Family Changes 257

 Growing Up Goulding 257

 The Tithing Story 259

 How the Wives Split the Work 260

 Stories of Baby Clara 261

 Summers on the East Fork Ranch 262

 How the Gouldings Made Shoes and Clothes 263

 The Story of the Gouldings' Candy Pull Parties 265

 The Story of Elijah's Exodus 265

 Giving Service to the End 267

14. Johnston's Army 269

 Conflict Forestalled 271

 Aftermath of the Army 272

15. Western Settlement and Homesteading Stories 275

 An Ancestral Connection Point: Archibald Gardner... 275

 Early Settler Days in Utah 276

 Joseph and Emma Christensen... 277

 Ancestors throughout the West.. 281

 The Goulding Family is Helped by Indians on the Way from California 281

 Karen Marie Hansen Christensen and the St. George Temple 281

 David Park and Walla Walla Jesus 283

 Kenion Taylor Butler and Olive Artemeshy Durfey Butler: Foster Parents and Early Settlers of Spanish Fork 285

 The Bryce Family 288

  Ebenezer Bryce and Mary Ann Park 288

    Ebenezer Bryce and the Upside-Down Ship Church 288

    Ebenezer Bryce and the Canyon 288

    Ebenezer Bryce and Bryce, Arizona 290

    William Henry Bryce, Rosanna Goulding, and Malinda "Aunt Lindy" Riggs 291

16. Organization of the Primary 293

17. Missions 299

    Six Generations Back from Janet 300

        John Goulding, Sr. 300

    Five Generations Back from Janet 300

        John Lowe Butler 300

        Caroline Farozine Skeen Butler 301

        Charity Skeen Butler 301

        Royal Durfey & Lydia Abell Durfey 301

    Four Generations Back from Alan 301

        Timothy Baldwin Clark 301

        Elizabeth Stevens Stevenson 301

    Four Generations Back from Janet 302

        Leven Simmons 302

        Kenion Taylor Butler 302

        Ebenezer Bryce 302

        Mary Ann Park Bryce 304

        Daniel Goulding 304

    Three Generations Back from Alan 304

        Ezra T. Clark 304

        Alfred Randall 305

        Mildred Elizabeth Johnson Randall 305

        Mads Christensen 309

        Jens Christensen Lamp 309

    Two Generations Back from Alan 309

        Edward Barrett Clark 309

        Joseph Mads Christensen 310

    Two Generations Back from Janet 310

        James Alma Simmons 310

    One Generation Back from Alan 312

- Walter Edward Clark 312
- Lela Willett Clark 312
- One Generation Back from Janet 312
  - Cecil Putnam "Mike" Ruppe 312
  - Alan C Clark 313
  - Janet Clark 313
  - Brenda Clark Sederberg 313
- Table of Missions Served 314

18. Conclusion **315**

19. Quilts through the Generations **317**

Works Cited **329**
- Clark 329
- Randall 332
- Christensen 332
- Ruppe 334
- Simmons 334
- Butler 335
- Bryce 335
- Goulding 335

Table of Figures

Figure 1: The author with Aunt Gladys Clark Farmer Fetzer and the Alice Randall Clark tribute book. 4
Figure 2: Alan, Brenda, Tom, and Janet in Rexburg. 15
Figure 3: Alan with some of his grandchildren: Mark, Maria, Rebecca, Matthew, and Timothy. 17
Figure 4: Pioneer ancestry of Alan C Clark. 35
Figure 5: Pioneer ancestry of Janet Lee Ruppe Clark. 36
Figure 6: Covered wagon sits next to natural spring water. 39
Figure 7: Joseph Smith family cabin, near Palmyra, New York. 41
Figure 8: Entrance to the Sacred Grove near Palmyra, New York. 42
Figure 9: The DuPage River in summer. 44
Figure 10: Interior of an old fort in Northern Illinois. 46
Figure 11: Ezra Thompson Clark. 47
Figure 12: St. Mary-le-Bow Church in London, the location of the Bow Bells. 48
Figure 13: Joseph Stevenson and Mary Stevens Stevenson. 49
Figure 14: Mary Stevenson. 51
Figure 15: Mississippi River scene. 53
Figure 16: Alfred Randall. 54
Figure 17: Margaret Harley Randall. 55
Figure 18: Karen Marie Hansen and Christen Anderson's wedding pictures. 56
Figure 19: Artist's re-envisioning of Karen and Christian. 57
Figure 20: Maren Christensen. 58
Figure 21: Mads Christensen. 59
Figure 22: Mads and Maren's house in Denmark. 60
Figure 23: Jens Christensen Lamp. 62
Figure 24: Images of the Jens and Trene Christensen family. 63
Figure 25: Jens Christensen home in Clarkston. 64
Figure 26: Cecil P. "Mike" Ruppe and his horse Blaze. 65
Figure 27: Leven Simmons. 66
Figure 28: Harriet Bradford Simmons. 66
Figure 29: Caroline Farozine Skeen. 67
Figure 30: John Lowe Butler (purported). 67
Figure 31: Royal Durfey and Lydia Abell. 69
Figure 32: Ebenezer Bryce. 70
Figure 33: David Park. 71
Figure 34: Ann Brooks. 71
Figure 35: David Park. 72
Figure 36: Daniel Goulding and Elizabeth Merrifield Pratten. 73
Figure 37: Elizabeth's mother, Diana Merrifield Pratten. 74
Figure 38: The Kirtland Temple 77
Figure 39: Alfred and Emmerette. 78
Figure 40: Purported image of John Lowe Butler and portrait of Caroline Farozine Skeen. 79
Figure 41: Three dollar note from the Kirtland Safety Society. 82
Figure 42: C. C. A. Christensen, The Battle of Crooked River. 83

Figure 43: C. C. A. Christensen, The Arrest of Mormon Leaders. 84
Figure 44: C. C. A. Christensen, Liberty Jail. 85
Figure 45: Orson Pratt. 86
Figure 46: Matthew, Tricia, Henry, Camilla, and Walter Sederberg in Adam-ondi-Ahman. 88
Figure 47: Purported image of John Lowe Butler. 89
Figure 48: The Nauvoo Temple as viewed from Old Nauvoo. 93
Figure 49: Camilla and Henry Sederberg near the reconstructed Nauvoo Temple. 94
Figure 50: Wilford Woodruff, circa 1849. 95
Figure 51: C. C. A. Christensen, The Nauvoo Temple. 96
Figure 52: Ezra and Mary Stevenson Clark. 96
Figure 53: Elizabeth Stevens Stevenson. 97
Figure 54: Alfred Randall, Emmerette Louisa Davis Randall, and Margaret Harley. 97
Figure 55: Leven and Harriet Simmons. 98
Figure 56: C. C. A. Christensen, Mormon Panorama Thirteen/Joseph Mustering the Nauvoo Legion. 99
Figure 57: Joseph Smith as Lieutenant General reviewing the Nauvoo Legion. 99
Figure 58: Purported image of John Lowe Butler. 100
Figure 59: Alfred Randall. 100
Figure 60: C. C. A. Christensen, Exterior of Carthage Jail. 101
Figure 61: Purported image of John Lowe Butler. 102
Figure 62: Ezra and Mary Stevenson Clark. 102
Figure 63: Harriet Bradford Simmons. 103
Figure 64: Ezra T. Clark. 103
Figure 65: Brigham Young, 1801–1877. 105
Figure 66: A traditional covered wagon. 107
Figure 67: C. C. A. Christensen, Leaving Missouri. 108
Figure 68: C. C. A. Christensen, Mobbers on the Missouri River. 109
Figure 69: C. C. A. Christensen, Burning of the Temple. 110
Figure 70: David Park. 111
Figure 71: C. C. A. Christensen, Pioneers Crossing the Plains of Nebraska. 112
Figure 72: Platte River, west of Omaha, Nebraska. 113
Figure 73: Devil's Gate, along the Mormon Trail. 115
Figure 74: Leven Simmons. 116
Figure 75: Alfred Randall and wives: Emmerette and Margaret. 116
Figure 76: Ezra T. Clark. 117
Figure 77: C. C. A. Christensen, Crossing the Mississippi on the Ice. 117
Figure 78: Mary Stevenson Clark. 118
Figure 79: Buffalo herd. 119
Figure 80: Elizabeth Stevens Stevenson. 120
Figure 81: C. C. A. Christensen, Entering the Great Salt Lake Valley. 121
Figure 82: Ebenezer Bryce. 121
Figure 83: The Salt Lake Valley. 122
Figure 84: Leven and Harriet Simmons. 123
Figure 85: Purported image of John Lowe Butler and image of Kenion Taylor Butler. Kenion would have been a young man of twenty when he crossed the plains. 124
Figure 86: Portrait of Caroline 125
Figure 87: Royal and Lydia Durfey. 125
Figure 88: Handcart pioneers struggle through a blizzard while crossing the Rocky Mountains. 126
Figure 89: Kenion Taylor Butler, rescuer for the Willie and Martin Handcart Company. 126
Figure 90: Historic statue memorializing handcart pioneers coming to Utah. 127
Figure 91: Members of the Christensen family crossed the Mormon Trail by handcart in 1857. 128
Figure 92: Karen Marie Hansen. 128

Figure 93: Handcart monument. 129
Figure 94: Purported image of John Lowe Butler, one of the first men to enter the practice of polygamy in Nauvoo. 135
Figure 95: Alfred wed second wife Margaret in Winter Quarters. 136
Figure 96: Leven Simmons. 137
Figure 97: Ezra T. Clark. 138
Figure 98: Daniel Goulding and second wife Fanny Pratten Goulding. 139
Figure 99: The Young Family residence. 140
Figure 100: Mads in later life. 141
Figure 101: Edward Clark and Alice Randall Clark. 142
Figure 102: Ezra T. Clark. 142
Figure 103: Edward Barrett Clark. 143
Figure 104: Mads Christensen. 143
Figure 105: Alfred Randall. 143
Figure 106: Daniel Goulding. 145
Figure 107: The Ezra and Mary Clark family. Back row: Edward, Hyrum Don Carlos, Amasa, and Wilford. Front row: Timothy, Mary (mother), Ezra, Mary Elizabeth (daughter), Charles, and Joseph. ... 149
Figure 108: Farmington, Utah. 151
Figure 109: Ezra T. Clark. 152
Figure 110: Susan, Ezra, and Mary. 155
Figure 111: Ezra's third wife Nancy Areta Porter Stevenson. 157
Figure 112: Ezra and Susan's family. Back row: Nathan, John, Sarah, Eugene. Front row: Susan Alice, Susan Leggett, Laura Blanche, Ezra, Horace, and Annie. 159
Figure 113: Views of the side of the Ezra T. Clark family home, as of 2021. 160
Figure 114: Front of Ezra T. Clark home, 2021. 161
Figure 115: Annie Waldron Clark lived on the "Underground" with Ezra and Mary for a time early in her marriage and gave birth to her first child at their home. She was the second wife of their son Charles Rich Clark. Pictured here with sons Myral and Carlos. 162
Figure 116: Mary Elizabeth Clark Robinson. 163
Figure 117: Ezra and Mary's oldest son, Ezra James Clark. 164
Figure 118: John Alexander Clark. 165
Figure 119: Joseph Smith Clark served as one of the primary Clark foremen for many years. 166
Figure 120: Edward B. Clark. 166
Figure 121: Brigham Young, 1801–1877. 168
Figure 122: John Taylor, third president and prophet of the Church of Jesus Christ of Latter-day Saints. 168
Figure 124: Great Salt Lake State Park. The Great Salt Lake was a regular relaxation spot for Ezra and his family. 169
Figure 123: Wilford Woodruff, circa 1849. 169
Figure 125: Antelope Island with clouds reflecting. Farmington is near the Great Salt Lake. 170
Figure 126: Portrait of Edward Stevenson. 170
Figure 127: Eliza R. Snow, second General President of the Relief Society. 171
Figure 128: Zina D. H. Young, third General President of the Relief Society. 171
Figure 129: Moroni statue at the Hill Cumorah. 173
Figure 130: Hyrum Don Carlos Clark, the model for the face of the Angel Moroni. 174
Figure 131: William O. Clark, brother of Ezra, performed Ezra and Mary's original wedding and came to Utah to officiate in the renewal of their vows for their Golden Anniversary. 175
Figure 132: Annie Clark Tanner home, 2021. 176
Figure 133: Edward and Wealthy. 181
Figure 134: Young Alice Randall Clark. 182
Figure 135: Logan Temple. 184

Figure 136: Quilt made by Alice Randall Clark for granddaughter Carol Clark Call. 187
Figure 137: Home of Alice Randall Clark in Georgetown. 189
Figure 138: Bear Lake 193
Figure 139: B.H. Roberts. 194
Figure 140: Alice with grandson Roland. 196
Figure 141: Wilford Woodruff Richards and Emily Randall Richards' young family...........................198
Figure 142: Wilford Woodruff Richards. 199
Figure 143: Wilford Woodruff Clark, on his favorite horse, Blaze. 200
Figure 144: Wilford Woodruff Clark and his twins. Woman is probably first wife Pamelia Dunn Clark. 201
Figure 145: Wedding picture of Wilford Woodruff Clark and first wife Pamelia Dunn Clark. 202
Figure 146: Charles Rich Clark. 202
Figure 147: Alice in old age with daughter Maurine and child. 203
Figure 148: Clark reunion. Edward, Wealthy, and most of Edward's children. 207
Figure 149: Edward in old age. 212
Figure 150: Alfred and wives. Back row: Mildred, Hannah, Elsey. Front row: Margaret, Emmerette, and Alfred. 216
Figure 151: Alfred and Margaret Randall family. Back row: Thurza, Margaret Ellen, Melvin, Emily, Alice. Front row: Mary, Orrin, Alfred, Margaret. 218
Figure 152: Centerville. 220
Figure 153: A gristmill. 222
Figure 154: Note to Alfred Randall by Brigham Young. 223
Figure 155: The Salt Lake Endowment House, circa 1855. An early building used to administer temple ordinances. 224
Figure 156: Whip used by Charles Franklin Randall during his time with the Pony Express. Item in possession of descendant Aaron John McMurdie. 225
Figure 157: This handgun, which belonged to Alfred Randall, has been passed down through the generations. The gun went to Emmerette's oldest son Charles Franklin Randall, then to Charles' youngest son, Lester, and then to Lester's daughter Norma Randall. Currently in the possession of Aaron John McMurdie, grandson of Norma 226
Figure 158: The house Alfred shared with fourth wife Hannah in North Ogden. 227
Figure 159: Autobiography of Alfred Randall in his own handwriting. 229
Figure 160: Maren Christensen. 232
Figure 161: Mads Christensen in his later years. 233
Figure 162: Hannah Christensen, second wife to Mads. 234
Figure 163: Purported image of John Lowe Butler. 240
Figure 164: Portrait of Caroline Farozine Skeen. 241
Figure 165: Caroline Farozine Skeen. 242
Figure 166: Fort Bridger. 244
Figure 167: Lovisa Hamilton. Seventh wife of John Lowe Butler. 246
Figure 168: Henrietta Blyth Butler. Eighth wife of John Lowe Butler. 246
Figure 170: Leven Simmons. 247
Figure 169: Harriet Bradford Simmons. 247
Figure 171: Leven Simmons. 248
Figure 172: Lydia Rebecca Fisher Simmons. 250
Figure 173: Elizabeth Merrifield Pratten. 256
Figure 174: Daniel and Fanny. 257
Figure 175: The Goulding family, circa 1886. 258
Figure 176: Fanny and Elizabeth Pratten Goulding. 259
Figure 177: The combined Goulding family. 260
Figure 178: Daniel and Fanny with daughter Phoebe and granddaughter. 261

Figure 179: Elizabeth and Henrietta "Retty." 262
Figure 180: Janet's ancestor Rosanna Susannah Goulding spent summers on the ranch with her mother. 263
Figure 181: First Henrieville Relief Society. 264
Figure 182: Elijah Goulding. 265
Figure 183: Sons of Daniel Goulding. 267
Figure 184: Mary Stevenson Clark. 272
Figure 185: Archibald Gardner. 275
Figure 186: Emma Christensen. 277
Figure 187: Trein Bendtsen Christensen, Emma's mother. 277
Figure 188: Joseph Mads Christensen. 278
Figure 189: Joseph Mads and Emma Christensen family. 279
Figure 190: Joseph Mads Christensen, June 1916. 279
Figure 191: Joseph Mads Christensen on steps of South Davis ward hall, circa 1830. 280
Figure 192: St. George Temple. 282
Figure 193: David Park. 283
Figure 194: William W. Davies and his two sons. Arthur was the Walla Walla Jesus. 284
Figure 195: The Davies Community's Main Compound. 285
Figure 196: David Park. 285
Figure 197: Kenion Taylor Butler. 286
Figure 198: Olive Durfey Butler. 286
Figure 199: Kenion Taylor Butler and siblings as adults. 287
Figure 200: Ebenezer Bryce and Mary Ann Park Bryce. 288
Figure 201: Janet Clark at Bryce Canyon. Ebenezer Bryce's mother's name was also Janet. 289
Figure 202: Bryce family cabin south of Tropic, Utah. 290
Figure 203: Bryce Canyon. 291
Figure 204: Rosanna Susannah Goulding. 292
Figure 205: William "Bill" Bryce and Malinda "Lindy" Riggs Bryce. 292
Figure 206: Eliza R. Snow. 293
Figure 208: The colorful sunset at the Great Salt Lake. 294
Figure 207: Mary Stevenson Clark. 294
Figure 209: Mads Christensen. 295
Figure 210: Ezra T. Clark. 295
Figure 211: The Salt Lake Railroad. 296
Figure 212: Aurelia S. Rogers, creator of the original Latter-day Saint Primary organization, beloved figure in Farmington, and friend of the Clarks and Mads Christensen. 297
Figure 213: Salt Lake City. 299
Figure 214: Purported image of John Lowe Butler. 300
Figure 215: Caroline Farozine Skeen. 301
Figure 216: Royal Durfey and Lydia Abell. 301
Figure 217: Kenion Taylor Butler. 302
Figure 218: Ebenezer Bryce. 302
Figure 219: St. George Temple. 303
Figure 220: Mary Ann Park Bryce. 304
Figure 221: Ezra T. Clark. 304
Figure 222: Mildred and Alfred served a mission together to Hawaii. 307
Figure 223: Mads Christensen. 309
Figure 224: Edward Barrett Clark. 309
Figure 225: Joseph Mads Christensen. 310
Figure 226: Letter of release to Elder Joseph Christensen, signed by Wilford Woodruff. 311
Figure 227: Walter Edward Clark. 312

Figure 228: Mike Ruppe and his horse, Blaze. 312
Figure 229: Alan and Janet Clark on a mission to England. 313
Figure 230: Brenda Clark Sederberg. 313
Figure 231: Quilt made by Alice Randall Clark for her granddaughter Carol Clark Call. 317
Figure 232: Enlarged segment of log cabin quilt by Reva Marie Simmons Ruppe. 318
Figure 233: Full log cabin quilt by Reva Ruppe. Brenda said Reva used polyester fabrics in many of her quilt designs, making them extremely hardy and long-lasting. 319
Figure 234: Quilt by Leila Willet Clark, second wife of Walter Clark. Leila had poor eyesight and Walter used to thread multiple needles for her to work with before he went outside. This quilt took her 650 hours to make. Quilt currently in the possession of Sarah Farmer. 320
Figure 235: Yarn-tied quilt by Janet Ruppe Clark. 321
Figure 236: Quilt by MaryLynn Olson, Alice's great-granddaughter and Brenda's cousin. 322
Figure 237: Art quilt by Rachel Farmer (Alice's great-grandchild). 323
Figure 238: Quilt by Maria Sederberg Longhurst, made for her daughter. 324
Figure 239: Rag quilt lap blanket by the author. 325
Figure 240: Quilt by Laura Sederberg Jaeger. 326
Figure 241: Quilt by Laura Sederberg Jaeger. 327
Figure 242: Quilt by Abby Sederberg. 328

1. Genealogy Charts for this Book / The Story Behind Last Names

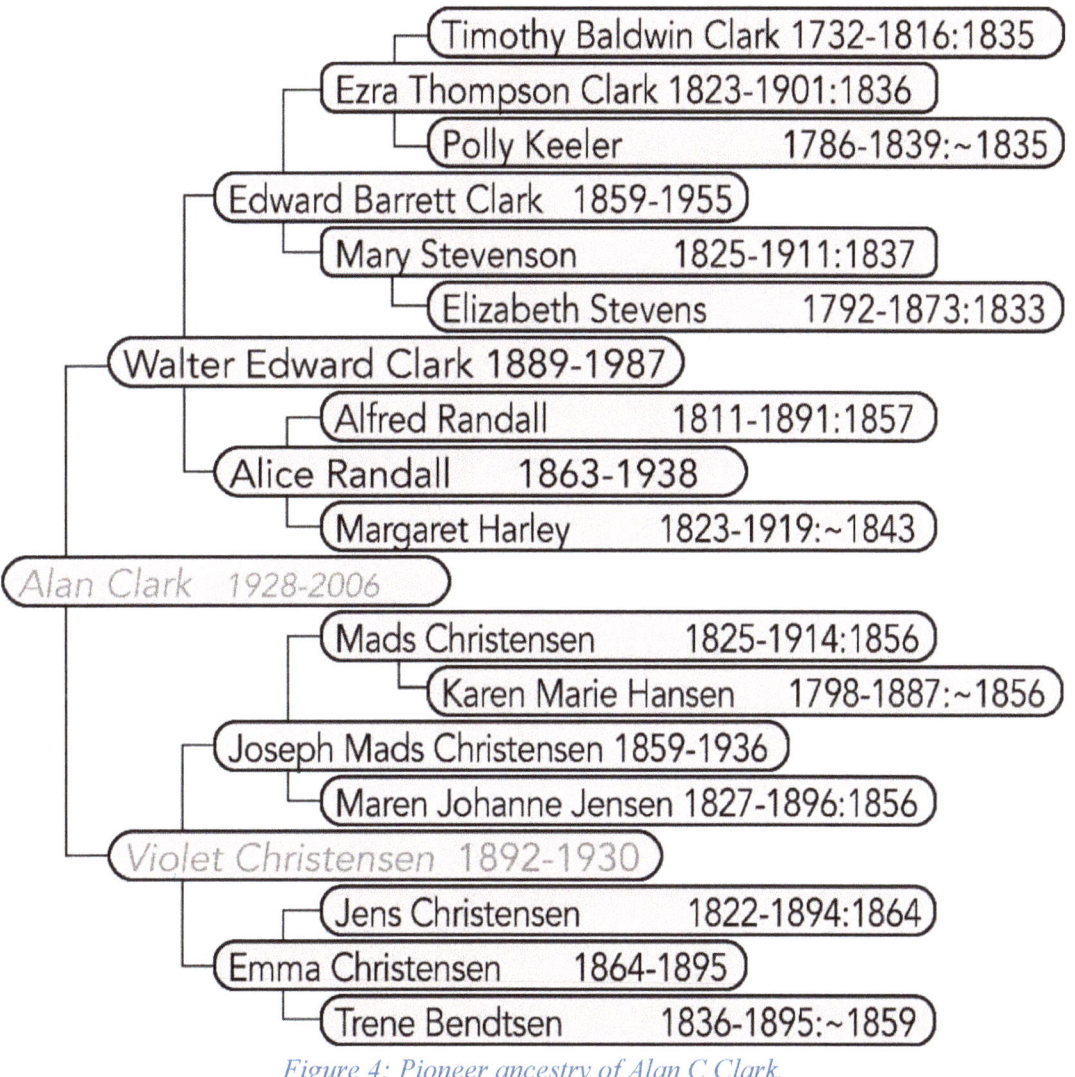

Figure 4: Pioneer ancestry of Alan C Clark.
Table created by Thomas Sederberg.

Names in gray are not a primary focus of this book.
Birth and death years follow each name.
The third year, if present, is the year of baptism for a convert.

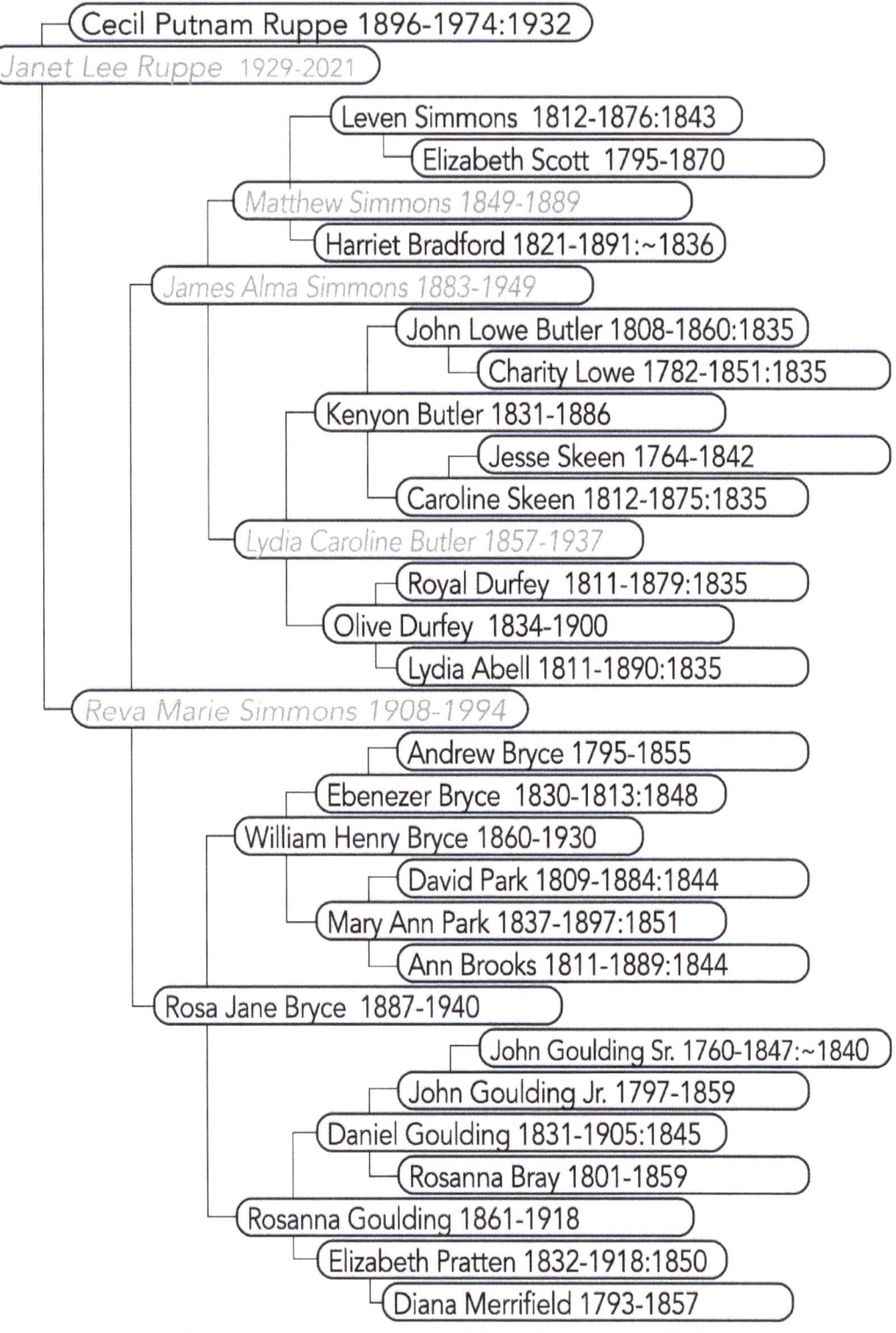

*Figure 5: Pioneer ancestry of Janet Lee Ruppe Clark.
Table created by Thomas Sederberg.*

Names in gray are not a primary focus in this book.
Birth and death years follow each name.
The third year, if present, is the year of baptism for a convert.

Where does the name of "Clark" come from?

The Clark families came from England in the 1600s. In English culture, newborn children received their father's last name. When a woman married a man, she gave up her maiden name (that is, her childhood last name), and adopted her husband's last name at that time.

The name "Clark" evolved from the word "clerk," which could mean a scribe, secretary, or religious scholar. When last names in England began to be used, the Clark family was probably engaged in one of these professions.

Let's learn more about the other last names on the Clark and Ruppe family tree.

Alan's matriarchal line goes through his mother, Violet.

You'll see Violet's matriarchal line, through her mother's mother's mother, has last names that change with each generation. But this isn't just due to marriage. Violet's family came from Scandinavia, where children historically received a last name based on their father's first name. This was called a "patronym." The last name changed with each generation for both sons and daughters.

Violet's maternal grandma was named Trene Bendtsen because Trene's father's name was Bendt. "Datter" or "sen" were used at the end of the father's name to mean "child of."

Can you find Trene on the family tree?

Why did families in many European countries give children the father's last name or a last name based on the first name of a father?

The answer is cultural. In English and other European cultures children typically needed to be born to a legally wedded father and mother to have social and religious legitimacy.

Because the last names of women are usually changed by generation or at the time of their marriage, sometimes this can contribute to making it harder to track their genealogy. However, their names and histories are still valuable to learn. Your mothers, grandmothers, and great-grandmothers did much to help establish, maintain, and care for their families and communities. Often the women were skilled farmers, frontierswomen, immigrants, midwives, nurses, healers, teachers, active mothers, and grandmothers. They had many exciting adventures during their lifetimes.

Your fathers, grandfathers, and great-grandfathers were teachers, scientists, immigrants, farmers, frontiersmen, members of the army or navy, and experienced in other ways. Many, many stories make up your family tree.

Historically, Western culture has recorded the stories of men more frequently than the stories of the women. The names of men in history have also been preserved and celebrated more often than the names of women in history. But our family has done work to preserve the stories of many of our ancestral women. They are a vital part of our ancestral family web. It is important for you to know the names and stories of both your grandfathers and your grandmothers.

Can you name the sequence of women for three generations back who are on Janet's matriarchal line?

The Power of Record-Keeping

Why can we trace some lines back further than others?

The answer is records.

Historical records such as births, baptisms, marriages, and deaths were kept by churches, governments, and occasionally other entities. Not all of these records have survived, and some places kept more careful records than others.

Our knowledge of our ancestors is found in the records we have access to—these records may include the dates outlining their lives as well as the stories of what they did and who they were.

Keeping records and writing down stories is a very important part of preserving our heritage.

Do you keep a journal?

That is one way you can keep your own record of your life.

Someday, someone else may read your stories and learn from what you recorded.

They may get new insight into how to solve a problem. They may feel less alone in something they've struggled with. Or they may be inspired to see that you have interests that they do too.

The people who read your story may be your own children and grandchildren, or they may be other people whom you choose to share with. Some people write a personal history or memoir and share it with the world! Then, many people might read it.

The stories we share help us make meaning out of our world. They help us recognize what is important and honor our experience as humans. They help us understand each other better, learn from the past, and decide what kind of future we would like to create.

They help us stay accountable to ourselves and to our roots.

If you want to gain a new skill or develop abilities in a field, reading a biography of someone who has already done that thing can help you gain confidence and a belief that you can do it, too. If you want to be inspired about your options in life and learn from others, biographies are a powerful place to look. It can be especially meaningful when there are stories from your own family you can be inspired by.

Sometimes people feel a closeness to their ancestors they may not feel to other historical figures. Your ancestors contributed to your heritage, influencing who you are today.

Reading their stories is a way to connect with their love and the legacy they've left, to honor them, and to learn from their life experiences.

Are you ready to read more?

Go to the next page to find out what in these stories reminds you of you.

2. Legends from the Pioneer Times

Figure 6: Covered wagon sits next to natural spring water.
© Crackerclips/Dreamstime.com

Have you ever wondered what the stories are behind the names on a family tree?
Every family lineage has a pathway through history.

Alan and Janet's family history is woven through with connections to significant pioneer and Church history. As the main body of Latter-day Saint pioneers migrated to the American West and sparked worldwide missionary efforts, many women and men dedicated their lives to building the kingdom—including many of Alan and Janet's ancestors.

The following chapters are a journey through some of the events that defined the early Church and the colonization of the American West. The lives and adventures of Alan and Janet's ancestors were intertwined with this history, and in some cases helped shape it.

In these chapters, most stories are of direct ancestors. A few stories are from others, such as extended family members or spouses. These stories illuminate the era and the history of the family.

Some ancestors do not have a biography or sketch easily available through my own library or through FamilySearch. For instance, Alice Randall Clark apparently has an autobiography—it is referenced in other family writings—but I have been unable to track it down. In cases such as Alice's and her mother Margaret's, neither of whom have an easily accessible known biography, I've looked to the writings of extended family in their near vicinity. Emily Randall Richards, younger sister of Alice, wrote a lovely life story that includes information about her mother, Margaret, as well as her sister Alice. I've drawn on her writing as well as stories from other close figures to flesh out the brief life sketches of Alice and Margaret that are easily available to the public. I have also drawn on the books in private personal collections, the David O. McKay Special Collections library at Brigham Young University, and other books that are less broadly available to the general public.

Where possible in this book, I have often used quotes and anecdotes from the ancestors themselves or their near relatives who knew these individuals and heard their stories personally. This gives us the opportunity to learn more of the stories of Alan and Janet's pioneer ancestors.

This book is merely a portion of what is available: a place to start. It will be enough for some readers to simply enjoy the stories here. Other readers, however, will want to read more. To you explorers—you may enjoy following the source notes to dive further into original books and manuscripts. You can also check the memories section of your ancestors in FamilySearch. As an easy next research step from there, you may find additional stories by checking the memory sections of your direct ancestors' family members, where you will sometimes find stories of direct ancestors that aren't included in the pages of the direct ancestors themselves.

The organization of this book is not a straight person-by-person recounting of family history. Instead, the stories here are woven into historical context to illuminate the intersections of family history with events in the broader world. Stories about a given ancestor or family are spread among chapters like a woven tapestry.

We start to see interesting intersections. For instance, we can see that the Clark and the Stevenson families began to build a relationship several years before Ezra T. Clark married Mary Stevenson.

In an extraordinary moment of Church history, Ezra's big sister Laura Clark Phelps got the Prophet's permission to attempt to rescue her husband and two other Church leaders from jail. Laura bravely rode with her younger brother John 160 miles to Columbia, where they successfully rescued Parley P. Pratt, King Follet, and Laura's husband Morris Phelps, though not without great difficulty.[1] [2]

Meanwhile, back in Clarksville near Charlestown, Elizabeth Stevens Stevenson took care of Laura's children during this difficult time, and she saw they were taken care of during Laura and Morris' daring travels. The fact that Elizabeth watched Laura's children shows that the Clark and Stevenson families knew each other well during the early years of the Church at Far West.

Let's follow the threads back through time to see what other stories unfurl . . .

---

[1] Parker Haddock, Edith, and Dorothy Hardy Matthews. "History of Bear Lake Pioneers." *Morris Charles Phelps*, Daughters of the Utah Pioneers, http://www.morrisphelps.org/history_of_bear_lake_pioneers.htm. Accessed 12 October 2020. (A. Charles Clark notes that Bruce Peterson, author of the Morris Phelps biography, has not been able to discover the origin of Morris having a middle name of Charles or any other name.)

[2] Clark, A. Charles, private correspondence with the author.

3. Early Latter-day Saint Origins: Conversion Stories

Figure 7: Joseph Smith family cabin, near Palmyra, New York.
Photo 56798 © Linda Bair/Dreamstime.com

At some point, each of the lines of Alan and Janet's parents or grandparents embraced The Church of Jesus Christ of Latter-day Saints. The earliest convert was within the first few years of the new religion—Elizabeth Stevens Stevenson (Alan's great-great-grandmother) was baptized in a lake on her property in Michigan in 1833. The most recent convert was Cecil P. "Mike" Ruppe (Janet's father), who was baptized 30 January 1932.

For these individuals, their newfound religion was often a joyous revelation. It elevated their spirits, gave peace to their souls, and helped them feel connected to a broader cause: building up Zion.

This new religion often brought challenges and sacrifice. Many were called to gather with the Saints, and some said goodbye to beloved family and friends forever.

The depth of their commitment to their faith often meant sacrifice, but by and large the ancestors found meaning in the practice of their faith. They sought spiritual growth and communion with others on a path of service to the Lord.

Alan and Janet took great pride in their ancestry and family connections, attending many, many family reunions over the years. They valued the stories of spirit, courage, service, and love found within their ancestral lines.

The Church was a primary force shaping generations.

Here are the stories of how Alan and Janet's ancestors found and joined The Church of Jesus Christ of Latter-day Saints.

Figure 8: Entrance to the Sacred Grove near Palmyra, New York.
Photo 56783 / Joseph Smith © Linda Bair/Dreamstime.com

The conversion stories are given in order from left to right as you'd look at Brenda Clark's family history, starting with the earliest ancestors on each line who accepted the gospel. Because the order is by lineage and not chronological, there is a little bit of a time jump between some of the entries, most notably Mike Ruppe, who was first of his line to be baptized, and who was converted in the 1900s, many decades after most of the others in these stories.

Timothy Baldwin Clark and Polly Keeler Clark

Timothy Baldwin Clark was a carpenter, a sometimes-soldier, and a partner in a sawmill in Illinois when he first heard the missionaries.

A descendant of the founders of Milford, New Haven, Connecticut, Timothy was born in 1778, and baptized at First Church in Milford on 10 May 1778.[3] His ancestors had come to the United States from England.

Timothy's wife, Polly Keeler Clark, was born in Connecticut on 13 February 1786. Her ancestry contains many interesting figures as well as some controversy. Most of Polly's ancestors came to America from England about five generations before her time.

Timothy had joined the Methodist faith at some point in his life, possibly in Connecticut or Ohio.

"So unpopular was the sect in Warren that to be a Methodist subjected the believer to both social and religious ostracism."[4] Timothy's membership obviously did not come about from him becoming swept up by a popular movement, and he demonstrated a willingness to embrace a minority cause, even one held in contempt by some. Early Ohio was populated largely by churchless frontier settlements. A general indifference or even outright hostility existed toward organized religion.

Evidence suggests that the Methodist Reverend Jesse Walker was a valuable figure to Timothy's religious life, and that for Rev. Walker, Timothy was willing to displace his family and move when called.

Timothy was an active lay leader in his local Methodist Church community. When the Reverend settled on the DuPage River 1828, Timothy moved to be near him, "in the place most recently designated as the new center of Methodist importance." When Rev. Walker moved in 1829 to a place soon to be known as Walker's Grove, Timothy and family followed him again.

James Emmett was a neighbor of the Clarks in Walker's Grove.[5]

---

[3] Most of the information on Timothy Baldwin Clark and family comes from articles about him on *FamilySearch* and the book *Timothy Baldwin Clark: A Narrative of the Life and Times of a Connecticut Yankee Gone Westward*, by A. Charles Clark.
[4] Clark, A. Charles. *Timothy Baldwin Clark*, p. 120.
[5] Ibid., p. 202.

Figure 9: The DuPage River in summer.
Photo 157359384 © James Andrews/Dreamstime.com

Rev. Walker retired with his wife to Chicago, picking Rev. S.R. Beggs as his successor. Soon after, in the 1830s, word came of a new religion, "Mormonites" being a name the practitioners were commonly known by at the time.[6]

Morris Phelps hosted elders from the new religion to preach in his home, leading to the baptism on the following day of James Emmett. James was confirmed to be an elder the same day.[7] He would soon become a missionary himself, and later come to convert and play a large role in the life of another of our ancestors, John Lowe Butler.

Daughter Laura Introduces Timothy and Polly to a New Religion

Daughter Laura Phelps had wed Morris Phelps, a fellow Methodist, on 28 April 1826.[8] She and Morris were baptized in August 1831 in Illinois, just a little over a year after the Church had officially been organized by Joseph Smith in western New York.

Timothy was a religious man, but he wasn't ready to jump into a new faith quite so quickly. A founding member of the Methodist Church congregation in Walker's Grove, Illinois, he enjoyed his

---

[6] Ibid., p. 203.
[7] Ibid., p. 204.
[8] Ibid., p. 173.

church there.⁹ Timothy and Polly may have also enjoyed being established in Illinois after having moved several times during the early years of their marriage. Their children were growing up. Maybe Timothy and Polly thought it would be nice to stay where they were.

Laura and Morris, on the other hand, were just starting out, with two young daughters. They were ready to commit to the new Church, and moved to gather with the Saints.

On 7 April 1832, Laura gave birth to her third child, in Lyman Wight's tent—the first Latter-day Saint girl born in Independence, Missouri. She named the child Harriet Wight Phelps, perhaps in honor of the Wight family. The young Phelps family settled in Little Prairie, Missouri. After fellow Saint John Murdock lost his wife shortly after she gave birth to twins in Kirtland, Ohio, the Prophet Joseph and his wife Emma, who had just lost twins of their own, famously took in the Murdock twins. John Murdock then moved to Missouri, where he was unable to adequately care for his remaining children. After John Murdock, Sr. was captured by authorities, Laura and Morris Phelps took in John, Jr., who was just older than their oldest child, Paulina. Laura provided him with protection and care. An intelligent young man, John was "a great help to Laura," who at that time ran a household dominated by young daughters. [10] [11] [12]

(John would eventually return to live with his father five years later, and was homesick for the Phelps family for some time.)[13]

Meanwhile, back in Illinois, Timothy and sons David Keeler and Barrett Bass served in the Black Hawk War in northern Illinois. Son William O. also accompanied his family to war, but given his young age he was kept back at the fort and not sent out on offensive actions. Abraham Lincoln also served in this conflict—it would be the future president's only military experience prior to the Civil War.[14]

A few years later, Morris Phelps returned to Illinois on a missionary assignment. William O. Clark was baptized by Morris on 13 April 1835 in the DuPage River. Morris would return in May accompanied by Charles C. Rich as his companion, with the goal of baptizing Timothy and the rest of his family.

---

[9] "Timothy Baldwin Clark." *FamilySearch*, Intellectual Reserve, https://www.familysearch.org/photos/artifacts/111063710?cid=mem_copy. Accessed 30 September 2020.

[10] John Murdock, Jr. would again interact with the greater Clark family in later years, as we shall see in an upcoming chapter.

[11] Phelps, Morris Calvin. "Laura Clark Phelps History - by Morris Calvin Phelps." *FamilySearch*, Intellectual Reserve, https://www.familysearch.org/photos/artifacts/104250413?cid=mem_copy. Accessed 3 October 2020.

[12] "John Riggs Murdock." *FamilySearch*, Intellectual Reserve, https://www.familysearch.org/tree/person/details/KWVG-GRF. Accessed 18 November 2020.

[13] Tanner, J.M. "A Biographical Sketch of John Riggs Murdock." *The Deseret News*, Salt Lake City, Utah, 1909.

[14] Monroe, R.D. "Indian Fighting and Politics in New Salem, 1831-1836." *Lincoln/Net*, Northern Illinois University Digital Library, https://digital.lib.niu.edu/illinois/lincoln/newsalem. Accessed 24 October 2020.

Figure 10: Interior of an old fort in Northern Illinois.
Photo 162146304 © Ej Rodriquez Photography/Dreamstime.com

Charles stayed with the Clarks for some time, helping on the farm with agricultural activities including repairing a gate, preparing soil and planting corn, and boot making. In total the visit of Charles C. Rich and Morris Phelps to the area spanned about six weeks from May to mid-June 1835.[15] Eventually, Timothy was baptized, on 7 May 1835.[16] Polly's baptism date is not known.

Timothy and Polly and family sold their land on the DuPage River to son Barret B. Clark,[17] and followed Laura to Independence, Missouri. By the time Timothy and Polly moved to Missouri, Rhoda and John Cooper had obtained property in Clay County, and Morris and Laura had been forcibly expelled from Jackson County with other Saints. Timothy's first property purchase was adjacent to the Coopers.[18] Six of Timothy and Polly's eleven children were eventually baptized: Laura, Rhoda, John Wesley, Ezra Thompson, Mary Ann, and William O.[19] Their other sons and daughters did not join the Church and

---

[15] Clark, A. Charles. *Timothy Baldwin Clark*, pp. 217–222.
[16] Rich, Charles C. "7 May 1835," *Journals, 1833–1862*, Charles C. Rich Collection, 1832–1908. CHL. MS 889, box 1. The Joseph Smith Papers, *Intellectual Reserve*, https://www.josephsmithpapers.org/person/timothy-baldwin-clark. Accessed 22 March 2022.
[17] Clark, A. Charles. *Timothy Baldwin Clark*, p. 225.
[18] Clark, A. Charles.
[19] Timothy and Polly's children which survived infancy in order of birth were: Sarah, Myra, Laura, Rhoda, David Keeler, Barrett Bass, William Oglesby, John Welsey, Homer Baldwin, Ezra Thompson, and Mary Ann.

remained in northern Illinois.[20] Sarah had married in Indiana and remained there, never joining the Church. Myra and John Sargent were married in 1825 while the family still lived in Southern Illinois. Myra and her husband perished by drowning in Louisiana in 1829.[21]

When the family arrived in Missouri in September 1835, Timothy purchased property near John Cooper—land that is now within the city boundaries of Excelsior Springs, Missouri.[22]

Ezra T. Clark

Ezra Thompson Clark was the tenth child of Timothy Baldwin Clark and Polly Keeler Clark.

He was still a boy living at home at the time that his parents met the missionaries and were taught by them.

After his parents were baptized, Ezra, along with the rest of the children still at home, relocated to live closer to the Saints.

Sometime after his family moved to Missouri, Ezra was baptized at age 12 in March 1836 by his brother William O. in Fishing River, Clay County, Missouri.

He came of age among the Latter-day Saint people and developed a devotion for his religion that continued throughout his entire life.[23]

Figure 11: Ezra Thompson Clark. Public domain via FamilySearch.

---

[20] Despite religious differences, the extended family remained cordial. Some of Ezra T.'s siblings who were not in the Church visited him while he lived in Utah. And Walter Edward Clark had a sister named Rhoda, named after one of Timothy Baldwin Clark's daughters who lived in the Midwest. This would have been the younger Rhoda's great-aunt.
[21] Clark, A. Charles.
[22] Clark, A. Charles.
[23] "Ezra Thompson Clark Life Sketch." *FamilySearch*, Intellectual Reserve, https://www.familysearch.org/tree/person/details/KW83-LG6. Accessed 30 September 2020.

Elizabeth Stevens Stevenson and Mary Stevenson Clark

Figure 12: St. Mary-le-Bow Church in London, the location of the Bow Bells.
Photo 75964333 © chrisdorney/Depositphotos

"Mother often told us children of her grandmother's [Elizabeth Stevens Stevenson's] deep spirituality, her devotion to her church, her gentle kind ways and her cultured, refining influence—all reflecting her personality."[24]—Clarice Stewart Anderson

Elizabeth was born in 1792 under the sound of the Bow Bells in London, which was significant, as according to old English tradition, only those born under the sound of the Bow Bells are "true Londoners."[25] At age 19, Elizabeth married Joseph Stevenson in London, and a few years later the young family moved to the British colony of Gibraltar, where Joseph accepted an appointment of Master Cooper in the ordinance department under the employment of the English government. The work was pleasant and paid well. Joseph built a shop next to the family home, where he worked in his leisure time. The family lived in Gibraltar for about fifteen years.

Elizabeth's daughter Mary wrote later that in Gibraltar, "Mother would go upstairs and reach out and wrap papers around the grapes

---

[24] Anderson, Clarice Stewart. "A Sketch of the Life of Elizabeth Stevens Stevenson." *FamilySearch*, Intellectual Reserve, https://www.familysearch.org/photos/artifacts/1008826?cid=mem_copy. Accessed 28 September 2020.
[25] The Bow Bells are the bells of the Church of St. Mary-le-Bow in London. To be born within the reach of their sound was the traditional definition of a Londoner or a cockney.

to keep the birds from eating them."[26]

Nolan Clark writes: "In 1827, Joseph Stevenson petitioned the Board of Ordinance for transfer to a North American British post. He was anxious to apprentice his four oldest children, all sons, to a trade, an opportunity that was not available in Gibraltar. (The Gibraltar climate also affected Joseph Stevenson with intermittent fevers.) After Joseph Stevenson's request was declined, Joseph quit his position with the Board of Ordinance and, in 1828, sailed from Gibraltar to New York."[27]

Elizabeth and Joseph immigrated to America on the ship *Constitution* in search of better opportunities for their sons to learn trades.

Figure 13: Joseph Stevenson and Mary Stevens Stevenson. Public domain via FamilySearch.

They eventually settled on wild land near Pontiac, Michigan, where Joseph built a two-story home. He purchased a farm, but died in 1832 at the age of 44 before he could implement planned improvements to the property.

In 1833, missionaries came to the area. One of their converts caused quite a stir: the deacon of the Presbyterian Church chose to be baptized. His family farm adjoined Elizabeth's, and the deacon's wife told Elizabeth she thought her husband was losing his mind.

Elizabeth asked, "Does he continue to pray?"

His wife replied that he was as devoted as ever, but for her part she considered the Mormon religion a delusion.

Elizabeth said, "Well, let us wait and see what will follow. If it is of God, it will stand. If not, it will fall."[28]

Soon after, Elders Jared Carter and Joseph Wood taught the gospel in a little schoolhouse near the Stevenson home. Elizabeth came to listen. When Joseph Smith himself

---

[26] Clark, Mary Stevenson. "Autobiography of Mary Stevenson Clark." *FamilySearch*, Intellectual Reserve, 20 June 2013, https://www.familysearch.org/photos/artifacts/1542747?cid=mem_copy. Accessed 30 September 2020.
[27] Clark, Nolan. "My Immigrant Ancestors."
[28] "Elizabeth Stevenson Clark - Pioneer Woman of Faith." *FamilySearch*, Intellectual Reserve, https://www.familysearch.org/photos/artifacts/104801730?cid=mem_copy. Accessed 31 October 2020.

taught at Pontiac, Elizabeth attended the gathering and felt peace. She was baptized in 1832 in a small lake on her property.

Her son Edward later wrote of the Prophet Joseph visiting their home: "In parting from under our roof the Prophet expressed a desire to have a loan of a large English Book of Martyrs, which we possessed, promising to return it to us when he should meet us again in Zion, in the State of Missouri, which he did, and on returning it he said, 'I have, by the aid of the Urim and Thummim, seen those martyrs.'"[29]

The Book of Martyrs was considered by many to be a holy book and was quoted over the pulpit in some churches like scripture.[30]

Elizabeth, whose husband had died by then, sold her property, receiving a small lump sum with a promise of more later. But nothing more was ever received, disappointing her greatly, and introducing a period of previously unexperienced hardship.

With her three youngest children, Elizabeth traveled with a group of Saints to Missouri. Over the following years, they moved with the Saints as events transpired that pressured the main body of Saints to move onward to a new homebase multiple times.

In Mary Stevenson Clark's autobiography, she recorded of the older siblings:

"My three oldest brothers did not receive the Gospel. They went to Cincinnati, Ohio, and worked at their trades, one a printer and the other two coopers. . . .

"I had a dream of seeing the Savior. He took me in His arms. We sat in a circle. He blessed us and kissed us. It was only the members who accepted the Gospel that sat in the circle. I told Mother my dream. She said it was a good dream and for me to be a good girl. I was about 7 years old."[31]

In Clay County, Elizabeth purchased a home, which was later lost during the mobbings. They later lived in Montrose, Iowa, across the river from Nauvoo, in a room adjoining Brigham Young's. From there they moved to Clarksville.

---

[29] Stevenson, Edward. *Reminiscences of Joseph, The Prophet, and the Coming Forth of the Book of Mormon*, p. 6. Project Gutenberg, 2017. *Project Gutenberg*, https://www.gutenberg.org/files/54337/54337-h/54337-h.htm. Accessed 14 October 2020.

[30] "Foxe's Book of Martyrs." *Wikipedia*, Wikimedia Foundation, https://en.wikipedia.org/wiki/Foxe%27s_Book_of_Martyrs. Accessed 14 October 2020.

[31] Clark, Mary Stevenson.

*Figure 14: Mary Stevenson.
Public domain via FamilySearch.*

Most of the Saints there were very poor.

Elizabeth and her daughters needed to work to support themselves. Her daughters Elizabeth and Mary worked for Gentiles who had money to pay for their efforts. Sometimes Elizabeth herself would hire out to help families also, leaving her youngest son, James, in the care of another family. Elizabeth was called on to care for the children of Laura Clark Phelps while she and her brother John W. Clark left the Nauvoo area for a number of days to rescue Morris Phelps, King Follett, and Parley P. Pratt from jail.

Elizabeth's daughter Mary later recorded of Elizabeth during this time in Nauvoo:

"My Mother was very handy with a needle and used to help the Prophet's wife and others of the Authorities, and so she was well acquainted and received much instruction and intelligence."[32]

In Mary Stevenson Clark's autobiography, she recorded:

"We lived in Missouri until the Saints were driven from there to Quincy, Illinois, and from there to Nauvoo. We moved over the Mississippi River to a town called Montrose, in Iowa. We lived in a room adjoining Brigham Young's. From there we moved to a settlement called Clarksville near a town called Charlestown. My brother Edward built a cabin and we went to work as best we could. My sister and I worked for the Gentiles for the Saints were too poor to hire us. My Mother was called upon to take care of the children of Sister Morris Phelps while she and her brother, John W. Clark, went to get her husband and others out of jail in Missouri, and she accomplished it for she was directed by the Spirit of the Lord. Mother took care and was a comfort to her children until they returned to their home.

"My sister Elizabeth and I were baptized when I was 12 years old, in Far West, Missouri by David Patten."[33]

---

[32] Clark, Mary Stevenson.
[33] Clark, Mary Stevenson.

Figure 15: Mississippi River scene.
© martyhaas/Depositphotos

Alfred Randall

Alfred Randall was born 13 June 1811 at Bridgewater, New York. In full adulthood, he was a well-built man, six feet tall, weighing about 200 pounds. He had a heavy head of hair and enjoyed telling and hearing clean humorous stories. He often laughed until tears ran down his cheeks. Similar good humor was evident in many of Alfred's children.[34] His ancestors came from England and had settled in New England a few centuries before Alfred's time.

You may have heard of a Clark relative who perished in the Salem Witch Trials; this was a woman in Alfred's ancestral family. His fourth great-grandaunt, Mary Ayer, was one of the nineteen people hanged during the Salem Witch Trials on 22 September 1692. She was condemned to death even though she denied she was a witch. Ironically, local people didn't kill the people who confessed to witchcraft, only those who were accused and wouldn't confess. Mary defended herself as well as she could in the trial, but it was to no avail. You can read more about her in a story referenced in the notes.[35]

---

[34] "Alfred Randall." *FamilySearch*, Intellectual Reserve, https://www.familysearch.org/photos/artifacts/91211035?cid=mem_copy. Accessed 2 November 2020.
[35] "Mary Ayer Parker." *History of American Women*, https://www.womenhistoryblog.com/2008/06/mary-ayer-parker.html. Accessed 14 October 2020.

Alfred came from an intelligent lineage and his extended family during his era had good connections. His cousin Samuel would serve as Speaker of the US House of Representatives during many of the early years that the Saints were establishing themselves in Utah, and was still serving in Congress during the years that the US government began to take more of an interest in dealing with the issue of polygamy then practiced by the Church.

When Alfred was nine years old, his family moved from New York to the Kirtland, Ohio area. Alfred helped clear timber from land where the Kirtland Temple would later be constructed. In 1830, Alfred moved to Munson, Ohio. Here he later married first wife Emmerette Davis in 1834, when he was 23 and she was 15. Along with her oldest sister, Roxanna, Emmerette at the time was "a believer in the Mormon religion and [Alfred] soon embraced the same faith for himself."[36] In 1838, Alfred and Emmerette moved to Chardown, Ohio, with their two children, and later to Quincy, Illinois, where Alfred became a carpenter.[37]

"Alfred was baptized a member of the Church in Quincy, Illinois in 1840 by Apostle Orson Hyde. He helped build the Nauvoo Temple and attended the first meeting held there."[38]

Margaret Harley Randall

Margaret Harley Randall was born and grew up in Pennsylvania. She was mostly of German and Swiss descent, and her ancestry has some notable interest in religion: her maternal grandfather and a paternal great-great-grandfather had both been reverends.

Here is an account of Margaret's conversion to The Church of Jesus Christ of Latter-day Saints, as told by her daughter Emily Randall Richards:

"Margaret Harley, daughter of Benjamin and Elizabeth Harley, was born January 13, 1823, in Chester County, Pennsylvania. Her mother died when Margaret was eleven years of age. She was always a delicate child, and it

Figure 16: Alfred Randall. Public domain via FamilySearch.

---

[36] "A Few Facts and Stories about Emmerette Davis Randall," Daughters of Utah Pioneers. *FamilySearch*. https://www.familysearch.org/photos/artifacts/40508208?cid=mem_copy
[37] "Alfred Randall."
[38] Randall, Helen Torney. "Life History: Alfred Randall." *FamilySearch*, Intellectual Reserve, https://www.familysearch.org/photos/artifacts/6107656?cid=mem_copy. Accessed 2 October 2020.

Figure 17: Margaret Harley Randall. Public domain via FamilySearch.

was said of her that she would not live to be twenty years of age. However, she lived to the ripe old age of ninety-six, dying 5 April 1919.

"The century in which Margaret lived saw the most wonderful advancement in the history of the world—the perfection and bringing into use of the steam boat, railroad, and telegraph, and the invention of the telephone and automobile and the improvement of the postal system.

"In their Pennsylvania home Margaret and her brother Edwin, four years her senior, were converted to the gospel of The Church of Jesus Christ of Latter-day Saints. Records are not available to show when and by whom they were baptized. Their father was a kind and loving man, but not being converted himself, felt sad to have his son and daughter join so unpopular a religion. Naturally, he would do nothing to help them join the Saints. However, he told Margaret to come back home when she found out her mistake.

"Margaret and her sister had been kind to a lonely old man who lived near, and when he died he left one hundred dollars to each of the girls. Margaret used her portion to take her to Nauvoo to join her chosen people, but did not arrive in that city until after the death of the Prophet Joseph Smith. She talked very little about her life and thus not much is known of the particulars of her travels and early experiences.

"At Nauvoo Margaret Harley hired out to work for Alfred Randall and his wife Emmerette Davis."[39]

This began Margaret's adventures as a member of The Church of Jesus Christ of Latter-day Saints.

---

[39] Richards, Emily Randall. "Margaret Harley Randall." *FamilySearch*, Intellectual Reserve, 1941, https://www.familysearch.org/photos/artifacts/24327746?cid=mem_copy. Accessed 2 October 2020.

Karen Marie Hansen

Figure 18: Karen Marie Hansen and Christen Anderson's wedding pictures. Public domain via FamilySearch.

Karen's granddaughter Annie Christensen Miller wrote a life sketch of Karen Marie Hansen that included her conversion experience:

"In the town of Stokkemarke, Maribo, on the island of Lolland, Denmark, Karen Marie Hansen was born on the 29th of September 1798. She was the daughter of Hans Bertelsen and Karen Henrichsen and was the oldest of seven children. . . .

"Though rather small in stature, Karen Marie was very rugged and wiry. She was a beautiful girl with large expressive deep blue eyes and dark hair and a rather high rounded forehead. Her lips and mouth denoted firmness and strength of character.

"She was married at the age of eighteen years to Christen Anderson of Blands, who was also a landowner and tiller of the soil. . . . She brought thirteen children into the world, but was called to part with six in early childhood. The remainder, however, grew to man and womanhood, married, and had large families and most of them lived to a ripe old age, past eighty years.

"In 1856 when the gospel message was brought to their village by the Mormon Elders, many people protested against a new creed coming into their midst. They, like their ancestors for many generations, had accepted the Lutheran faith, and now, why allow another religion to be presented to the members and especially that of the despised Mormons. The feeling of hatred was engendered and some persecution followed. Some of the Elders were tarred and feathered; others were flogged. Grandmother's standard of right was to protect the innocent from violence so long as their actions were upheld by the laws of that land and did not injure their fellow men. She therefore opened her door to the Mormon missionaries, gave them food and shelter and listened to their gospel message and the testimony they bore. She knew they had the truth, she believed what they said, but she did not know what attitude her husband would take towards the Elders when he found out they had been to their home and that she believed their message. She would wait and pray that the Lord would soften his heart and open his eyes that he might see the gospel as she saw it.

"In the meantime, one of her married sons had met the Elders and was investigating their doctrines and felt favorably impressed. This was a great comfort to grandmother. She often went to his home to converse on the principles of the gospel. They rejoiced together in the new light, which they had received, and were a strength to each other.

"As time went on, Karen became thoroughly convinced of the truthfulness of the gospel and had constantly prayed that her husband might also believe it. Later he did believe, but the gospel did not have so responsive appeal to his heart as it had to hers. No sacrifice was too great for her to make, the gospel was all to her, she was willing to live up to every requirement. Not so with her husband. He believed the gospel, understood that by humbly living its principles, a man could be uplifted and better able physically and mentally to retain the spirit of God and finally go into his presence, but he felt the sacrifice was too great for him to make. He had acquired habits in his youth that he thought he could not overcome, and he did not have sufficient faith in the Lord to ask for divine help in overcoming these habits.

"The Elders preached the Word of Wisdom to all investigators and made it very emphatic that none could be baptized unless they gave up the use of coffee, tobacco, and strong drinks.

"So when grandmother and two of her sons, one daughter, and a daughter-in-law were all baptized into the fold of Christ, grandfather stood aloof, lacking courage, feeling that the spirit was willing, but the flesh was weak. But he did not become embittered, nor did he oppose in any way, grandmother or her plans, for she and the members of her family that had joined the church worked to one end, that of getting ready to migrate to Utah. The way opened up to them just a few months after their baptism so that they had the means necessary for their immigration. As the time of parting came, grandmother had no regrets for the step she had taken. But the pull on her heartstrings was hard when she thought of leaving her husband, the father of her children, never to see his face again, and three sons and one daughter who would not accept her faith. She knew she was leaving dear ones, flesh of her flesh, friends of her youth, and friends of her mature years—the home of her youth, the home that her husband and she together had made, where their children were all born, where their happiest and their saddest days were spent. Now she was to leave all, but she was brave and bore up wonderfully.

Figure 19: Artist's re-envisioning of Karen and Christian. edisoncarerra/Fiverr

"She kissed her loved ones goodbye, placed her trust in the Lord, and turned her face westward to the land of Zion, where she would spend the remainder of her days with the people of God.

"They left their native shores on the 18th day of April 1857. Karen was in her 59th year. She knew they had a long, hard journey before them. They were on the water six weeks and one day and landed at Philadelphia. From there they went by rail to Florence where they joined a company of saints who were enroute to the Salt Lake Valley."[40]

---

[40] Miller, Annie Christensen. "Sketch of Karen Marie Hansen." *FamilySearch*, Intellectual Reserve, https://www.familysearch.org/photos/artifacts/3335590?cid=mem_copy. Accessed 2 October 2020.

Mads Christensen and Maren Johanne Jensen

Figure 20: Maren Christensen. Public domain via FamilySearch.

Maren Johanne Jensen Christensen was born 21 May 1827 to Jens Rassmussen and Adriene Marie Fabricuis at Sandbjerg, Lolland, Denmark. According to family history, Maren's mother, Adriene Marie, came from a family that had worked in universities and served as church reverends, but Adriene fell in love with a farmer and chose a very different life.[41]

Jens and Adriene were well-to-do and owned their own home and farm. Maren helped with taking the geese to pasture from a young age. As was the custom in Denmark, from age 7 to 14 Maren went to a school where she and the other students were taught mainly out of the Bible. They memorized a lot of scriptures.

Maren loved the outdoors and had a close relationship with her father.

"When as a child she came home from school, how she loved to go out into the field where her father was at work and tell him all that had happened while she was gone. He always listened attentively to all she said. . . . And when his day's work was done, how glad she was to go home hand in hand with him, tripping merrily along by his side."[42]

As she grew older, Maren helped her father a great deal on the farm. When he passed away, she was devastated. Within a few years, Maren's mother had to hire her out to other families. Starting at age 15, Maren would work for other households and be paid $15 to $20 plus room, clothes, and board for a whole year's work. She could come home only one Sunday per month. Maren's mother Adriene

---

[41] Miller, Annie C. "Sketch of My Mother, Maren Johanne Jensen Christensen," p. 92.
[42] Miller, Annie C. "Sketch of My Mother, Maren Johanne Jensen Christensen." *Short Life Sketches of Our Ancestors*, Ruth C. Ashby, 2002, p. 84. *FamilySearch*, https://www.familysearch.org/photos/artifacts/39847618?cid=mem_copy. Accessed 5 October 2020.

eventually remarried, and Maren came home for only a year. Though her new stepfather was kind, Maren felt that she was old enough and capable enough now that she needed to make her own way in the world.

Mads Christensen was born 24 March 1825 to Christen Andersen and Karen Marie Hansen, in Blands Maribo, Denmark, on the Isle of Laaland (now called Lolland). His parents were farmers who struggled sometimes. To keep the grain crop from being entirely spoiled in wet rainy seasons in Blands, the farmers would cut heads from the grain by hand, dry them as best they could, and thresh them. This was a poor method, but they needed the bread.

From age 7 to 14, when he was confirmed, Mads lived with his Aunt Anne and Uncle Christen Jorgensen Hovmand. They cared for him kindly and oversaw him getting a good education and religious training in the teachings of Martin Luther. A religious child, Mads firmly believed in the power of prayer. He prayed that he may live to see the Lord's power manifested on Earth as it had been in the days of the Savior.

Figure 21: Mads Christensen. Public domain via FamilySearch.

Upon completing his common schooling, Mads moved home to his parents and began to learn the craft of carpentry, starting with small projects and eventually becoming skillful at building homes and furniture. Mads built a home for his married brother and began one for himself. His mother encouraged him to finish it and get married, but Mads replied he didn't think he'd keep the property long anyway, as he had a feeling he was going far away. His mother was upset by this, but Mads did finish the house and Karen's fears subsided.

*Figure 22: Mads and Maren's house in Denmark.
Public domain via FamilySearch.*

Maren met Mads at a house party near her mother's house. They formed an attachment and eventually were married on 24 November 1854. They moved into Mads' new house together.

But just a few months after Mads and Maren were married, missionaries for The Church of Jesus Christ of Latter-day Saints arrived in the area. The doctrine they preached interested Mads immediately, as he felt it was a direct answer to his childhood prayers. Mads came to firmly believe in their message.

Despite the negativity of many of the local residents toward the missionaries, Mads embraced the gospel. Maren was more reluctant to embrace this new faith, as her family had been Lutheran for many generations. Still, she would feed the missionaries, and thought a great deal about the message they taught, though she said little. She was pregnant with her first child, and had been taught to pray when pregnant. She prayed to know the Lord's will. Mads also prayed—he prayed that they might embrace the gospel together.

One of their daughters later recorded this story from that era:

"As the days went on, persecution increased [against the Elders]. . . . One day a mob gathered, determined to flog one of the Elders. He ran to Mother's home, the mob following after. As he entered the door, he asked her to let him hid[e] somewhere. She was all alone, but she locked the outside door, took him to her wardrobe closet, opened the door, and after he had stepped inside she locked it and put the keys in her pocket. By this time the mob had surrounded her house. They knew they had no right to break in as the law would severely punish such an offense, so they kept trying to get her to open the door long enough for them to get the Elder; they told her they would not harm her, they only wanted him. She told them firmly and fearlessly that she would not open the door, that that was her home and they had no right to enter without her permission. They said they would bring an officer to compel her to. She deliberately and quietly told them that she respected the laws of her country and if the proper officer came she would unfasten the door to them, but she would not uphold mob violence or lawlessness. They stood around for some time talking among themselves, and finally when they found they could not frighten her into opening the door, they departed. After they had gone, the thought flashed to Mother's mind, "Have I smothered that man to death by fastening him in that tight place?" She hurriedly unlocked the door, and to her great delight he was not the worse for his close confinement, and was very grateful to her for the protection she had given him."[43]

After Maren's baby was born, she asked Mads when they should take him to the Lutheran church to be christened.

Mads replied, "Never."

Maren felt almost crushed by his answer.

Mads explained that the Latter-day Saints named and blessed their children in a different way.

Some weeks passed and Maren thought and prayed a great deal. One day to Mads' great joy, when he came home from work Maren told him she was ready to be baptized and accept the gospel.

On a cold 23 January 1857, ice was broken for the baptism of Mads and of Maren, who neither hesitated nor caught a cold.

Mads and Maren soon after left Denmark on 18 April 1857 with Mads' mother, Karen Marie Hansen, to join the Saints in America. Maren's mother wept and offered to care for Maren and her child in her own home if they would stay.

But Maren told her mother, "The Gospel that I have accepted means more to me than earthly possessions. I shall go with my husband and share the hardship that comes to us and trust in the Lord for protection."[44] [45]

---

[43] Miller, Annie C. "Sketch of My Mother," p. 83.
[44] Miller, Annie C. "Sketch of My Mother," p. 83.
[45] Christensen, Phillis. "Life Sketch of Mads Christensen." *Short Life Sketches of Our Ancestors*, Ruth C. Ashby, 2002, pp. 74–80. *FamilySearch*, https://www.familysearch.org/photos/artifacts/42728048?cid=mem_copy. Accessed 5 October 2020.

Jens Christensen Lamp and Trene Bendtsen

On 6 February 1822, Jens Christensen was born to Christian Lamp and Johanne Margrethe Jensdatter in what was called the hunter's house, in a forest at Ondense Amy Fyn, Denmark. His siblings were Hans, Peter, Christian, and Lena. Jens' father, Christian, had been born in an area of Prussia that was disputed between Denmark and Prussia. His family had moved to Denmark when he was about two, where they had grown up as Danish citizens. Jens and his siblings received their father's Prussian surname Lamp as a surname, but their Danish patronymic of Christiansen was included before Lamp.[46]

As an adult, Jens stood about 5'11 and weighed about 170 pounds. Jens worked as a coachman for a minister and served as a soldier in the Danish–German war in 1848–50. He had two children by other women prior to marrying Trene, and one of his sons lived with Jens' parents while he served in the military. Jens enjoyed good clean jokes and singing war songs.

Trene Benson Christensen was born in Tommerupe, Tårnby, Denmark, on 14 November 1836 to Bengt Neilsen and Martha Swenson. Her siblings were Seend, Thønnes, Niels, Marchen, Emma, and Peder Bendtsen. Her family, who lived in a thatched-roof home surrounded by a garden of vegetables and sweet-smelling flowers, made their living by farming and market gardening (relatively small-scale farming). Each day Trene picked peonies and sold them in the city.

Figure 23: Jens Christensen Lamp. Public domain via FamilySearch.

As an adult, Trene was about five feet tall—nearly a foot shorter than her husband—and weighed 140 lb. She was of medium complexion with gray eyes.

Trene and Jens met during the time when Jens was stationed with the army. They married 25 June 1856 when Jens was 34 and Trene was 19. The couple began their married life in the home where Trene had grown up; their first four children were born there. After marriage, Jens worked as a carpenter and a night watchman. They went on to have a total of ten children together; two died as infants but the rest survived to adulthood: Johanne (Hannah), Margrethe, Maratha (Martha), Emma, James, Joseph George, Petra Willardine, Eliza Brighamine, and Josephine Hansine.

---

[46] Rogers, Tamara C. "Christian Lamp." *FamilySearch*, Intellectual Reserve, 2 March 2019, https://www.familysearch.org/photos/artifacts/78248864?cid=mem_copy. Accessed 19 October 2020.

Their daughter Emma would become the mother of Violet, who was Alan's mother. Emma's oldest sister, Johanne, would become the second wife of Mads Christensen, Alan's great-grandfather.

Jens was a family man. He did not drink or use slang or profanity. Trene was a good housekeeper and took loving care of her garden. She was very sensitive and of a spiritual mind.

*Figure 24: Images of the Jens and Trene Christensen family.
Public domain via FamilySearch.*

When Trene and Jens' oldest child, Johanne, was about 10 years old, Trene's sister Marchen joined The Church of Jesus Christ of Latter-day Saints, and emigrated to Utah. Trene also believed in this new religion.

It would be five years before Jens came to also believe.

Emma was born during this time. Her parents decided to have her "sprinkled" as this was how little children were baptized in the faith of their parents. That night, however, Trene developed inflammatory rheumatism and was unable to get up from her bed. Jens attempted to find another woman to take her place at the sprinkling and failed. So, he declared Emma wouldn't be sprinkled. They joined The Church of Jesus Christ of Latter-day Saints shortly thereafter and had all their children blessed in the tradition of their new religion.

After Jens and Trene were baptized, missionaries taught at their home regularly, and Jens and Trene also hosted them for bi-weekly Tuesday evening prayer meetings. The family walked eight to ten miles to attend church, and traveled there and back on Fast Sunday without eating until after coming home. Trene, who loved to talk about the gospel, taught in one of Copenhagen's first Relief Society organizations.

Figure 25: Jens Christensen home in Clarkston. Public domain via FamilySearch.

The family decided to go to America and gather with the Saints in Zion. The older children went ahead first, and then Trene and Jens came with the youngest four in October of 1880. After living in Farmington, Utah for two years they moved on to Kanesville for a decade and then lived on a farm east of Clarkston, Utah.

Jens chewed tobacco for a time after he joined the Church, until one night when he dreamed that President Brigham Young came to him and rebuked him for using it. Jens said he saw the error of his ways and stopped using chewing tobacco.

In their later years, Trene and Jens adopted their granddaughter Clara, who was the child of their daughter Martha.

Jens, who sustained injuries from a runaway team of horses that he never recovered from, died in Clarkston 13 February 1890.

Trene died in Clarkston 13 May 1895. Both Jens and Trene are buried in the Clarkston cemetery.[47][48]

---

[47] "Jens Christensen." *FamilySearch*, Intellectual Reserve, 9 July 2013, https://www.familysearch.org/photos/artifacts/1661839?cid=mem_copy. Accessed 5 October 2020.

[48] Bunn, Celeste. "Trein Bendtsen." *FamilySearch*, Intellectual Reserve, 27 June 2013, https://www.familysearch.org/photos/artifacts/1508929?cid=mem_copy. Accessed 5 October 2020.

Cecil P. "Mike" Ruppe

Figure 26: Cecil P. "Mike" Ruppe and his horse Blaze. Image via FamilySearch.

Cecil Putnam "Mike" Ruppe was born in his Grandfather Brabb's log cabin in Ogallah, Kansas, on 16 October 1896, to John Boyer Ruppe and Ella Antonette Brabb.

Mike earned his childhood spending money by shooting rabbits and trading in the ears for five cents. He supplied his family with "stubble ducks" (prairie chickens) for them to eat.

Mike was a high school football player; his team never lost a game in two years. He served in the navy during World War I, spending most of his time, including during the pandemic years, on the battleship *North Dakota*. Most of his military service was served off the coast of the United States, and he apparently never saw conflict. Some of the happiest moments in his military service as recorded in his journals included the times his mother Ella mailed him some of her fried chicken from Kansas.[49]

After the war years, Mike became acquainted with Reva Simmons when she was working with his extended family on their homestead in Blue Mountain, Colorado.

Reva's first impression of Mike was less than favorable: "He smoked a dirty, old stinky pipe with Prince Albert tobacco. I didn't think much of him."

She dated his friend for a while, but eventually Mike won her over.

Before Reva left Blue Mountain, Mike visited Reva one morning. "I went into her tent one morning and talked to her, and she gave me the first kiss, so, you see, I knew then that she was my own if I could manage it."

He asked Reva if he could write to her, and she agreed, not knowing how interesting his letters would be.[50]

His family had not liked the Latter-day Saints, but Mike ended up marrying a girl of that faith. Mike and Reva were married in 1928, and they spent their honeymoon picking fruit in Oregon, California, and Idaho. Mike was baptized on 30 January 1932. Reva and Mike were sealed in the Salt Lake Temple on 9 June 1932.[51]

---

[49] Ruppe, Reva, et al. *Side by Side*, p. 30. Rexburg, Ricks College Press, 1994. *FamilySearch*, https://www.familysearch.org/photos/artifacts/32861979?cid=mem_copy. Accessed 19 October 2020.
[50] Ruppe, Reva, Janet Clark, and Brenda Sederberg. *Side by Side: The Life Story of Cecil Putman "Mike" Ruppe and Reva Marie Simmons Ruppe,* p. 37.
[51] Bunn, Celeste. "Cecil Putnam Ruppe." *FamilySearch*, Intellectual Reserve, 20 May 2013, https://www.familysearch.org/photos/artifacts/1081584?cid=mem_copy. Accessed 12 October 2020.

Leven Simmons Sr. and Harriet Bradford

Figure 27: Leven Simmons. Public domain via FamilySearch.

Figure 28: Harriet Bradford Simmons. Public domain via FamilySearch.

Leven Simmons was born 1 August 1812 to Samuel Simmons and Elizabeth Scott, in Meads County, Kentucky. His parents loved adventure and had helped establish the small settlement where they lived. Leven's father, Samuel, was killed in a runaway (horses) accident in early 1820. In 1833, Elizabeth Scott Simmons moved with her four sons to Illinois, where they remained for many years and three of the four sons married, including Leven.

Harriet Bradford was born 30 March 1821, in Jefferson County, Illinois, the oldest of five children of George Bradford and Sarah Hood Bradford. In her adult life, "Harriet was a small, thin, frail-looking little woman, but her looks were deceiving. She was as strong as an ox. She was resourceful, extremely industrious, and loved children, her own and anyone else's who were near. She had one name by which she referred to all children—'Sugar' or 'Little Sug.'"[52]

When Elizabeth Scott Simmons moved to Illinois from Kentucky, they settled near the Bradfords, and Leven and Harriet met. They married on 27 February 1836 in Hancock County, Illinois, and lived on a farm about twelve miles away from Nauvoo.[53] After learning of the Church, they became interested in it and were baptized by Stephen Markham. Leven was baptized on 24 June 1842, and Harriet was probably baptized at the same time.[54]

Harriet's two cousins Elizabeth Hood Atchison and Nancy Hood Caldwell were also baptized, but the rest of their family members were horrified that they joined.[55]

Harriet had a strong testimony that would sustain her through many upcoming trials.[56]

Leven and Harriet received their endowments in the Nauvoo Temple, and they were sealed after they arrived in Utah, on 4 December 1856, in the Salt Lake City Endowment House.[57]

---

[52] Olsen, Gary Lamar. "Life History of Harriet Bradford Simmons." *FamilySearch*, Intellectual Reserve, 7 January 2018, https://www.familysearch.org/photos/artifacts/46276814?cid=mem_copy. Accessed 3 December 2020.

[53] Olsen.

[54] Simmons Jr., Benjamin Franklin. *Biography of Levan Simmons and Wives Harriet Bradford and Lydia Rebecca Fisher*, p. 1. *FamilySearch*, https://www.familysearch.org/photos/artifacts/32269379?cid=mem_copy. Accessed 5 October 2020.

[55] Olsen.

[56] Olsen.

[57] Simmons Jr.

Charity Lowe & John Lowe Butler I[58] and Caroline Farozine Skeen

Figure 30: John Lowe Butler (purported). Public domain via FamilySearch.

Figure 29: Caroline Farozine Skeen. Public domain via FamilySearch.

Charity Lowe, mother of John Lowe Butler, was born 13 January 1782 in Surry, North Carolina, to William Lowe and Margaret Farr. She married James Butler in 1802 in a ceremony performed by Charity's father, William Lowe.

Family legend says that Charity's husband James Butler was a frontiersman and also probably a blacksmith, who was a friend of Daniel Boone. He held Daniel Boone in such high esteem that he took the steel straps from one of Boone's pack saddles and melted them down to make fire tongs, which were passed down through generation; descendant Ross E. Butler wrote about owning them.[59]

Charity and John had fourteen children, ten of whom lived to adulthood. James and Charity raised their family in the Methodist faith.

James taught his sons the blacksmith trade, but due to childhood illness his son John Lowe Butler was better suited to studying books (though John did also learn blacksmithing and ended up using that skill quite a bit as an adult). John questioned the Methodists' teaching and considered joining the Baptists. His father, concerned, went to the lengths of getting a Methodist minister to baptize John by immersion. But John got teased for being different and ended up joining the Baptists.

---

[58] There is some debate as to whether John lived to have a photograph taken of him. This purported image of John Lowe Butler is found in Tueller, Margaret. *Your Simmons Lybbert Family Tree*. FamilySearch, 2016. *FamilySearch*, https://www.familysearch.org/photos/artifacts/24310561?cid=mem_copy. Accessed 5 October 2020.

[59] Butler, Elder Ross E. "Charity Lowe Butler." *FamilySearch*, Intellectual Reserve, 24 September 2013, https://www.familysearch.org/photos/artifacts/2654806?cid=mem_copy. Accessed 5 October 2020.

John worked as a teacher as a young adult, and he married a woman from across the river who lived on a plantation in Tennessee: Caroline Farozine Skeen.

After the death of James Butler in 1835, missionaries for The Church of Jesus Christ of Latter-day Saints taught in the area.

John and Caroline joined the Church in 1835.

Charity confronted John: "You were not satisfied with the Methodist, and you joined the Baptists; you were not satisfied with the Baptists, and so now you join the Mormons; now what will you do next?"

Just a few weeks later, Charity heard the missionaries preaching at the home of her brother, John Lowe, who was something like a justice of the peace in Simpson County. John Lowe was esteemed by the community, had a strong sense of fairness and honor, and could be very clever about promoting law and order among the sometimes wild-and-rough people of Kentucky. John Lowe did not join the Church, but he protected the reputation and safety of his family members who did.

When Charity heard the missionaries teaching, she felt strongly that what they were teaching was true. The missionaries left before she could be baptized and she wept to have missed her opportunity. But then the missionaries returned and both Charity Lowe Butler and Charity Skeen, sister of John's wife, Caroline, were baptized.

In the spring of 1836, John and Caroline moved from Kentucky to Clay County, Missouri, by ox team, joined by John's mother, Charity, his younger brothers, and his younger sister. In Missouri, they joined the gathering of the Saints. Charity would have been about 56 years of age at this time. In Nauvoo, Caroline lived in her own home, on the north end of town. She and daughter-in-law Caroline both joined the Nauvoo Relief Society. Her sons John Lowe, Edmund Ray, James Morgan, and Lorenzo Dow looked after their mother. Lucy Ann soon left home, marrying Reuben Allred. During the Nauvoo period, Lorenzo was called on a mission to England.

Charity began the migration west with her family, but passed away in North Pigeon Creek, Iowa, in 1851 during a period when the extended Butler family was living there prior to crossing the plains to Utah.[60]

---

[60] Tueller, Margaret. *Your Simmons Lybbert Family Tree*. FamilySearch, 2016. *FamilySearch*, https://www.familysearch.org/photos/artifacts/24310561?cid=mem_copy. Accessed 5 October 2020.

Royal Durfey and Lydia Abell

On 16 March 1811, Royal Durfey was born to Jedediah Durfey (also spelled Durfee) and Lydia Dean in North Crosby, Johnstown, Leeds, Upper Canada. Royal grew up in Upper Canada, in what is today Ontario.

Three days later, on 19 March 1811, Lydia Abel was born to William Roberts Abell and Louise Merry in North Crosby, Leeds, Ontario, Canada.

In about 1833 Royal Durfey and Lydia Abel married. On 28 June 1834, their first child, Olive Durfey (who would later marry Kenion Taylor Butler and who would be Janet's great-great-grandma), was born in North Crosby, Upper Canada. Just two years later, in July 1835, Royal and Lydia converted to The Church of Jesus Christ of Latter-day Saints.

Sometime after the birth of second daughter Emma Durfey, on 22 August 1836, the family moved to New York, where third daughter Sarah Durfey was born 13 August 1838.

The family moved to the Nauvoo area at some point between the birth of Sarah and the birth of their son, Alma Durfey, who was born 8 February 1844 in Montrose, Lee, Iowa. The family stories do not record whether they lived in Winter Quarters before crossing the plains.[61] [62]

Royal would pass away in 1878 in Salem City, Utah, and Lydia would pass away in 1879 in Salem City, Utah.

Figure 31: Royal Durfey and Lydia Abell. Public domain via FamilySearch.

---

[61] Davis McQuivey, Dorene. "Royal Durfey 1811 - 1879 Family records and Salem Springs Compiled by Dorene Davis McQuivey GG Granddaughter." *FamilySearch*, Intellectual Reserve, 4 April 2014, https://www.familysearch.org/photos/artifacts/6295317?cid=mem_copy. Accessed 5 October 2020.
[62] Tueller.

Ebenezer Bryce

Figure 32: Ebenezer Bryce. Public domain via FamilySearch.

In Dunblane, Perthshire, Scotland, Ebenezer Bryce was born on 17 November 1830, to Andrew Bryce and Janet Adams, the third consecutive son and third child of their eight children. The name "Ebenezer" also belonged to his father's older brother, who died as a young man. At about eighteen months old, Ebenezer with his family relocated to Tullibody, Clackmannanshire, where his parents had five daughters. Only four of Andrew and Janet's children lived to maturity (two sons and two daughters). Ebenezer's sister Margaret would eventually move to America and live in Massachusetts, where she was married to Peter Wright.

Ebenezer began working at the shipyards at age ten, becoming an apprentice at age 15. When Ebenezer was about 17, in the spring of 1848, he became interested in The Church of Jesus Christ of Latter-day Saints, but neither his father nor his family and friends were supportive of his new religious interests. His father would attempt to prevent him from attending meetings by locking up his clothes. Despite this, Ebenezer was baptized that April and determined to emigrate to Utah.

"His father followed him on board a ship to persuade him not to go. But he was still intent on going, so his father took his hand and said if he would promise to be responsible for his own sins he could go. Ebenezer agreed and his father returned home. They never saw each other again."[63]

Ebenezer arrived in New Orleans on board the *Erin's Queen* from Liverpool with 232 souls, as a member of the John Sharp Company, in October 1848. Ebenezer worked his way from New Orleans to St. Louis (earning the $2.50 river fare), and also worked in Paducah, Kentucky. In St. Louis, where he did carpentry and lived at a boarding house, one evening he went to town with some of the other men. They returned to find that their landlady had died of cholera.

Also in St. Louis, Ebenezer was ordained a member of the 31st Quorum of the Seventy, on 27 February 1849. His membership in this quorum would continue while in the Salt Lake Valley.[64]

---

[63] Bryce, Wendell A. "EBENEZER BRYCE." *FamilySearch*, Intellectual Reserve, 13 January 2015, https://www.familysearch.org/photos/artifacts/12688101?cid=mem_copy. Accessed 5 October 2020.
[64] Bryce.

Figure 33: David Park. Public domain via FamilySearch.

Figure 34: Ann Brooks. Public domain via FamilySearch.

David Park and Ann Brooks

David Park was born 12 June 1809 in Cambuslang, Lanarkshire, Scotland, to James Park and Marion Allen.

Ann Brooks was born 3 May 1811 in Cambuslang, Lanarkshire, Scotland, to James Brooks and Barbara Newbigging.

David and Ann married in March 1830 and immigrated to Canada with four of David's brothers.

Three of the Parks brothers, including David, joined The Church of Jesus Christ of Latter-day Saints sometime between 1843–45, converted by Elder John Borrowman, who later married David's niece Agnes Park. A small branch established near Warick was attended by many families in the extended Park clan, the extended Gardner family, John Borrowman's family, and a few other families as well.

During the winter of 1845–46, John A. Smith visited their branch to inform them the Saints were being driven from Nauvoo and told them that if the members of the branch wanted to travel with the Saints to the Rocky Mountains, there was no time to lose.

The fifteen families of the branch went to work disposing of their property as best they could for the 1,500-mile journey to Nauvoo, in some cases selling at a loss. In March 1846 they left Canada.

Figure 35: David Park. Public domain via FamilySearch.

A close friend of the Parks family had a narrow escape, and the Parks and others helped transport his family and belongings after he left. Archibald Gardner sold his mills for twenty cents on the dollar. His business partners did not want him to leave and swore out a warrant for his arrest to attempt to keep him in town. Archibald, who felt he'd done no wrong, left town at night, chased by a posse, and crossed a half-frozen mile-wide St. Clair River into the United States. From there he traveled alone to Nauvoo.

David and Ann and their family traveled with some of David's brothers, leaving within a week of Archibald's departure and traveling by ox team.

They made a new road when leaving the area—trimming miles off their route. The road became known as the "Nauvoo Road," connecting two main county roads near northwestern Alvinston.

John Gardner, Jr. accompanied the Parks families to the St. Clair River to help them cross. The posse that had chased Archibald came to attack these teams to attempt to gain Archibald's property, but no one in the group would tell them which wagon belonged to Archibald. Robert talked with them, and learned they "were working at a big scare, and they thought they had done it. They said they would go and get out papers for me to sign and when I signed them, they would let the teams go. I told them I would look at their papers after they got them. While they were gone . . . some of the men and boys of the town . . . threw down the fence where our teams and wagons were corralled and told us to drive out. . . . I got [Archibald's] team first on the boat . . . and the rest of the Company soon followed."[65]

The group of Saints that included the Parks and the Gardners became known as the Canadian Company, a name that would stay with them all the way to Utah.

They traveled in small groups until they were a few days out of Nauvoo. There they gathered and on 6 April 1846 arrived in Nauvoo, where they found many vacant homes available.

"We could have brick, frame, log or stone houses without cost. The Saints had nearly all left who were able to go, and their homes were standing empty and unsold. They had been driven out and what could not readily be disposed of was left behind. Some had furniture in—chairs, bedsteads, etc. Here for three weeks we fitted up outfits and secured supplies, which included flour, parched corn, cornmeal and seed for planting, then started west in companies of ten wagons to the company."[66]

John Goulding, Sr.

John Goulding Sr., Janet's fourth great-grandfather on her mother's side, was baptized in 1840 by Parley P. Pratt in England. He was a coal miner as were other generations of his family. Five years after John's baptism, his grandson Daniel heard the missionaries and joined the Church as well at age 14.

---

[65] Egbert, Martin W. "PARKS, David and Ann Brooks (compiled by Martin W. Egbert, 3rd Great Grandson)." *FamilySearch*, Intellectual Reserve, 2013, https://www.familysearch.org/photos/artifacts/3522451?cid=mem_copy. Accessed 5 October 2020.

[66] Egbert.

Daniel's parents were not pleased with this decision, so Daniel lived with grandparents John and Sarah Baylis Goulding until after Sarah passed away. At that time, accounts are mixed as to whether Daniel and his grandfather went to live with Daniel's other set of grandparents[67] or to live with Daniel's parents.[68] [69]

Daniel Goulding and Elizabeth Merrifield Pratten

Daniel Goulding was born 31 March 1831 in Winterbourne Down, Gloucestershire, England, to John Goulding, Jr. and Rosanna Bray. The Goulding family had been working as colliers (miners) in coal mines for at least a few generations. Starting at age six, Daniel went into the mines and worked next to his father.[70]

In Westerleigh, Gloucestershire, England, extensive coal works were carried on under the direction of the lords of the manor. The small coal harvested from this mine entirely wastes and leaves no cinder.[71]

Daniel heard the missionaries when he was 14 years old, and converted to The Church of Jesus Christ of Latter-day Saints. He was baptized in 1845, which displeased his parents so much that he went to live with his grandparents.

At the age of 17, Daniel was made the presiding elder of the Wintersburn Branch, and served there until his marriage at the age of 19 to Elizabeth Merrifield Pratten.[72]

Figure 36: Daniel Goulding and Elizabeth Merrifield Pratten.
Public domain via FamilySearch.

---

[67] LeAnne Clark Bunn has pointed out that records place Sarah's death at the time when Daniel would have been six years old. So, some part of that story has probably not been handed down accurately.
[68] Monson, Harold. "Daniel Goulding - Stalwart Mormon Pioneer." *FamilySearch*, Intellectual Reserve, 4 November 2014, https://www.familysearch.org/photos/artifacts/11352704?cid=mem_copy. Accessed 23 September 2020.
[69] "GOULDING, Daniel and PRATTEN, Elizabeth Merrifield." *FamilySearch*, Intellectual Reserve, 30 December 2013, https://www.familysearch.org/photos/artifacts/4192428?cid=mem_copy. Accessed 5 October 2020.
[70] "A Few Tidbits of Daniel's Life." *FamilySearch*, Intellectual Reserve, https://www.familysearch.org/photos/artifacts/47118511?cid=mem_copy. Accessed 24 October 2020.
[71] "Goulding, John Sr by James A Goulding." *FamilySearch*, Intellectual Reserve, https://www.familysearch.org/photos/artifacts/87113575?cid=mem_copy. Accessed 24 October 2020.
[72] Farnsworth, Mint. "History of John Goulding Sr. & Daniel Goulding as Told to Mint Farnsworth by James A. Goulding." *FamilySearch*, Intellectual Reserve, https://www.familysearch.org/photos/artifacts/108653189?cid=mem_copy. Accessed 24 October 2020.

Figure 37: Elizabeth's mother, Diana Merrifield Pratten. Public domain via FamilySearch.

Elizabeth Merrifield Pratten was born 16 May 1832 in High Littleton, Somerset, England, to Thomas Pratten and **Dinah/Diana Merrifield**. Elizabeth's father died when she was 15.

As an adult, Elizabeth was a small, dainty woman.

Her granddaughter-in-law Sofe recalls: "Until she was about 60 years old she wore a size 3 shoe. Her hair was so dark it was almost black and I remember her beautiful dark brown eyes."[73]

When Elizabeth heard the missionaries, her heart was touched, so she was baptized. Her sister Fanny would later be baptized, too.[74]

Daniel and Elizabeth met at the local Church branch and were married 19 February 1851, when he was 19 and she was 18. Elizabeth worked in the home of Daniel's parents, who did not like the Church and also may not have looked kindly on a household employee marrying their son, so Daniel and Elizabeth kept their wedding a secret for a time.

Daniel and Elizabeth created a home together that was often visited by the missionaries.

A family story is told that one elder told Elizabeth: "Sister Goulding, I promise you in the name of the Lord, if you never waste anything you will never want."

As the story concludes: "This wonderful promise was literally fulfilled, for while life was never easy, neither did she have to go hungry."[75]

In 1853–54, after the birth of their first child, Daniel and Elizabeth sailed to Australia, which was then a popular destination for settlers who wanted to build wealth by working in the gold mines. They sailed with Elizabeth's brother Elijah Pratten, and he paid their way. The difficult sea journey lasted several weeks.[76] In Australia, Daniel and Elizabeth thought they might earn money to take to Utah. It took them eight years to earn enough to travel to California. Daniel and Elizabeth settled in New South Wales, and Daniel, who had prior mining experience, found work in the mines. The family moved to Tarago sometime between 1859 and 1861, where they founded a branch of the Church. Here, once again, Daniel presided over the local Church.[77]

---

[73] Johnson, Sofe Wasden. "Physical traits as told by grand-daughter in-law, Sofe Wasden Johnson." *FamilySearch*, Intellectual Reserve, https://www.familysearch.org/photos/artifacts/41787505?cid=mem_copy. Accessed 5 October 2020.

[74] Johnson, Zina E. Goulding. "Fanny Pratten Goulding (written by her daughter Zina E. Goulding Johnson when Fanny was 81 years old.)" *FamilySearch*, Intellectual Reserve, https://www.familysearch.org/photos/artifacts/72131151?cid=mem_copy. Accessed 19 October 2020.

[75] Bunn, Celeste. "Elizabeth Merrifield Pratten." *FamilySearch*, Intellectual Reserve, 25 June 2013, https://www.familysearch.org/photos/artifacts/1487305?cid=mem_copy. Accessed 5 October 2020.

[76] Clark, Janet Lee Ruppe. "Goulding," *The Jim & Janey Simmons Story*, p. 14.

[77] Farnsworth.

Both of Daniel's parents passed away back in England while Daniel and his family lived in Australia. A couple years later when Daniel and Elizabeth's next child was born, they named her Rosanna Susannah. "Rosanna" had been the first name of Daniel's mother.[78] "Susannah" was the name of a sister of Elizabeth's who had passed away. Rosanna Susannah Goulding is a great-grandmother of Janet Ruppe Clark. Daniel and Elizabeth had six babies while living in Australia, three of whom would survive to settle in Utah with them. In 1868, their family set sail for America, crossing the Pacific and arriving in California, where they would stay for a few years before continuing onward to Nevada and then Utah.

These are the stories of how the ancestors of Alan and Janet found and joined the Church. Most of them were baptized during the earliest days of the Church, and became pioneers who would gather to be with the Saints. In the next chapters, we'll see where these ancestors lived and stories of what they were doing during subsequent early Church history.

---

[78] "Daniel Goulding Timeline." *FamilySearch*, Intellectual Reserve, https://www.familysearch.org/tree/person/timeline/KWN2-ZKM. Accessed 24 October 2020.

4. The Gathered Saints

Figure 38: The Kirtland Temple
© James Dalrymple/Shutterstock

Kirtland, Lake County, Ohio (Headquarters of the Church, 1831–1837)

Kirtland, Ohio, was one of the first gathering places for the Saints of the new religion founded by Joseph Smith.

In those early first days, the Church was called "The Church of Christ." It would have a few other names before the leadership settled on "The Church of Jesus Christ of Latter-day Saints."

Outsiders of the religion called the members "Mormons," and at times, members called themselves that as well. This name came about as a nickname based on the Book of Mormon.

Kirtland was the site of the Church's first temple, and several significant events in early Church history took place there. Joseph Smith sent out a call asking converts to the Church to gather together, and Kirtland became the earliest gathering destination for many new Saints.

Alan's ancestor Alfred Randall and his wife Emmerette Louise Davis didn't have to travel far to join the saints in Kirtland, as they already lived in the area.

Alfred Randall and Emmerette Louise Davis in Kirtland

Figure 39: Alfred and Emmerette. Public domain via FamilySearch.

Emmerette met Alfred when she was a teenager and he was a young man. Alfred's parents had moved their family to the Kirtland area in about 1820, when he was nine. Emmerette's family lived in the area as well.

Alfred and Emmerette married on 8 January 1834 in Munson, Ohio.[79] Alfred was 22 and Emmerette was 15 at the time of their marriage.

The Kirtland Temple, dedicated 27 March 1836, was built on land Alfred had helped to clear as a young person after his parents moved their family to Kirtland.

Alfred had not yet become a member of the Church when the temple was built. He was baptized on 12 May 1840 by Orson Hyde.

Independence, Jackson County, Missouri

In 1831, members of the Latter-day Saint movement began settling in the area of Jackson County, Missouri. Joseph Smith designated a spot near Courthouse Square as a temple of the New Jerusalem, in anticipation of Christ's Second Coming.

The peace that the Saints hoped to find in the area did not last long, as tension grew with the local citizens of Missouri. Things escalated to the point that the Saints evacuated the area in 1833. Conflict continued to build between the Saints and the other citizenry until things escalated into the 1838 Mormon War.

Over the succeeding decades, multiple splinter groups, which had broken away from the mainstream Latter-day Saint movement, returned to Independence, including the Community of Christ (initially known as the Reorganized Church of Jesus Christ of Latter Day Saints), the Church of Christ (Temple Lot), The Church of Jesus Christ (Cutlerite), and the Restoration Branches.[80]

---

[79] "Emmerette Louisa Davis." *FamilySearch*, Intellectual Reserve, https://www.familysearch.org/tree/person/memories/KWJB-JNS. Accessed 26 October 2020.
[80] "Independence, Missouri." *Wikipedia.* https://en.wikipedia.org/wiki/Independence,_Missouri

Timothy Baldwin Clark and Polly Keeler in Independence

In September 1835, the Timothy Baldwin and Polly Keeler Clark family joined the Latter-day Saint Church and moved to join the Saints in Independence, Missouri.

Here, they encountered a very different version of neighborhood than what they had seen in Ohio. In Ohio, friendly neighbors joined with settlers in the construction of a log cabin, with no payment for help offered or expected other than whiskey on hand for the men to drink. New settlers who had received such help were later expected to pay the favor forward to others.[81] However, in Missouri, neighborhood meant drunken behavior, Sabbath breaking, swearing, and general irreligious conduct.[82]

John and Caroline Butler Family Moves to Missouri

Caroline Skeen grew up on a Tennessee plantation in a slave-owning family. Caroline never combed her own hair until after she was married, because an enslaved Black woman did it for her. Despite this sheltered upbringing, she later resourcefully survived in the more primitive environments of the Mirabile Settlement and Nauvoo, the Emmett Expedition, and pioneer life in wagons and settlements.

The father of the Skeen family, Jesse, had given John and Caroline two slaves as a wedding present; John did not believe in slavery and freed them within just a day or so. This led to a rift between John and Jesse. Jesse was a man with a temper that he didn't always manage well. He disliked John and Caroline's choice of new religion so much that he actively spread negative stories about them. The aggression of Jesse and some of the other local men got so bad that John's maternal uncle, John Lowe, a justice of the peace, stepped in and intervened multiple times.

Figure 40: Purported image of John Lowe Butler and portrait of Caroline Farozine Skeen. Public domain via FamilySearch.

John recalled of his uncle: "The Judge was a first rate good man. He did not believe in Mormonism but he believed in folks having their rights."[83]

This good uncle used the leverage of his position, and threatened to levy heavy fines on any who had harassed John and the other Mormons and did not apologize for their actions and right their wrongs. The mischief-makers respected John Lowe enough that they acknowledged their wrongdoings, and would always make things right. On one occasion, John Lowe required Jesse to sign an admission that stories he had been spreading about John, Caroline, and their new religion were untrue; on another occasion John Lowe rode out to confront a man who had thrown rocks at John Lowe Butler and a fellow Saint and retrieved an expression of remorse from him.

---

[81] Clark, A. Charles. *Timothy Baldwin Clark*, pp. 102–103.
[82] Ibid., pp. 237–238.
[83] Hartley, William G. *My Best for the Kingdom*, p. 386. C. L. Dalton Enterprises, 1993.

When Jesse caught wind of the idea that John and Caroline may be leaving the area and going to join the Saints, he sent word three times that if John decided to go, Jesse would shoot him.

John wrote back that he had a good rifle and could shoot as good as Jesse could and that if Jesse came to his house when he was going to leave or before, John would shoot Jesse first if he could.

John Lowe once again intervened for the family's wellbeing.

He showed up at the Butler home when young Keziah was about a month old and the family was just a day or two away from leaving.

"Caroline, bring me John's rifle quick, there is a flock of turkeys and I want to kill one," he said, promising to bring it back directly.

When John returned, he asked "Where is my rifle?"

Caroline told him that Uncle John Lowe had borrowed it to shoot turkeys.

John said, "Suppose the old man should come to kill me. I should have no weapon to defend myself with at all and that will be a good go."

"But," said Caroline, "Do you think he will come?"

"I cannot tell," said John.

The family eventually left their home, starting out on their move without the rifle. The road led past Uncle John's.

Uncle John Lowe came out to tell the family goodbye, rifle in hand. He handed it to John, who saw it was still loaded.

John Lowe explained he had only wanted to get it out of John's possession and into his own. "For John, I should not like to see you kill the old man."[84]

John Lowe Butler and Jesse Skeen both survived John leaving town with his family, thanks to the wise uncle.

John and his family moved to Northern Missouri, where they initially settled in the Mirabile Settlement.

The Clarks in Far West, Caldwell County, Missouri

Far West was founded in 1836 by W.W. Phelps and John Whitmer.

Morris Phelps along with his wife, Laura Clark Phelps (sister of Ezra T.), bought a farm just outside of Far West in the summer of 1837. Trouble in the area was brewing.

One day, Joseph Smith and his brother came running and Laura hid them in her house, behind the clothes curtain.

The mob was soon after them.

Their leader said, "Where are they? We know they are here; we saw them come."

Laura answered calmly, "No, gentlemen, they are not here, but you are welcome to look all you want to."

She tried to appear neutral as the mob hastily searched her home.

After they left, Joseph emerged from the hiding place and commented, "Sister Laura, there are black lies and white lies and that certainly was a white one that came from your lips."[85]

---

[84] Hartley, pp. 386–387.
[85] Phelps, Morris Calvin. "Laura Clark Phelps History - by Morris Calvin Phelps." *FamilySearch*, Intellectual Reserve, https://www.familysearch.org/tree/person/memories/KWJB-M16. Accessed 3 October 2020.

On 18 August 1836, Timothy Baldwin Clark purchased land in Caldwell County. On October 11, Timothy claimed 40 additional acres in Mirabile Township.[86] The extended Clark family were major land holders in Caldwell County. Timothy, his sons, and his sons-in-law owned a cumulative total of about 600 acres.[87]

As of 1838, Timothy was designated as a priesthood holder, so he was ordained in that year or a previous year. He served in the Teachers Quorum and was called "Father Clark" in Missouri. He was acting president of the Teachers' Quorum at the Second Quarterly Conference held on 6 July 1838, two days following the cornerstones of the Far West Temple Site, at which he may also have been a participant.[88]

Tensions escalated between the Saints and the Missourians during the time the Clarks lived there. On 27 October, Governor Boggs responded to reports of "Mormon Depredations" with orders that members of the Church be "exterminated or driven from the state." The ongoing conflicts eventually culminated in a militia of approximately 3,500 led by Maj. Gen. Samuel D. Lucas assaulting the Saints, destroying animals, stealing property, and generally wreaking havoc. Among the properties targeted by the militia was the Clark farm. Timothy and his sons were imprisoned.

Timothy later gave the following affidavit to an Iowa justice of the peace 7 January 1840:

"This is to certify that I was at work on my farm on the last of October, 1838, when an armed company under General Lucas, came and took myself and my three sons prisoners, and threw down my fences, opened my gates, and left them open, and left my crops to be destroyed, and while I was prisoner, they declared that they had made clean work in destroying the crops as they passed through the country, and took from me two yoke of oxen, and three horses and two wagons, and compelled me and my sons to drive them loaded with produce of my own farm, to supply their army.

"I had in possession at the time, four hundred and eighty acres of land, and rising of a hundred acres improved, with a small orchard and nursery, the necessary buildings of a farm, etc.; and in consequence of my imprisonment my fences remained down, and most of my crops were destroyed; and further this deponent saith not."[89]

The W.W. Phelps / Clark Connection

"Phelps" is a famous last name in early Church history. W.W. Phelps was a prominent early Church leader and author of several hymns, including "Gently Raise the Sacred Strain," "Now Let Us Rejoice," "Praise to the Man," and "The Spirit of God Like a Fire is Burning."

W.W. Phelps was a distant cousin of Morris Phelps (Laura Clark Phelps' husband), and also a distant relative of Alan's in various ways, none very close.

In an interesting twist, however, W.W. Phelps is Janet's second cousin four times removed through her father's line, though he was the first of his direct ancestry to join the Church.

---

[86] Clark, A. Charles. *Timothy Baldwin Clark*, p. 240.
[87] Ibid., p. 246.
[88] Ibid., pp. 251–252.
[89] Ibid., pp. 255–259.

Figure 41: Three dollar note from the Kirtland Safety Society.
© Everett Collection/Shutterstock

Kirtland Safety Society

In 1837, Joseph Smith and Sidney Rigdon set up the Kirtland Safety Society, which operated like a bank. It was a time of economic turmoil, and within a year the Safety Society failed.

Alfred Randall was not yet a member of the Church at that time, so he probably did not participate as a member of the Safety Society, but Joseph Smith did later give him a unique memento from the venture.

Alfred had among his possessions a three-dollar note from the Kirtland Safety Society.

Writing on the back said: "This was given to Alfred Randall, by Joseph Smith. He said that if he would keep this he would never be broke."[90]

A Daring Rescue by Laura Clark Phelps

Laura Clark Phelps[91] was the daughter of Timothy Baldwin Clark and older sister to Ezra T. Clark. She was first in her family to be baptized in the Church, and though she had a relatively short life, she was a very brave woman.

One of the most powerful stories we have from her life is the tale of how she rescued her husband (Morris C. Phelps), King Follet, and Parley P. Pratt from jail after they had been imprisoned for several months.

---

[90] "Kirtland Safety Society Three Dollar Note." *FamilySearch*, Intellectual Reserve, https://www.familysearch.org/tree/person/memories/KWNN-5FW. Accessed 26 October 2020.
[91] Laura Phelps is not a direct ancestor, but she was a favorite extended family member of Brenda Clark Sederberg. Laura's stories are included here for the benefit of Brenda's grandchildren who would like to know some of the family history stories that their grandma particularly found heroic.

*Figure 42: C. C. A. Christensen, The Battle of Crooked River.
Public domain via Wikimedia Commons*

Here is the tale of how that came to happen.

As tensions rose between the Saints and their opponents, a series of conflicts came up.

In October 1838, at the Battle of Crooked River, the Saints faced off against a combination of the militia and the mob. Many church leaders were taken prisoner, among them Joseph Smith, his brother Hyrum, Parley P. Pratt, Morris C. Phelps, and Timothy B. Clark.[92]

Timothy B. Clark was shortly after released, but the others were held for a much longer time.

---

[92] Phelps.

*Figure 43: C. C. A. Christensen, The Arrest of Mormon Leaders.
Public domain via Wikimedia Commons*

When the mob came to Morris and Laura Phelps' yard, they shot the animals. When Laura's daughter Harriet tried to protect her pet pig, the mob was going to shoot the girl. Laura came to the defense of her daughter, saying, "Shoot all the animals you desire but leave my little girl alone."

During this battle, Brigadier General Doniphan was ordered to shoot Joseph Smith and the other leaders. He refused and instead the prisoners were taken to Ray County and jailed at Richmond. There, the men were bound with irons and treated harshly.

One night, the men couldn't sleep due to the guards' loud, shocking language. The Prophet stood, and Morris later recalled the words he spoke as being close to the following:

"Silence, ye fiends of the infernal pit, in the name of Jesus Christ I rebuke you, and command you to be still. I will not live another minute and hear such language. Cease such talk, or you or I will die this instant!"

The guards begged his pardon and quieted down for the night.

Figure 44: C. C. A. Christensen, Liberty Jail.
Public domain via Wikimedia Commons

Joseph, Hyrum, and some of the others were moved to Liberty Jail, but Parley P. Pratt, Morris Phelps, and others continued to be held in Richmond Jail, where they dealt with hardships for six months. Laura came to visit Morris and hoped they would release him. But she had to leave finally because Governor Boggs had expelled the Saints from Missouri and she needed to move her family. She relocated them to a location seven miles west of Montrose, Iowa, where she settled near her father, Timothy Baldwin Clark.

On 4 February 1839, Laura received a patriarchal blessing from Joseph Smith, Sr., in which he commended her for her integrity.

On 27 February 1839, Laura's mother, Polly Keeler Clark, passed away. Her last words were: "O, do not weep for me. I sure am going home; I am going home."[93]

Laura's new house in Montrose had formerly been used to stable horses. The family cleaned it thoroughly, whitewashed it, and made it a home.

Meanwhile, while Morris was tried in court, he was told that if he would denounce the Mormon Bible, he would be set free. He refused, and was kept in captivity.

Morris wrote a letter to Laura calling her to his star. She decided to go to him and be there to support him during his trial. She rode about 150 miles through hostile Missouri with her younger brother John Clark. When they arrived at the jail, both Morris and Parley P. Pratt were sick and in despair after eight long months of confinement. Orson Pratt had also come to support them. Since no one appeared

---

[93] Clark, A. Charles. *Timothy Baldwin Clark*, p. 263.

Figure 45: Orson Pratt. Public domain via Wikicommons.

against the prisoners in court, their case was continued again, and they were returned to jail, where the jailer and his wife said several of their prisoners had died of old age as their cases continued indefinitely.

Faced with this difficult situation, a dream of a way to escape came to both Parley P. Pratt and to Laura Clark Phelps.

The group decided to act on it.

John Wesley Clark (more commonly known by his middle name of Wesley) and Orson Pratt left the jail, taking Laura's horse with them, and seemed to head for home, explaining to the jailer that Laura wished to stay and be with her husband for longer.

Actually, John and Orson were taking the horse for Brother King Follet. John had instructed Laura not to touch the prisoners or assist in any way.

When the jailer opened the door to bring the evening meal, King Follet seized the door. Parley and Morris escaped, reaching the bottom of the stairs to the kitchen—through which they must pass in order to escape. King Follet and Parley reached the outdoors, but Morris was caught by the jailer and his wife, who called out loudly, alarming the town.

Laura believed she was praying silently, but her husband later said she shouted, "Oh Lord God of Abraham, Isaac, and Jacob, deliver thy servant!"

Morris felt as strong as a giant when he heard these words, and pushed the jailer and his wife off his chest, and got away.

The enemy had captured King Follet. Morris was spent, and John helped him onto his horse. The group separated and got away.

Orson and John made the journey to Quincy on foot. Parley went by foot, and then by horse, then by foot again. With no food, he was greatly weakened by the time he reached safety.

Morris, for his part, had gone but a few miles and had lost his hat when he was surrounded by horsemen in pursuit of him. He was in sad shape.

The men cried out, "Say, stranger, God damn you. What is your name?"

Morris replied, "You damn rascals, what is yours?"

On finding Morris could swear as well as they could, the men concluded he could not be Mormon, while his fearless manner made them believe he was not fleeing for his life. He talked with them and learned King Follet had been recaptured, but the pursuers were more interested in Parley and himself.

Morris went on, a free man, traveling all night. When morning came, he begged for a straw hat from a farmhouse.

Though a very strong and athletic man, by the time Morris reached Quincy, he was suffering with chills and fever, the weakened state from his long confinement, and his recent traveling without food. Friends cared for him as he lay sick in bed.

His chief worry was for Laura, for no one knew how she fared.

After the escape of the men, the jailer and his wife cursed and railed at Laura, threatening her with death. They turned her out of doors to face dusk and an abusive mob, which had gathered. Another crowd came, and with them the recaptured King Follett on Laura's horse and side saddle. The abuse from the mob grew.

After threatening to burn King Follett alive, the mob eventually lost interest in this violence, and sent him to the lower dungeon. As he was elderly and not a Church leader of interest to the mob, he was a few months later released.

Laura, for her part, was left with the mob. A young son of a family surnamed Richardson, seeing Laura's plight, ran home to get his mother, who, with her son and husband, went to the courthouse yard.

When Mr. Richardson saw the state Laura was in, he said to his wife, "Elizabeth, you take this lady to our home. If her husband was the greatest murderer in the world, we could not see anyone in our town treated with such cruelty as this."

Laura called the Richardsons true friends, and stayed with them for ten days.

After recovering Laura's saddle, Mr. Richardson, who was a saddler, fixed it up better than new. He also recovered her horse, caring for it until it was in good shape again.

Laura told these good people of her religion, gave them a Book of Mormon, and sang hymns for them.

After ten days with no news of her husband, Laura couldn't stand it any longer. Mr. Richardson arranged for Laura to travel toward her home in the company of the mail boy for the first sixty miles. After Laura left the mail boy, she soon struck the Mississippi River, which she traveled next to for fifty miles. The next portion of her journey would take her into thick woods, and her courage failed her. With six miles to go before she'd reach a hotel, a lonesome, dismal feeling came over her.

As she looked into the woods, a man emerged on horseback. It was King Follet's son.

"I wonder if you are not the woman I am looking for?" he asked.

Laura replied, "I believe you are the man I am looking for."

He carried a note from Morris saying he was all right. Mr. Follet escorted Laura safely to the hotel, and the next day they reached Quincy, where Morris was.

After two more days of recovery there, the couple was able to travel the remaining miles to Montrose, Iowa, to be reunited with their family.

The widow Elizabeth Stevens Stevenson had watched the Phelps children at Laura's house while Laura went to go and rescue Morris.

In the wake of this daring escape, it was decided that it would be wise for the escaped men to leave the area for a while. So, they were called on missions. Morris and Laura with little Joseph left in August for Kirtland, Ohio, where they could visit Morris' parents. With Morris' health broken, he needed time and space to recuperate. The Phelps' daughter Paulina stayed at Mr. Foote's place, and John Murdock, Sr. took Mary Ann and Harriet. Morris' parents never were baptized, but he always spoke well of their good character. Laura had another baby while accompanying Morris on this mission—her son was born in Indiana at the home of William and Sally Coles, Laura's oldest sister. They returned to Nauvoo in July. This baby would later die by scalding.

Laura was a midwife and practical doctor, working day and night in all weather to help her people. Overexertion and exposure took a toll on her health.

In 1841, during a peaceful time, Laura saw a vision. She saw many killed by the mob and the Saints being driven from Nauvoo, traveling in great groups and facing great suffering. The way was blotted out and she could not see where they were going.

Afterwards, she spoke often of this vision and said she could not endure the suffering that waited ahead.

Sickness came to her, and Laura died 2 February 1841, at age 34.

She was buried in the old graveyard at Nauvoo. The Prophet Joseph Smith and Heber C. Kimball preached her funeral sermons.

Joseph said her life had been short in years, but full of noble accomplishments, and that her exaltation was assured. Heber C. Kimball authored her obituary for the "Times and Seasons," and Joseph Smith noted Laura's passing in his diary.

"The last hymn Laura sang as she gathered her family around was 'Lead Kindly Light.'

Adam-ondi-Ahman (Diahman), Daviess County, Missouri

John Lowe Butler was among the Saints who lived for a time in the area they called Diahman, also known as Adam-ondi-Ahman.

Saints had settled in the area starting in the 1830s.

Joseph Smith had taught his belief that Adam-ondi-Ahman was the place Adam and Eve went after their exile from the Garden of Eden. On 25 June 1838, the Church settlement at Adam-ondi-Ahman was formally established, and within just a few months, its population grew to about 1,500.

Missourians grew worried that the Latter-day Saints would seize political control of Daviess County, and on an Election Day in August, conflict between the Missourians and the Church members came to a head. John Lowe Butler would play a key role in the events leading up to the conflict boiling over, and it is the event that put him into the history books.

Figure 46: Matthew, Tricia, Henry, Camilla, and Walter Sederberg in Adam-ondi-Ahman.
Photo © Matthew Sederberg. Used with permission.

John Lowe Butler and the Gallatin Election Day Battle[94]

Figure 47: Purported image of John Lowe Butler. Public domain via FamilySearch.

Saints tended to vote as a block, giving rise to concerns that votes by Church members would control election outcomes. Talk was heard around Gallatin that Church members might be prevented from voting. A few weeks prior to the election, John D. Lee[95] and Levi Stewart learned from Judge Josiah Morin at Millport that "it was predetermined" by locals "to prevent the 'Mormons' from voting, and thereby to elect Col. Wm. P. Peniston who led the mob in Clay County."

He warned Lee and Stewart to come armed to the polls. But the Saints dismissed such warnings and rather than going to the polls in groups and with arms, they went unarmed and individually.

On Election Day morning, 6 August 1838, John and a neighbor—Brother McGee—rode together for thirteen miles on a winding road to reach Gallatin, a tiny village of about ten cabins on the west bank of the Grand River. The polling place was a small frame house on the square's southwest corner, twelve by fourteen feet, where a large crowd of dozens of Missouri voters had already gathered, waiting for the polls to open at 11:00 a.m. Some men who were members of the Church stretched out on the grass nearby, heavily outnumbered by the Missourians.

Voting was by voice rather than by secret ballot.

Upon the opening of the polls, there was a rush as the Missourians went quickly to vote.

John blamed the initiation of the fight on William Peniston, an influential man from a family of original settlers in the county, who did not want the votes of the members of the Church to defeat his efforts to win the office of state representative. Peniston stood on a whiskey barrel and made what John considered to be an inflammatory speech against the Saints, and apparently called the Church leaders "horse thieves, liars, [and] counterfeiters" who claimed to work miracles but could not.

Missourians asserted that if the Saints did not vote to suit them, they must not vote at all.

The Saints did not like the idea of being deprived of their vote, so some determined to go put in their vote.

"Now for my part I felt like backing every one for it was our right," John recorded later, in his autobiography.

Peniston passed whiskey around to his friends, and John retreated to behind the grocery.

Dick Weldon started cursing at Church member Samuel Brown when Samuel tried to vote, and then struck him. Samuel defended himself with an umbrella, Abraham Nelson tried to pull Weldon off, and a half-dozen men attacked him and ripped his clothes. Things escalated quickly from there, with Hyrum Nelson joining the melee to strike Missourians with the butt of his whip.

John, who was away from the crowd, was startled by the rising noise of commotion. He could hear the fighting.

"I felt at first not to go in amongst them, for I did not want to have any trouble," he later wrote. "[I] wished to vote and thought after voting I would start home immediately, for I did not like the spirit manifested."

---

[94] See Hartley, chapter 6.
[95] Later of the Mountain Meadow Massacre.

When John stepped around the building, he saw members of the Church under attack from Missourians carrying sticks, clapboards, and shakes. "[E]very one of the Missourians trying to get a lick at a 'Mormon.'" He noticed "four to a dozen mobbers" thrashing one Mormon and "damning 'em."

As a Danite and a militia captain, John was obligated to defend his fellows. Running into the fight, he "hollowed out at the top of my voice saying 'O yes, you Danites, here is a job for us.'"[96]

John snatched up a large stick from a mound of split oak logs, which John D. Lee described as "clubs":

"[T]here was a lot of oak timber, which had been brought there to be riven into shakes or shingles, leaving the heart, taken from each shingle-block, lying there on the ground. These hearts were three square [three-sided], four feet long, weighed about seven pounds, and made a very dangerous, yet handy weapon; and when used by an enraged man they were truly a class of instrument to be dreaded."

As John held the stick, he later recalled: "Many thoughts ran through my mind. First I remembered that I never in my life struck a man in anger, had always lived in peace with all men and the stick I had to fight with was so large and heavy that I could sink it into every man's head, that I might chance to strike. I did not want to kill anyone, but merely to stop the affray, and went in with the determination to rescue my brethren from such miserable curs at all hazards, thinking when hefting my stick that I must temper my licks just so as not to kill. Furthermore, when I called out for the Danites, a power rested upon me such as one as I never felt before."

As he called for the men to quit fighting, John began "tapping them as I thought light," but to his surprise "they fell as dead men, their heads often striking the ground first." He struck none "except those who were fighting the brethren."

The fight continued for some time.

"Captain Butler was then a stranger to me," another Saint said in his account, "and until I saw him give the Danite sign of distress, I had believed him to be one of the Missouri ruffians, who were our enemies. . . . Capt. Butler was attacked from all sides, but, being a powerful man, he used his oak club with effect and knocked a man down at each blow that he struck, and each man that felt the weight of his weapon was out of the fight for that day at least. Many of those that he came in contact with had to be carried from the field for surgical aid."

The fight was intense but short.

John said the fight, which he thought lasted two minutes from first to last blow, was a minor affair when compared to the election fights in Kentucky, with opponents "fighting through each other for six or eight minutes with clubs, knives, [and] brickbats."

After the fight, "Captain Butler called the Mormons to him, and as he stood on a pile of building timber, he made a speech to the brethren. He said that his ancestors had served in the war of the Revolution to establish a free and independent government—one in which all men had equal rights and privileges; that he professed to be half [hale?] white and free born, and claimed a right to enjoy his constitutional privileges, and would have his rights as a citizen, if he had to fight for them; that as to his religion, it was a matter between his God and himself."

After Missourian reinforcements began to show up in small groups, swearing and armed, the Saints knew it was time to head to safety.

Samuel Smith, the brother of Joseph and a neighbor of John's, came to John and

---

[96] The Danites were an early Mormon vigilante group tacitly approved by Church leadership to help protect the Saints.

said, "let us go home." Samuel took John to the Smith home, approximately three miles from the Butler home.

Meanwhile, Brother Gee returned John's team to his home. Caroline, outdoors, saw the wagon coming and went to meet it, noting only one man was in it, standing and whipping the horses.

Caroline met the upset driver. "Why Brother Gee," she asked, "what in the world is the matter? Where is Mr. Butler?"

"Why, isn't John Butler come home?" he asked. "I thought that he would have been home by this. He has killed five or six men at the Election."

Gee stopped at the house and started for home, leaving the horses for Caroline to unhitch.

"She took them off the wagon and fed them," John said, "and then waited anxiously for my return," though John did not return that night.

When votes were counted, Peniston was defeated.

The following day, word of the Gallatin Election Battle spread to the two nearby settlements of Church members, though initial reports were not entirely accurate.

That morning, John made his way to Far West to visit the Prophet Joseph Smith himself, who recommended that John retrieve his family from the area as they might come to harm from the Missourians.[97]

The Mormon War of 1838

In the wake of the Gallatin Election Day Battle, escalating conflicts led the Governor of Missouri to eventually call out 2,500 state militiamen to put down a "Mormon rebellion," and to issue an extermination order to rid the state of members of the Church.

As the terrified members fled their homes in the face of violence, they sought protection in Far West, where they found themselves under siege.

In October 1838, Smith, Young, Kimball, and other leaders dedicated a temple square on the highest point of the bluff in Diahman.

On 1 November 1838, Joseph Smith, Jr. and Sidney Rigdon (among others) surrendered themselves, hoping to relieve the other members from persecution. They were put on trial, and the main body of the Church was forced to sign over their property in Far West and Caldwell County to pay for the militia muster and then leave the state.

Afterwards, Nauvoo, Illinois, became the new gathering place.[98]

Today, about 3,000 acres of Adam-ondi-Ahman is maintained as a Church historic site. It largely remains as undeveloped farmland.

Timothy Baldwin Clark and a Secret Meeting at Far West

Timothy hosted the apostles at a special meeting at his home in Far West on April 26 of 1839. The main body of the Saints had already moved on, but the apostles were following a mandate from the Prophet Joseph to gather at the Temple Site in Far West. Timothy may have been left alone by the mob due to his age as he lingered, living in Far West after most of the other Saints had left.

---

[97] Hartley, p. 51 and following.
[98] "1838 Mormon War." *Wikipedia*. https://en.wikipedia.org/wiki/1838_Mormon_War

The Church leaders gathered in two groups—a group with Brigham Young met at Timothy Baldwin Clark's home, which was located about a mile from the designated temple lot, and a group including Wilford Woodruff met at the home of Morris Phelps, whose home was located a mile further away.

At about midnight, Brigham Young and his party met at Timothy's home.

Heber C. Kimball later recorded seeing "a beautiful, clear moonlight . . . all seemed still as death."

Brigham recorded: "Early on the morning of the 26th of April, we held our conference, cut off 31 persons from the Church and proceeded to the building spot of the Lord's house."

According to Wilford, "The 'Mission of the Twelve' was sung, and we repaired to the southeast corner of the Temple ground."

Upon arriving at the building spot, after singing, the men rolled a stone "upwards of a ton weight, upon or near the southeast corner."

After the laying of the cornerstone, Wilford Woodruff and George A. Smith were ordained members of the Quorum of the Twelve Apostles, and the apostles individually prayed to the Lord, kneeling on the cornerstone one at a time to pray.

After the prayers, "Adam-ondi-Ahman" was sung, and the group disbanded.

Two sons of Timothy Baldwin Clark were present with this group: William O. and John W.

Following the disbanding of the group, Heber C. Kimball recounts:

"The brethren wandered among our deserted houses, many of which were in ruins, and saw the streets in many places grown over with weeds and grass . . . we went to Father Clark's, breakfasted, and before sunrise departed."[99]

Soon after the events of that night, Timothy and his family, animals, and possessions would soon be on the move, eventually settling near Montrose, Iowa, across the river from Nauvoo, Illinois.

The Saints in Nauvoo

John Lowe Butler, Life Guard to the Prophet

John Lowe Butler had strength and intelligence, and a natural leadership ability that Church leaders called on constantly, both to serve as a protector to the Saints and their leaders and to support Church interests and aid group cohesion. Because of his strength and quick thinking, John was given a number of dangerous assignments. He served as a life guard (body guard) to Joseph Smith, in addition to his responsibilities as a Danite and a militia leader.

Joseph Smith and the Butler Family Cloak

With sickness common in Nauvoo, Joseph Smith often administered to the sick. Sometimes he blessed cloth articles, which others could then use to bless the sick. For the Butler family, Joseph blessed John's large broadcloth cape or cloak. For the rest of John and Caroline's lives, this cloak was wrapped around ill family members.

---

[99] Clark, A. Charles. *Timothy Baldwin Clark*, pp. 270–273, and p. 291.

Figure 48: The Nauvoo Temple as viewed from Old Nauvoo.
© K. Bradley Washburn/Dreamstime.com

In the following generation, it was given to John Lowe Butler, Jr., and it was used with his family to bless the sick; according to family accounts it did seem to have a healing effect. When the cape became old and shabby, it was cut into ten pieces and distributed to the ten children of John Lowe Butler, Jr.[100]

Timothy Baldwin Clark across the River from Nauvoo
Timothy Baldwin Clark settled across the river from Nauvoo in Lee County, Iowa.
Ezra's wife Mary would later record in her autobiography: "When we lived seven miles west of Nauvoo, my husband's father (Timothy Baldwin Clark, father of Ezra T. Clark) had a good supply of animals, and we went often to attend Conferences and Fourth of July celebrations in Nauvoo and reviewed the Nauvoo Legion in their marching. It was a beautiful sight to see the Prophet Joseph on his prancing black horse that seemed to keep time with the music of the band. We would sometimes attend

---

[100] Hartley, p. 114.

meetings in the Grove. We witnessed the laying of the cornerstone of the Temple and later attended the Conference held therein and received our Endowments there on New Year's Day 1846."[101]

During the Nauvoo period, Timothy's son Ezra became great friends with Wilford Woodruff, who would later become fourth President of the Church. When Wilford went on a mission, his pregnant wife Phebe eventually came to stay with Timothy Baldwin Clark. She gave birth to her baby in a home on Timothy's property during the time that her husband was away.

To quote from *Timothy Baldwin Clark,* by A. Charles Clark:

"As the aging father of 11 children, and without a spouse, Timothy may have been especially sympathetic to Phebe's plight. She was young, without a husband, an infant to watch, pregnant with another, impoverished and sickly."

In Phebe's own words, she went to Father Clark's "into a small house of his in the same door yard, just before I was confined. I chose to go there that I might be more retired. I had everything at that time that was necessary to make me

Figure 49: Camilla and Henry Sederberg near the reconstructed Nauvoo Temple.
Photo © Matthew Sederberg. Image used with permission.

comfortable and have been much blest of the Lord…father Clark says that you need not be concerned about me until you return, only pray for me. He is very kind."

Phebe stayed with the Clark family for most of a year.

"[H]e has made me welcome to stay here until you return;" she wrote to her husband. "Would it not be for the best think you, they are a very kind family. He says he wants me to feel at much as home as at my father's house."

---

[101] Stevenson Clark, Mary. "Autobiography of Mary Stevenson Clark." *FamilySearch*, Intellectual Reserve, https://www.familysearch.org/photos/artifacts/1542747?cid=mem_copy. Accessed 3 October 2020.

Figure 50: Wilford Woodruff, circa 1849. Public domain via Wikicommons.

Phebe wrote several letters to Wilford, detailing the great care she received from Timothy and the rest of the Clark family. Her stay with them lasted ten months, until she eventually moved to Maine, apparently with family members, returning to stay in the state of her birth.[102]

Timothy's grandson, Edward B. Clark, wrote in his autobiography:

"My remembrance of what I have heard my parents say of Timothy Baldwin Clark is that he was kindhearted, generous and of a religious mind . . . the Prophet Joseph Smith was often in the home."[103]

Another significant experience of Timothy's during the Nauvoo era came after the introduction of baptism for the dead. Timothy was baptized by proxy for his mother, his father, and his brother, Joseph, in 1841.[104] [105]

Timothy was also present 24 May 1844 when Brigham Young placed the capstone of the Nauvoo Temple in a special celebration.[106]

---

[102] Clark, A. Charles. *Timothy Baldwin Clark*, pp. 291–293.
[103] "Genealogy of Ezra T. Clark," *The Autobiography of Edward B. Clark.* http://ezratclark.org/familyfile_AEBC_genealogy.asp
[104] Clark, A. Charles. *Timothy Baldwin Clark*, p. 297.
[105] Black, Susan Easton, and & Harvey Bischoff. *Annotated Record of Baptisms for the Dead, 1840 - 1845*, Vol. 2. The Center for Family History & Genealogy, Brigham Young University Press: Provo, Utah, 2002, pp. 796–797.
[106] Ibid., p. 313.

*Figure 51: C. C. A. Christensen, The Nauvoo Temple.
Public domain via Wikimedia Commons.*

Ezra T. Clark and Mary Stevenson Clark in Nauvoo

*Figure 52: Ezra and Mary Stevenson Clark.
Public domain via FamilySearch.*

According to the 1840 Census, these names were listed in order, implying they were neighbors:

Widow Stevenson

The Woodruff Family

Timothy B. Clark

During the era of Joseph Smith's Nauvoo, when young Ezra lived on his father's farm, across the river from Nauvoo, Ezra enjoyed being part of the excitement of a new religious movement. Ezra and his friends, who would have included Edward and Mary Stevenson, enjoyed going to activities such as dances and parades in Nauvoo.

At the time that Joseph Smith requested donations for the Nauvoo Temple, Ezra gave the Prophet all that he had.

Joseph told him: "Young man, you will never lack for the necessities of life nor for money."

This comment turned out to be prophetic.[107]

---

[107] Tanner, Annie Clark. *A Biography of Ezra Thompson Clark*, p. 6.

Figure 53: Elizabeth Stevens Stevenson. Public domain via FamilySearch.

Elizabeth Stevens Stevenson and Family in Nauvoo

Elizabeth Stevens Stevenson and her daughters, who had come to know the Prophet Joseph when he was a guest in their home back in Michigan, joined the Saints in the period when they lived in Nauvoo.

"Ever on the move, the Saints were never allowed to remain in one place long at a time. Enemies of Mormonism were determined to destroy them. Eventually, they reached Nauvoo.

"Most of the Saints were destitute. Everyone tried to earn a little. Elizabeth's two daughters worked in the homes of Gentiles. The Saints had no money to pay for help. Elizabeth was an excellent seamstress, and often sewed for Emma Smith, so again she was associated with the Prophet."[108]

Alfred Randall, Emmerette Louisa Davis, and Margaret Harley in Nauvoo

Figure 54: Alfred Randall, Emmerette Louisa Davis Randall, and Margaret Harley. Public domain via FamilySearch.

Once Alfred joined the Church, he was a stalwart member. He accepted callings to Church service, and was frequently in the company of leaders, including Joseph Smith.

Alfred was ordained a deacon 13 February 1841 by Jacob Crouse. Shortly after, he and Emmerette moved with their children to Nauvoo, where Alfred helped build the Nauvoo Temple. Alfred was ordained an elder in 1842 by President Fredrick L. Williams, who later presided over the Reorganized Church. Alfred received a patriarchal blessing from John Smith.

He also attended the Nauvoo Temple's first meeting, overseen by Joseph Smith. Alfred knew and loved Joseph, and was frequently in the company of the Prophet and other Church leaders.

On 7 June 1841, Joseph Smith recorded in his journal that Alfred accompanied him to Monmouth, Warren County, Illinois, along with a Mr. King, Charles C. Rich, Amasa Lyman, and others.

"We traveled very late, camping by the roadside about midnight," Joseph recorded.

This journey was to attend one of Joseph's trials.

In Alfred's biography, it is written: "Alfred has said that no sooner was one trial over than he [Joseph] would be summoned to another for stealing a cow, a horse, or some other trumped-up charge which they would say he had committed, however, none of them was proven to be true and he was released, only to be called to others until his life was unbearable."[109]

While the Saints were gathered at Nauvoo, Margaret Harley gathered to join them from Pennsylvania, where she had been baptized. She looked for a family she could hire on to help with. Alfred

---

[108] "A sketch of the life of Elizabeth Stevens Stevenson, arrived in Salt Lake Valley October 1847, Written by Clarice Stewart Anderson." *FamilySearch.* https://www.familysearch.org/tree/person/memories/KWJT-JWW

[109] Kofoed, Lucy Randall. *The True Story of Alfred Randall, Pioneer.*

and Emmerette were well enough off that they hired Margaret to help in their household. At the time, the family probably had three children.

Margaret must have been very appreciated by the family, as Emmerette named her fourth child "Margaret" in about 1848.

The Randall home was always well stocked with provisions, and Alfred was a jovial host, entertaining Brigham Young, Ezra Benson, and others at Nauvoo, Winter Quarters, and elsewhere.

Heber C. Kimball ordained Alfred to the Fifth Quorum of Seventy in 1845.[110]

The Simmons Family in Hancock County

Figure 55: Leven and Harriet Simmons. Public domain via FamilySearch.

Leven Simmons met Harriet Bradford in Hancock County, Illinois, where they were married 27 February 1836, when Harriet was 14 and Leven was 23.

They farmed about twelve miles from Nauvoo, and lived there for several years.

While in the Nauvoo area, Harriet gave birth to her first five children, starting with George Washington Simmons, who was born to Harriet when she was 15 years old and who lived just a few years. Harriet would go on to have a baby every few years from age 15 through age 45, eventually having a total of twelve babies, ten of whom would live past childhood.

---

[110] "Alfred Randall." *FamilySearch*, Intellectual Reserve, https://www.familysearch.org/tree/person/memories/KWJB-JNS. Accessed 26 October 2020.

Figure 56: C. C. A. Christensen, Mormon Panorama Thirteen/Joseph Mustering the Nauvoo Legion. Public domain via Wikimedia Commons.

John Lowe Butler and the Martyrdom of Joseph Smith

Following the destruction of the Nauvoo Expositor printing press, on Monday, 25 June 1844, Governor Ford sent orders that Joseph go to Carthage by 10:00 a.m. without escort, or Nauvoo and all her inhabitants would be destroyed.

Joseph, in the company of eighteen others charged with riot, headed out on the twenty-mile ride to Carthage. John Lowe Butler was one of Joseph's bodyguards who started with the group.

At the site of the temple, Joseph paused, commenting, "this is the loveliest place and the best people under the heavens."

Figure 57: Joseph Smith as Lieutenant General reviewing the Nauvoo Legion. © Everett Collection/Shutterstock.

Figure 58: Purported image of John Lowe Butler. Public domain via FamilySearch.

Just four miles from Carthage, they were met at Albert Fellows' farm by about sixty Illinois militiamen, with orders for the Nauvoo Legion to surrender all state arms that had been issued to them.

Joseph countersigned the order and told John and his other companions, "I am going like a lamb to the slaughter."

After Joseph and the company returned to Nauvoo to ensure the arms surrender, fifteen men, including Joseph and John, rode back toward Carthage. At 9:00 p.m. they stopped again at Albert Fellows' farm, pausing for half an hour. The guardsmen had to leave Joseph there.

Joseph told Hyrum that he wanted him to return with the bodyguards.

The bodyguards "begged of him to let us stay with him and die with him, if necessary," John later wrote, "but he said, no, we were to return to our home. And Brother Hyrum said that he would stay with Brother Joseph."

And so, Joseph would not go on alone.

Hyrum rode with his brother to Carthage, and the others retreated silently.

"For my part," John would later write, "I felt that something great was going to transpire. He blessed us and told us to go. We bade them farewell, and started. We had twenty miles to ride, and we went the whole distance without uttering one word. All were dumb and still and all felt the spirit as I did myself. I cannot express my feelings at that time for they overpowered me. I felt like the Prophets of the Lord were about to be taken from us and that they were going to await their doom, the same as the Lord his when He was here upon the earth. We went to our homes like so many sheep that had lost their shepherd, knowing not what to do." Many years later one of John's daughters told her own daughter that John often said he was "never so loath to do anything in his life as he was to leave the prophet."

It was late Monday night.

Figure 59: Alfred Randall. Public domain via FamilySearch.

On Thursday, June 27, at 5:15 p.m., Joseph and Hyrum were murdered at Carthage Jail.[111]

The Martyrdom of Joseph and Hyrum—Alfred Randall's Story

Family stories place Alfred Randall close to events leading up to the Martyrdom of Joseph and Hyrum this way:

On 24 June 1844, Alfred Randall accompanied Joseph Smith to Carthage Jail. He was made to leave, being forced downstairs backwards at the point of a bayonet. Though this makes for a great story, a closer examination of the details reveals that the text referenced as being the source for this record does not mention Alfred Randall by name.

It is possible that a different official source document at the Church might hold this story and the original authors used an incorrect title, or it is also possible that this is an embellished story.

However, Alfred did swear an affidavit years later as to his experience of certain other events that night:

At about 10:00 p.m., Alfred was standing near troops in the square, who were stationed there by Governor Ford.

---

[111] Hartley, p. 130.

He heard one soldier say, "I calculate to see old Joe dead before I leave."

Another wondered whether any Mormons might be listening in.

Another soldier, near Alfred, said, "If I knew there was, I would run my bayonet through him."[112]

Alfred heard other soldiers saying that this would be the last of the Mormons.

As he wandered through the people that night, Alfred saw Governor Ford standing by the fence at Harbleton's Hotel.

"He heard a soldier tell Governor Ford: 'The soldiers are determined to see Joe Smith dead before they leave here.' Ford replied harshly 'If you know of any such plot, keep it to yourself.'"[113]

Figure 60: C. C. A. Christensen, Exterior of Carthage Jail. Public domain via Wikimedia Commons.

After a mob stormed the jail, Joseph and his brother were murdered.

Two days later, their bodies lay in state in the Nauvoo Mansion House, where mourners could stream by and pay their last respects. John Lowe Butler played a role in helping to provide security for the body of the Prophet and his brother after the martyrdom.

John Lowe Butler and the Aftermath of the Martyrdom

In gloomy Nauvoo after the martyrdom, it took time for many to accept the deaths, as they had seen Joseph delivered from danger many times.

---

[112] "Alfred Randall."
[113] Kofoed, p. 9.

Friday morning, General Dunham ordered the entire Nauvoo Legion, of which John Lowe Butler was a member, to gather on the parade ground east of the Nauvoo Temple at 10:00 a.m.

They met, and were then counseled not to let their violent feelings get the better of them. Legion officers counseled together and about noon rode out to meet the hearse-wagon coming from Carthage, which carried the bodies, covered with brush to block the sun.

When the caravan was a mile east of the temple, it evolved into a formal funeral procession, which was led by the City Council and Joseph Smith's staff, including John.

Other Legion officers followed, along with scores of citizens, moving along Mulholland Street with a stream of solemn lamentations and wailings.

Figure 61: Purported image of John Lowe Butler. Public domain via FamilySearch.

The bodies were taken inside the Mansion House. A crowd of thousands gathered, and Church leaders urged them to be peaceful and not to retaliate.

On the following day, June 29, thousands moved through the Mansion House to solemnly grieve and view the martyr's bodies. The Butlers were there, and daughter Charity Artemesia, later recounted experiencing gloom and deep sorrow.

The night following the viewing, John didn't return home, apparently helping to secretly bury Joseph's body within the walls of the unfinished Nauvoo House.

The Nauvoo Legion remained on guard, watching against an attack of the mobs, but nothing immediately came.

John would later recount the experience of those in Nauvoo following the martyrdom: "The Saints all felt it when Brother Joseph was killed. They could not tell the reason why it was, but their hearts seemed to melt within them and they mourned and knew not what for."[114]

Mary Stevenson Clark Reflects on the Martyrdom of Joseph Smith

"We passed through the sad afflictions of the Saints in the assassination of our dear Prophet and his brother. My Mother walked the dooryard in lamentation. But with all the persecutions we had passed through, we were driven again toward the wilderness."[115]

Ezra T. Clark and Mary Stevenson Clark after the Martyrdom

Unmarried at the time, Ezra and Mary were among the vast weeping throng that went to meet the bodies of Joseph and Hyrum.[116]

Figure 62: Ezra and Mary Stevenson Clark. Public domain via FamilySearch.

---

[114] Hartley, p. 130.
[115] Stevenson Clark.
[116] Clark, Antone, *Noble Pioneer: A Biography of Ezra T. Clark,* 2002, p. 92.

After the Martyrdom: Transfiguration of Brigham Young Witnessed by Ancestors

Harriet Bradford Simmons

Harriet later told her descendants of the unrest among the Saints after the death of Joseph Smith. Much speculation centered around who the next leader would be and how he would be chosen. A meeting was called to discuss the matter, which Harriet attended.

After several brethren spoke, Brigham Young, then President of the Quorum of the Twelve Apostles, rose to speak.

One descendant recounted Harriet's experience: "As he stood before them, the mantle of the Prophet fell upon him and his countenance underwent a change and the members of the congregation saw before them a perfect likeness of the Prophet Joseph Smith. When he began to speak, his voice was that of the Prophet. She said that the entire assembly witnessed and testified as to what had happened, and everyone knew that God had chosen a leader for his people. That she actually witnessed this miracle was something Harriet never got over, and testified of it often, the rest of her life."[117]

Figure 63: Harriet Bradford Simmons. Public domain via FamilySearch.

Another descendant wrote of Harriet's experience: "She said the people knew without a doubt who was to lead the Church and everyone felt that a miracle had happened before their eyes."[118]

Figure 64: Ezra T. Clark. Public domain via FamilySearch.

Ezra T. Clark's Account of the Transfiguration

"Before I left Nauvoo, I heard the Prophet Joseph say he would give the Saints a key whereby they would never be led away or deceived, and that was: the Lord would never suffer the majority of this people to be led away or deceived by imposters, nor would he allow the records of this Church to fall into the hands of the enemy.

"I heard Joseph say this, and I also heard him say that he would roll the burden of the Apostleship upon the quorum of the Twelve.

"I heard Joseph preach many times; heard him, in the last sermon he ever delivered, bear testimony to the truth of the work that God had called him to; also that the Lord had never suffered him to be slain by his enemies, because his work had not been done, until a short time ago.

"He had now laid the foundation of this work, and rolled the burden of the priesthood upon the Twelve; and, having given them their washings and anointings, they would now bear off this work triumphantly, and it would roll on faster than ever before; and, if the Lord was willing to accept of him, he was willing to go.

"This he spoke to the people.

"I was one who heard his voice, and know that he spoke like an angel from heaven. I never heard him speak with more power than then, and I heard him many times. I was satisfied. I knew him to be a

---

[117] Olsen, Gary Lamar. "Life History of Harriet Bradford Simmons." *FamilySearch*, Intellectual Reserve, 7 January 2018, https://www.familysearch.org/photos/artifacts/46276814?cid=mem_copy. Accessed 4 December 2020.
[118] Huff, Elizabeth F. "Harriet Bradford (1821-1890)." *FamilySearch*, Intellectual Reserve, https://www.familysearch.org/photos/artifacts/35018993?cid=mem_copy. Accessed 4 December 2020.

prophet of God. I had heard him prophesy many times, and had seen his prophecies fulfilled, and had also shaken hands with him, and he had blessed me, and I had felt the influence and power of the Lord upon him and upon me, and I have never forgotten that blessing from that day to this, and I never shall.

"Two days later the Prophet was martyred, and two or three weeks later, when the saints held a conference, and Brigham Young arose as leader of the Church, I want to bear record that he spoke as Joseph used to speak; to all appearances, the same voice, the same gestures, the same stature. I bear this record to all the world, to my children and to my children's children, and also bear record that this work is God's work, and that it will roll on as it has done from that day to this."[119]

---

[119] Clark, Antone, pp. 91–92.

Figure 65: Brigham Young, 1801–1877.
© Everett Collection/Shutterstock

5. Mormon Trail

If we all love tales of pioneers, it is because from the time we are weaned to the time we die, life is pioneering. —*Harry Emerson Fosdick*[120]

Figure 66: A traditional covered wagon.
© LPeak/Depositphotos

---

[120] As quoted in *One Man's Journey in Search for Freedom,* by Obert Tanner Clark, p. 4.

As is quoted in Alfred Randall's biography, after the death of Joseph and Hyrum and the transfer of leadership power to Brigham Young, Brigham said, "We have tried to live in peace; to fight back would only complicate our problems, not solve them. We must be patient. . . . We can go voluntarily or be driven, but go we must. . . . To the West we must go."[121]

As the Saints neared the end of their time in Nauvoo, mobs and ruffians bothered the Saints. Some homes were burned, and it was a time of unrest as a few groups left the Church under leaders who felt that they, rather than Brigham Young, were the next true authority to lead the religion after the death of Joseph Smith.

Through tenacity and determination, however, a large party of Saints rallied together and readied to depart Nauvoo and head west.

Figure 67: C. C. A. Christensen, Leaving Missouri.
Public domain via Wikimedia Commons.

Abandoning Nauvoo

Leven Simmons and Harriet Bradford Simmons Face the Mob

In 1845, mobs burned the Simmons' crops, which drove the family into Nauvoo for protection. Leven outfitted his family to go west with the first company leaving Nauvoo, but ended up giving his team to Orson Pratt, who lacked one and couldn't go without one. As the violence continued, Leven sold

---

[121] Kofoed, Lucy Randall. *The True Story of Alfred Randall, Pioneer.*

his $1,500 farm for $250, bought a new team, and in spring of 1847 the family fled to Pisgah, camping there in covered wagons.[122]

While in Pisgah under rough living conditions, Harriet feared for the life of her baby, who had become very sick with an ear infection.

Figure 68: C. C. A. Christensen, Mobbers on the Missouri River. Public domain via Wikimedia Commons.

One cold day, a neighbor woman ran to her wagon, saying "Come quickly, the mob is coming. We'll go in our wagon. I'll take the children."[123]

Harriet wanted something to wrap her sick baby in to guard against the cold. She picked up the large warm "flapjack," or pancake, she'd prepared for Leven's supper, and tied it around the baby's head with some cloth, then wrapping him up with what else she could grab, got away just in time in the neighbor's wagon. Harriet's resourcefulness proved to be just what was needed. The moist heat of the baby's flapjack head wrap brought relief to his infected ears.[124] [125]

The baby in question probably would have been little Leven Simmons, Jr., who was born in Winter Quarters on 1 October 1847.

---

[122] Simmons, Jr., Benjamin Franklin. "Biography of Levan Simmons and wives Harriet Bradford and Lydia Rebecca Fisher." *FamilySearch*, Intellectual Reserve, https://www.familysearch.org/photos/artifacts/101996849?cid=mem_copy. Accessed 4 December 2020.
[123] Simmons, Jr.
[124] Olsen, Gary Lamar. "Life History of Harriet Bradford Simmons." *FamilySearch*, Intellectual Reserve, 7 January 2018, https://www.familysearch.org/photos/artifacts/46276814?cid=mem_copy. Accessed 4 December 2020.
[125] Huff, Elizabeth F. "Harriet Bradford (1821-1890)." *FamilySearch*, Intellectual Reserve, https://www.familysearch.org/photos/artifacts/35018993?cid=mem_copy. Accessed 4 December 2020.

In Winter Quarters, Leven's services were needed making barrels, buckets, and churns, mending wagons, and handling any other job that came to his hands.[126]

From Winter Quarters, Leven and Harriet went to Little Pigeon, Iowa, and from there back to Springfield, Missouri. They planted crops wherever they went, knowing that the food would be helping those who followed them as they'd have to move on before a harvest came.[127]

Ezra T. Clark and Mary Stevenson Clark Marriage and Sealing

Ezra T. Clark and Mary Stevenson were married at her home by his brother, William O. Clark, on 15 May 1845.

They were later sealed in the Nauvoo Temple on 6 February 1846, on the last day of recorded ordinances in the Nauvoo Temple, in a ceremony officiated by Brigham Young.[128]

The Alfred Randall Family's False Start

During the last days in Nauvoo, Alfred Randall and family were visited by members of the mob at their home. The men offered Alfred $7.50 for his farm, and told him he'd better take it, and that he had only seven days to be there. Alfred told Emmerette to hand him his gun, and the men ran away. In the end, the Randall family abandoned their farm when they left, and didn't get even the $7.50 for it.[129]

Figure 69: C. C. A. Christensen, Burning of the Temple.
Public domain via Wikimedia Commons.

---

[126] Huff.
[127] Olsen.
[128] Clark, Antone. *Noble Pioneer: A Biography of Ezra Thompson Clark*, p. 99.
[129] Kofoed, p. 11.

David Park and Ann Brooks Park Find Abandoned Nauvoo

Figure 70: David Park. domain via FamilySearch.

David Park and Ann Brooks Park had joined the Church in Canada, during the early years it was founded. Upon hearing that the Saints were called to move westward to Zion, the Canadian group wholeheartedly decided to sell their possession and come along.

Of the group's arrival in Nauvoo on 6 April 1846, David's friend and fellow traveler Archibald Gardner reported, "We found that the twelve [Apostles] had started (beginning Feb. 4, 1846) for the Rocky Mountains. There were plenty of homes open to us. We could have brick, frame, log or stone houses without cost. The Saints had nearly all left who were able to go, and their homes were standing empty and unsold. They had been driven out and what could not readily be disposed of was left behind. Some had furniture in— chairs, bedsteads, etc. Here for three weeks we fitted up outfits and secured supplies which included flour, parched corn, cornmeal and seed for planting, then started west in companies of ten wagons to the company. We crossed the Mississippi, passed Montrose (Iowa) and camped on the Bluffs a few miles north. The downpour that night brought water around the wagons up to our boot-tops and during the storm a son named William was born to Robert Gardner Jr.'s wife, May 22, 1846. The next morning the mother and baby were made as comfortable as possible and the Canadian Company moved on. We were endeavoring to catch up with the (earlier) companies from Nauvoo who were ahead."

The Canadian group stopped at Winters Quarters, where they made preparations for the coming bitter winter. David and Ann Brooks Park stayed in Missouri three years, raising money for their trek west.[130]

Timothy Baldwin Clark Stays Behind

Timothy, a widower since the passing of his wife, Polly, chose not to cross the plains to Zion but instead to spend his last years living near three of his sons and their families near the DuPage River, in Northern Illinois. By then, all his children were grown.[131]

Beforehand, however, Timothy and his married sons in the Church had the opportunity to attend the Nauvoo Temple, on Thursday, 1 January 1846, among the eighty-nine people who received ordinances that day.[132]

Timothy's son Ezra T. Clark and daughter-in-law Mary Stevenson Clark traveled on without him. But Mary's mother, Elizabeth, did go along with their company.

Timothy may have decided not to cross the plains with the Saints because he had some reservations about the practice of polygamy, though other possibilities as to why he may not have chosen to cross the plains could include his advanced age, the differences in religious choices by his children

---

[130] "Parks, David, and Ann Brooks." *FamilySearch.*
https://www.familysearch.org/photos/artifacts/3522451?cid=mem_copy
[131] Clark, A. Charles. *Timothy Baldwin Clark*, p. 303.
[132] Ibid., pp. 313–314.

following the death of Joseph Smith,[133] financial difficulties, or feeling worn out from the many moves that he had already made during his lifetime.[134]

Figure 71: C. C. A. Christensen, Pioneers Crossing the Plains of Nebraska. Public domain via Wikimedia Commons.

The Harsh Threats of the Trail

The Mormon Trail extended from Nauvoo, Illinois, through the states of Iowa, Nebraska, and Wyoming, all the way to Salt Lake City.

Heading out on the trail was a risky proposition, and presented many challenges for the pioneers, some of which included:

Indians,[135] which were sometimes hostile, and sometimes friendly. Indians could steal supplies and might kidnap people. Sometimes Indians demanded a toll for safe passage. When Indians were around, the pioneers would go on alert.

Wildlife, which roamed the prairies freely could sometimes present a threat, most noticeably in the form of buffalo stampedes.

---

[133] William, and probably Rhoda's family, joined a splinter group, but Ezra went west with the Saints.
[134] Ibid., pp. 318–319.
[135] A note on the political correctness of the word "Indian": I've researched different angles and have decided in this book to use the word "Indian" rather than "Native American," both to fit with historical usage and also to reflect the usage of many current elders of these nations. Where an individual tribe's name is known, it is used instead. Here is an article which explores this matter more: https://www.huffpost.com/entry/the-name-indian-and-polit_1_b_67593

Weather, which during the summer could be hot and strain vulnerable pioneers, and which during the fall and winter could bring life-threatening snow and cold.

Cholera, a disease that caused 40 percent of pioneer deaths. The Mormon Trail followed along slow-moving rivers like the Platte and Sweetwater. In the spring, the rivers moved fast and were swollen with snow melt. This was their safest season of the year. The companies traveling earlier in the year had healthier water. But as temperatures rose in the summers and hundreds of travelers trekked along the rivers, using them for bathing and toileting as well as for cooking and drinking water, the rivers grew contaminated by sewage and became hosts for lethal cholera.[136][137]

Leaving early in the season was the best bet for survival. Having a well-stocked wagon and good leadership for the company also made for better travel.

Figure 72: Platte River, west of Omaha, Nebraska.
© Suzanne Tucker/Dreamstime

---

[136] "When Mormon Pioneers Left Often was a Life or Death Proposition," *Deseret News.* http://www.deseretnews.com/article/865607624/When-Mormon-pioneers-left-often-was-a-life-or-death-proposition.html?s_cid=Email-4

[137] Hertzel, Anna Lenz. "Vardis Fisher: Marriage, children and adult life." *FamilySearch*, Intellectual Reserve, 13 June 2014, https://www.familysearch.org/photos/artifacts/7811206?cid=mem_copy. Accessed 3 December 2020.

Timeline and Stories from the Mormon Trail

Boldface line entries indicate events in the Latter-day Saint Church and US political sphere.
Regular type indicates events in families in Alan and Janet's ancestry.
(Only ancestral families who were part of the Mormon Trail migration are included in this timeline.)

Acronyms of the ancestral pioneer families are as follows:
AR = The Randall family. Alfred Randall crossed the plains with first wife Emmerette and second wife Margaret Harley Randall.
EB = Ebenezer Bryce.
ESS = Elizabeth Stevens Stevenson, who crossed the plains with the Ezra T. Clark family.
ETC = The Ezra Thompson Clark family. Ezra Thompson Clark and first wife Mary Stevenson Clark.
JLB = The Butler family. John Lowe Butler and wives Caroline Farozine Skeen Butler and Sarah Lancaster Butler crossed the plains together with Caroline's children.
LSS = The Simmons family. Leven Simmons Sr. and first wife Harriet Bradford Simmons.
MC = The Mads Christensen family. Karen Marie Hansen Andersen (mother of Mads Christensen), Mads Christensen, and first wife Maren Johanne Jensen Christensen.
RD = The Durfey family. Royal Durfey and Lydia Abell Durfey.

Other Ancestral Pioneer Families:

The Goulding family of Daniel and Elizabeth Goulding came to Utah via a different route: They left England via a ship and stopped in Australia for several years, where Daniel worked as a miner and served in Church leadership and Elizabeth had a few children, including our ancestor Rosanna Susannah Goulding. Eventually they saved up enough money to take a ship to San Diego, from whence they eventually traveled eastward and settled first in California, then in the Big Muddy area in Nevada, before moving up into Pleasant Grove, Utah, and then to Garfield County.

The Park family of David Park and Ann Brooks Park have a part of their story told earlier in this chapter, of how they came to Nauvoo. Their names are not discoverable in the Mormon Overland Trail database, and the dates and company name for their journey were not found among the family histories I examined. However, they must have crossed in about 1850, as there is record of them living in Salt Lake City, Utah, that year. From there they went with their family to Nevada, where David would pass away in 1884 and Ann in 1889, both in Mottsville.

It is presumed that Jens Christensen Lamp, and wife Trene Bendtsen Christensen, immigrated around 1880, after the First Transcontinental Railroad was complete, though it is not known whether they took the train to Utah. Their daughter Emma, who is our ancestor, immigrated in 1879 at the age of 15 and worked in people's homes to help raise money for the rest of her family to immigrate.

Figure 73: Devil's Gate, along the Mormon Trail.
© Ffooter/Depositphotos

Timeline of the Pioneer Trail[138] (Offered in present tense.)

ESS 3 February 1846: Elizabeth Stevens Stevenson receives her endowments. She will later receive a sealing to her late husband Joseph in the Salt Lake Endowment House.

Winter Quarters

1846: Mormon Battalion organized, composed of 550 men and 33 laundresses. It is believed to be the only religiously based unit in US military history.

AR 1846: In Winter Quarters, Alfred Randall is called as bishop to some of the families whose men serve in the Mormon Battalion.[139]

ETC 1847 November 21: Timothy Baldwin Clark is born to Ezra and Mary Clark in Winter Quarters. He is named after his grandfather.

---

[138] Present tense is used rather than past tense in the timelines of this book.
[139] Kofoed, pp. 11–12.

ETC 1846–1848: At Winter Quarters, Ezra T. Clark crops for the Saints until spring of 1848, when he plants a crop he will not be there to harvest and prepares to go west.

Mormon Trail

1847: The first company prepares to leave to go to Utah.

Figure 74: Leven Simmons. Public domain via FamilySearch.

Leven Simmons 1847?

LSS 1847: According to the records of the Daughters of Utah Pioneers, Leven Simmons comes to Utah in 1847 with Captain Howell's Ox-Team Company #76, though his name does not appear to be listed on their official roll. According to the DUP account, Leven "walked all the way and helped pick the trail the pioneers followed." The Simmons family history, however, recounts that Leven came to Utah in the year 1854 with his family. It's possible he went west in 1847 and returned to bring his family later. But family history places the Simmons, including eight children, family wintering in 1847 at Winter Quarters, then living at Little Pigeon Creek, Iowa and Springfield, Iowa before immigrating to Utah.[140]

The Alfred Randall Family 1848

Figure 75: Alfred Randall and wives: Emmerette and Margaret. Public domain via FamilySearch.

AR 1848 January 29: Alfred Randall marries second wife Margaret Harley. Brigham Young officiates.

AR 1848 June 7: The Heber C. Kimball Company of 662 individuals, including Alfred, Emmerette, and Margaret, and Emmerette's children, depart Winter Quarters for the Mormon Trail. Joseph F. Smith and his mother, Mary Fielding Smith, are also part of this company.

AR 1848 Summer: Howard Egan records a buffalo stampede the Heber C. Kimball Company experiences:

"[O]ne day we had camped for noon. . . . Mother caught her boys, and . . . we landed in the wagon, and she followed, and just in time, for a stampeded herd of buffalos was coming straight for the camp. They divided just a little way from the camp, some passing the back, some the front of the corral. . . . the part that passed the back end struck and broke a hind wheel of the last wagon in our wing. We staid there to repair damages till next day."

Alfred Randall, with his carpentry skills, may have been called on to help repair wagons in situations like these.

---

[140] Daughters of the Utah Pioneers. "Biography of Levan Simmons." *FamilySearch*, Intellectual Reserve, https://www.familysearch.org/photos/artifacts/32269379?cid=mem_copy. Accessed 3 December 2020.

Ezra T. Clark 1848

Figure 76: Ezra T. Clark. Public domain via FamilySearch.

ESS, ETC 1848 July 3: The Willard Richards Company, comprising 526 individuals, departs Winter Quarters for Utah. Ezra T. Clark, Mary Stevenson Clark, sons Ezra and Timothy, and Mary's mother, Elizabeth Stevens Stevenson, travel in this company, among the group captained by Apostle Amasa Lyman, whose accompanying family includes Ezra's niece Paulina Eliza Phelps Lyman (second of Amasa's wives), and her first child. Ezra and Mary will later name a son after Amasa.

Nancy Aretta Porter Mattice (a different Nancy than the one who later weds Ezra) later recounts: "The first incidents were pushing the [wagons onto] flat boat or raft when we crossed the Missouri River. . . . I can see the large cake of ice that come floating down the river and the men took poles to push them away so they would not strike the boat."[141]

Mary shares a few remarkable incidents from the migration westward in her autobiography:

Figure 77: C. C. A. Christensen, Crossing the Mississippi on the Ice. Public domain via Wikimedia Commons.

---

[141] Mattice, Nancy Aretta Porter. "A Sketch of the Life of Nancy Aretta Porter Mattice." *Church History*, Intellectual Reserve, https://history.churchofjesuschrist.org/overlandtravel/sources/19152/a-sketch-of-the-life-of-nancy-aretta-porter-mattice-1-4. Accessed 18 May 2021.

Mary Stevenson Clark 1848

Figure 78: Mary Stevenson Clark. Public domain via FamilySearch.

"The Prophet Joseph Smith said, before his death, that we would go to the Rocky Mountains. My brother, Edward Stevenson, went with a company in 1847. My husband and I and babe in June 1848. But before starting, my sister's husband, Job Bailey, was not ready to go with us. But he said he would come in two years. His father had joined the Strangites (an apostate group) and so there was no sign of my sister's coming as her husband was preparing to go with his father. My brother, Edward, when with my husband in Illinois working for breadstuff would kneel upon the ground and pray to Our Father in heaven to deliver our sister from apostasy and open the way for her. All of a sudden, her husband was taken violently ill and passed away the day her baby was born. The Doctor sent a note to my husband who went back and settled her business and brought her and her two little girls in time to start with us. We got along nicely.

"I will mention what looked like a sad accident: My husband was driving three yoke of oxen. I tried to jump out of the moving wagon but did not jump far enough and fell back in front of a hind wheel. My husband, as quick as thought, grabbed that wheel and held it from turning. My Mother, who was in the wagon, jumped out and ran to the leads and stopped them. He raised the wheel and said: 'Get up if you can.' He was as white as a sheet. I got up and got the camphor for I thought I was fainting.

"We lived two winters at Winter Quarters where my second child was born. From there we started in June 1848 and saw many herds of buffalo and many Indians. We were not frightened. I had all I could do caring for our children and cooking. We used buffalo chips for fuel. We would stop a day, once in a while and cook up all we could and do our washing. Evenings we would milk the cow and put dried bread in the milk and had this for supper. We were happy. We would get around our campfires. We felt we were going to a place of safety where we would not be mobbed and driven from one state to another as we had been. We were poor and had not time to get clothing and food for our needs before starting, that we really needed."[142]

---

[142] Stevenson Clark, Mary. "Autobiography of Mary Stevenson Clark." *FamilySearch*, Intellectual Reserve, https://www.familysearch.org/tree/person/memories/KWJ6-HKP. Accessed 3 October 2020.

Figure 79: Buffalo herd.
© dmbaker/Depositphotos

Elizabeth Stevens Stevenson 1848

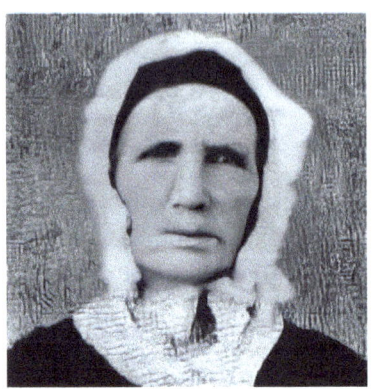

Figure 80: Elizabeth Stevens Stevenson. Public domain via FamilySearch.

Of Elizabeth Stevens Stevenson's experience with the wagon train, a granddaughter later writes: "In spite of privations and suffering the Saints seemed to be happy. . . . There were many interesting experiences during the long, hard trek to the valleys of the mountains. Sunday, of course, was their sacred day. They halted their traveling to rest themselves and their animals, and to worship. . . . In the evenings around their campfires, visiting, singing, dancing were enjoyed."[143]

One of Elizabeth's great-granddaughters later recounts: "Mother often told us children of her grandmother's deep spirituality, her devotion to her church, her gentle kind ways and her cultured, refining influence— all reflecting her personality. A lovely lady, indeed. Among my most treasured possessions is a dainty silk neckerchief brought across the Plains by Elizabeth. She used to wear it around her neck, pinned under her chin with a lovely brooch. She must have loved to wear it, for it is almost threadbare."[144]

The Willard Richards Company Encounters Indians

One woman in the Willard Richards Company records a particular Indian encounter on the trail:

"One evening, the company was eating dinner, a group of Indians had gathered nearby. One old squaw asked for and was given permission to hold a pioneer woman's baby. The squaw then turned and ran with the baby as fast as she could into the gathered Indians, who closed around her making a lot of noise. Chaos erupted among the pioneers, with a woman screaming, others scolding the mother, and still others trying to console her.

"The captain climbed up on his wagon tongue, calling for order. Everything fell quiet.

"'Let the Sioux listen to the white man,' he said. 'Bring that baby back or there will be war right now, the white man will fight for his children.'

"In an undertone, he added, 'Every man to his guns.'

"Every man got into line.

"The Indians were in a huddle seeming to council what to do. After a while and it seemed such a long time to us here come the squaw with the baby (saying) Here take it, here take it. I can just see him now, in his little pink apron and his hair flying in the wind and (laughing) we were a thankful family to get our baby back."

Mattice records that the Indians do not bother the company again after this event.[145]

Ezra T. Clark is one of the men in this company. The men help keep their families safe on the trails.

AR 1848 September 24: The Heber C. Kimball Company arrives in the Salt Lake Valley.

---

[143] Anderson, Clarice Stewart. "A sketch of the life of Elizabeth Stevens Stevenson." *FamilySearch*, Intellectual Reserve, 14 May 2013, https://www.familysearch.org/photos/artifacts/1008826?cid=mem_copy. Accessed 11 May 2021.

[144] "A sketch of the life of Elizabeth Stevens Stevenson, Arrived in Salt Lake Valley October 1847, Written by Clarice Stewart Anderson." *FamilySearch*. https://www.familysearch.org/tree/person/memories/KWJT-JWW

[145] Mattice.

ESS, ETC 1848 October 10: The Willard Richards Company arrives in the Salt Lake Valley.

Figure 81: C. C. A. Christensen, Entering the Great Salt Lake Valley.
Public domain via Wikimedia Commons.

Figure 82: Ebenezer Bryce.
Public domain via FamilySearch.

Ebenezer Bryce 1850

EB 1850 June 11: The James Pace Company, comprised of 264 people and 100 wagons, departs Kanesville, Iowa. Ebenezer Bryce, age 19, travels with them. He comes as a single man, having left his family behind in Scotland.

EB 1850 Summer: In the first several weeks of their journey, the James Pace Company sees several deaths due to cholera. Many are buried in their temple clothes, without coffins, in unmarked graves. Due to the high number of deaths in the company, the group fragments, falling into segments and following different leaders. Fear of deaths is high, and the people in the group are uncertain about who best to follow. There is an absence of leadership strong enough to keep the group cohesion.[146]

EB 1850 July 19: A few people in the James Pace Company are baptized for their health.

EB 1850 September 22–23: The James Pace Company arrives in the Salt Lake Valley.

Figure 83: The Salt Lake Valley.
© marzolino/Depositphotos

---

[146] Pace, James. "James Pace Papers." *Church History*, Intellectual Reserve, https://history.churchofjesuschrist.org/overlandtravel/sources/5788/james-pace-papers-1846-1861-autobiographical-sketch-circa-1861-9. Accessed 18 May 2021.

Leven Simmons and Harriet Bradford Simmons 1852

Figure 84: Leven and Harriet Simmons. Public domain via FamilySearch.

LS 1852 Spring: Leven Simmons and Harriet Bradford Simmons with their seven children depart for Utah with Captain Howell's ox team company. With wagons heavily loaded, everyone walks who is able, with Harriet carrying baby Levi all the way to Utah in a sling made of her apron to keep her hands free.

The book *Simmons Family History* gives the following account from their journey:

"The Sweetwater River in Nebraska was too swollen to ford, and it was anticipated that it would take three weeks for the water to subside. Captain Howell's company was told that if they traveled upstream a few days, they would find a place where the water divided into several streams, which would be crossable. They were told they would find plenty of buffalo that way, but they would have to keep a lookout for Indians.

"They decided to go north and take this route.

"One night, an Indian and his little boy came to their camp, which was in a rocky place. The pioneer men bought elk meat from them. 'When the Indians got a short distance from camp they were attacked by a group of Indians of another tribe, with whom they were at war.' The Indians which had traded with the pioneers were killed. The captain ordered the company to hitch their teams and move on, fearing trouble. A short distance away, they met the wife of the dead Indian, and when she asked what had happened, they told her and she went away.

"The next morning early, someone thought they saw something move on the hillside; all at once a whole band of Indians raised up out of the brush and came toward the camp. Harriet put a baby's nightgown on a whip stock and they waved it for a truce. The Indians came into camp and they were four hours talking through an interpreter before they could convince them that they did not kill their man. They wanted to know what the wagons were loaded with; they were loaded with arms and ammunition in this company and they had been warned not to tell the Indians. Grandfather told them they were loaded with food and he went and got them some and the Indians went away."

The company also have an unexpected encounter with Orson Hyde:

"Orson Hyde came through carrying the mail. The Indians had caught him and taken his horse and all of his clothes. Leven gave him a horse and they fitted him up with some clothes and he went on his way."[147]

JLB 1852 July 4: The Eli B. Kelsey Company departs Kanesville, Iowa. Among the members of the company are John Lowe Butler, his first wife and their children, and the first twenty-eight Scandinavian immigrants to cross the Mormon Trail. There are some orphans traveling with the group as well: some children whose parents have recently died of cholera, and some orphans who survived the terrible tragedy of the riverboat *Saluda*, which had been chartered to transport immigrants up the Mississippi River but which had its boilers explode, killing two dozen Saints. Kenion Taylor Butler, then called Taylor, and his father John are called on to use their cattle and wagon skills to help the Scandinavians, who do not have

---

[147] Burch, Annie Fergusson. *Samuel Simmons and Elizabeth Scott: Their Ancestors and Descendants,* Salt Lake City, 1965, pp. 16–17.

prior experience with oxen. Kenion and John are called upon to help lead that group, despite not speaking the same language as the Scandinavians.

John Lowe Butler and Kenion Taylor Butler Help Danish Immigrants 1852

Figure 85: Purported image of John Lowe Butler and image of Kenion Taylor Butler. Kenion would have been a young man of twenty when he crossed the plains. Public domain via FamilySearch.

John's official company assignment is blacksmithing. At the beginning of the journey, however, though John and his family speak no Danish, he and son Taylor help the Danish immigrants learn to drive ox teams, being called on to replace Christian Raven—the original captain of the Danish group of "ten" (ten wagons)— who lacked driving skills.

"Danes disliked the American method of putting oxen in yokes, so they made harnesses in regular Danish fashion. But once harnessed, the oxen became frightened and 'struck out in a wild run.' . . . As John told it, 'None of them had ever driven an ox team before and they could not get along at all.' . . . For him and son Taylor, it was 'a fine [difficult] job to fix them. They had yoked up their cattle some one way and some another. Some of their [wagon cover] bows were too large, some too small.' Butler father and son 'went to work and fixed up the yokes and bows,' John said. Then they 'paired the cattle as well as we could.' After that, the company 'got along a great deal better, but they were still green about driving.' John taught the foreigners other basics of 'ox-teamology.'"

On July 24, the Butlers celebrate Pioneer Day with the rest of the Kelsey Company, along with another company that is traveling nearby.

The Kelsey Company suffer little from cholera, but they do face other stresses of the trail.

On one occasion, they encounter a buffalo stampede. A few of the animals are felled by men in the company with rifles, and the pioneers appreciate this as it provides extra provisions for the trail.

On August 18, Indians come to the camp—about two hundred Sioux men, women, and children, along with horses, dogs, and furniture.

John recounts other trials from the trail:

"One day we were driving along and there was a storm coming up. There was a flash of lightning struck the ground, the man said just ahead of his oxen. They [the oxen] turned out and started to run [and] with that frightening the other team behind him and it started. That started some more, so they stampeded and broke four wagons down, some spokes broke out, felleys [rims] broke out, points off from axle trees, and tongues out, reaches [connecting rods] broke, and there it was, all smashed up together. I had the job to fix them all up."

As Hartley writes in his biography of John Lowe Butler: "Hammer, anvil, and stubborn iron created clanging that rang through the high plains camp, while John's fuel and bellows produced fire hot enough to soften iron sufficiently to be reforged."

Caroline Farozine Skeen Butler 1852

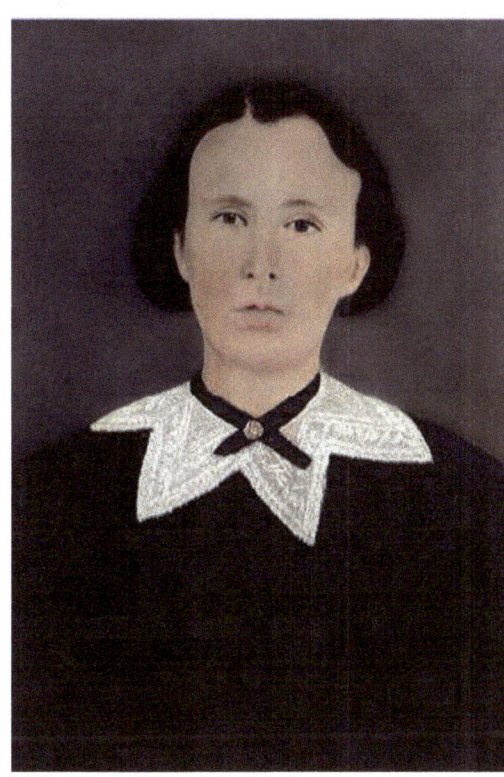

Caroline is skillful in making soap, a useful skill among pioneers. She cooks fat gathered from dead animals along the way and marrow from bones in water that holds soaked cottonwood ashes. As Caroline boils it together, the mix becomes soft soap, which she stows in a barrel in the back of the wagon for women to use on wash day.

One day, Caroline gets some flour from fellow travelers and makes her children each a biscuit, a special treat. Daughter Sarah wants to save hers for later and accidently drops it in the soap barrel, "but she fished it out, washed it, and ate it anyway." Flour and biscuits are rare,[148] and not to be wasted.

Caroline is 40 years old at the time she crosses the Mormon Trail. She crosses the plain with her oldest ten children, who at the time range in age from Kenion Taylor Butler, age 20, down to young Thomas, who is just a year old. The older children are a great help on the plains. A few years after reaching Utah Territory, Caroline will give birth to her last child, Alveretta Farozine Butler, in 1854.

My Best for the Kingdom, by William Hartley, gives many more details of the adventures of the Butler family on their journey west.

Figure 86: Portrait of Caroline Farozine Skeen. Public domain via FamilySearch.

Royal and Lydia Durfey 1852

RD 1852 July 8: The Henry W. Miller Company departs the outfitting post at Kanesville, Iowa, with 229 individuals and 63 wagons. Royal Durfey is 41, Lydia is 41, Olive Artemisia is 18, Sarah is 13, and Alma is 8. Richard Bentley recounts of this speedy trek: "We made good time, passing all the companies along the road down to the 7th. The cholera was very bad on the plains that year, but only one or two died out of our company. Captain Miller would not stop in one camp long enough for the people to get sick and die. It was very sorrowful to see so many graves by the roadside."[149]

RD 1852 September 10: The Henry W. Miller Company arrives in the Salt Lake Valley, the Durfey family among them.

LSS 1852 September 26: The Simmons family arrives in Utah, pauses to rest, and then moves on to settle in Springville.[150]

Figure 87: Royal and Lydia Durfey. Public domain via FamilySearch.

---

[148] Hartley, pp. 242–249.
[149] "Kenion Taylor Buter." *FamilySearch*. https://www.familysearch.org/tree/person/memories/KWJY-DQ8
[150] Based on the accounts by Olsen and Huff.

Figure 88: Handcart pioneers struggle through a blizzard while crossing the Rocky Mountains. © Everett Collection/Shutterstock.

Figure 89: Kenion Taylor Butler, rescuer for the Willie and Martin Handcart Company. Public domain via FamilySearch.

JLB 1852 October 14–16: The Kelsey Company, including the Butlers, arrives in Utah.

Kenion Taylor Butler and the Willie and Martin Handcart Companies

1855 August: The Willie and Martin Handcart Companies leave late in the season to cross the plains to Utah.

JLB 1855 December: Rescuers from Spanish Fork are among the last called in to help the Willie and Martin Handcart Company. Bishop John Lowe Butler sends a company of five wagons and teams along with thirteen young and able-bodied men. He sends his son Kenion Taylor Butler as the assistant captain of the company. After Taylor's return, he recounts his experiences with John, who records in his autobiography:

"[Taylor] told me how he found the Saints, and how the road was. He said that there were teams that reached nearly from the City to

*Figure 90: Historic statue memorializing handcart pioneers coming to Utah.
Photo 249912628 © Dallas Golden/Dreamstime.com*

Fort Bridger. They had to have men shoveling out snow and breaking the road, and in some places the snow was up above the wagon bows on each side. And they found the Saints in an awful condition. Some with their feet froze and some with their fingers froze, and they had no food to eat, and he said that he never saw such a sight before. It was dreadful, and he said that they [the rescued] were so over-joyed they did not know what to do hardly. Deep snow not only made it hard for men to keep the trail open, but it blocked off easy access to firewood: They were all picked up and fed [the people] and clothes given to them. When they camped at night, there were a whole lot of the boys would break a road to a tree and cut it down for firewood. And when they were coming back, they never saw the sun for six days, and it snowed all the time, and they had to break the road over again. And in coming down the Big Mountain they never locked a wheel but gee'd off and let the hub of the off wheel drag in the snow, and so they came down."[151]

---

[151] Hartley, p. 295.

Mads and Maren Christensen 1857

Figure 91: Members of the Christensen family crossed the Mormon Trail by handcart in 1857. Images are public domain via FamilySearch.

MC 1857 June 15: A party of Christensen family members depart Iowa City, Iowa, in the Christian Christiansen Handcart Company, consisting of 330 individuals, 68 handcarts, and 3 wagons.

Mads and Maren Christensen travel with their son, Rasmus, and Mads' mother, Karen Marie Hansen Christensen, and others of Karen's family.

On the trail, Maren almost dies of cholera, but a blessing from Mads helps save her.[152]

MC 1857 Summer:

Karen Marie Hansen 1857

Though Karen is 58 at the time she crosses the plains, she has the endurance to walk through sun and rain.

"Her faith was in the Lord; if he spared her life to reach the Valley of Salt Lake, she would praise his name. If she died by the wayside, she would die unto him. . . . She said, 'The Lord blessed us each day, kept us from harm, and made our journey more easy.'"

She later recalls one day when the company was out of water. They'd given all the milk to the young children, who still cried for a drink. The grown people prayed to find water.

Figure 92: Karen Marie Hansen. Public domain via FamilySearch.

"The sky had been clear all day and was still clear except for one small cloud that suddenly seemed to hover over them. Then the rain began to pour down, so that the chuckholes in the road filled with water and the saints set pans and buckets out to catch the rain, and some dipped up the water from the chuckholes and strained it through a cloth and drank it. They all had a drink and went on their way rejoicing, feeling the Lord had heard their prayers and had sent the rain especially to quench their thirst."

---

[152] Bunn, Celeste. "Maren Johanne Jensen." *FamilySearch.* https://www.familysearch.org/photos/artifacts/1497291?cid=mem_copy

Figure 93: Handcart monument.
Photo 5897605 © Margiew/Dreamstime.com

    The company wades across streams when there is no bridge, removing shoes and stockings and carrying these across tied together and hung over their shoulders. The women walk into the water holding up their skirts. Though the currents are sometimes strong, they always reach the other side in safety, and gratefully put back on their stockings and shoes.

    The steep mountains are hard on the elderly, who sometimes climb on hands and knees to the top, then use sticks and canes to brace themselves on the way down.

    The company peacefully passes Johnston's army on the way to Utah, wondering what would happen if the army entered Utah Valley. They trust in the Lord.

    Karen is often very tired when night comes, ready to sleep on the ground when the call comes to retire, thankful to be another day closer to the end of the journey, and thankful to still be alive.[153]

1857: The Saints receive word that Johnston's Army is heading toward Utah.

ETC 1861 June 1: Susan Leggett, age 22, departs Florence, Nebraska, in the David H. Cannon Company, numbering 225 individuals and 57 wagons. The future second wife of Ezra T. Clark, Susan's sense of finery and grace endure even in the face of challenges of the trail. She travels with a young family in

---

[153] Miller, Annie Christensen. "Karen Marie Hansen Life Sketch." *FamilySearch*, Intellectual Reserve, https://www.familysearch.org/tree/person/memories/L5D2-KFW. Accessed 2 October 2020.

exchange for help with the children, and embroiders yards of fine muslin for her future babies' wardrobes, tying her work to the wagon bow. All ten of her children will later be blessed in those first baby clothes.[154]

ETC 1861 August 11–16: The David H. Cannon Company reaches the Salt Lake Valley.

AR 1862 July 24: Hannah Severn, age 21, (future fourth wife of Alfred Randall) departs Florence, Nebraska (now Omaha), in the John Riggs Murdoch Company, comprising 700 people and 65 wagons. John Riggs Murdoch, now age 35, was fostered by the Clark and Phelps families for a few years after the death of his mother. His twin siblings had been adopted by Joseph and Emma Smith. John lived with and helped Morris and Laura Clark Phelps and their children, and later stayed with Timothy Baldwin Clark while Laura worked to get her husband out of jail. John Riggs Murdoch and Ezra Thompson Clark had guided the family cattle from Independence, Missouri, to Nauvoo, Illinois. John goes on to a long career of Church service.[155]

AR 1862 September 27: The John Riggs Murdoch Company reaches the Salt Lake Valley.

1869 May 10: The transcontinental railroad is completed when the Golden Spike is driven into the ground at Promontory Summit, Utah, opening Utah to rail service and ending the era of the traditional pioneers.

---

[154] "Biography of Susan L. Clark." *Family Search*, Intellectual Reserve, https://www.familysearch.org/photos/artifacts/7929293?cid=mem_copy. Accessed 13 May 2021.
[155] Brenda Clark Sederberg enjoyed noting the life connections of John with both the Joseph Smith family and her ancestors.

6. Polygamy Pathways

"Polygamy . . . was something many just 'didn't talk about'" wrote one of Daniel Goulding's descendants. [156]

Called "the peculiar practice," polygamy started quietly with Joseph Smith in Nauvoo, and was initially offered only to particularly loyal Saints such as John Lowe Butler, estimated to be among the first twelve men to enter the practice when he married Charity Skeen as his second wife on 24 December 1844.[157]

In the early days, people who were invited to practice polygamy often had one of two reactions—denounce it and leave the Church, thereby being branded apostate, or embrace it. Some, such as Brigham Young and Heber C. Kimball, initially expressed displeasure but later spoke of it as an encouraged spiritual practice for their time.

Polygamy could be a hot button issue for outsiders.

Its practice indirectly led to Joseph Smith's death. After the Nauvoo Expositor newspaper's only issue took a stand against polygamy, Joseph and the Nauvoo city council ordered the press to be destroyed. Arrested on charges of riot, Joseph was later assassinated at Carthage.[158]

The practice of polygamy had been slowly expanding to include more people, among them Margaret Harley, who married Alfred Randall as his second wife at Winter Quarters in 1848.

---

[156] RVTwitch. "A few tidbits of Daniel's life—comments." *FamilySearch*, Intellectual Reserve, https://www.familysearch.org/photos/artifacts/47118511?cid=mem_copy. Accessed 22 November 2020.

[157] Hartley, William G. *My Best for the Kingdom: history and autobiography of John Lowe Butler, a Mormon frontiersman*, p. 136. C. L. Dalton Enterprises, 1993.

[158] The Church of Jesus Christ of Latter-day Saints. "Nauvoo Expositor." *The Church of Jesus Christ of Latter-day Saints*, Intellectual Reserve, https://www.churchofjesuschrist.org/study/history/topics/nauvoo-expositor?lang=eng. Accessed 21 November 2020.

The Saints went west to live their religion, including polygamy, free of persecution. In 1852, polygamy was made public to the Church as a whole.

During the 1856–57 Mormon Reformation,[159] "the principle" was fervently encouraged. One woman observed, "This is the greatest time for marrying I ever knew."[160]

In 1857, John Lowe Butler, then a bishop, married four new wives, bringing his lifetime total to eight, though the most in his household at any one time was six.[161]

Leaders were especially encouraged to practice polygamy. But spiritual devotion didn't always equal prosperity, and with no recommended model of polygamous family living to follow, families were left to their own ingenuity to determine how to live and structure their family.

In some families, such as Ezra T. Clark's and the Gouldings, all wives and children shared resources as a giant family. They worked hard together, lived close together, and financially thrived. In others, such as Edward B. Clark's, the Randalls, and the Christensens, plural wives operated somewhat as single women or single mothers, with the father living with the first wife, a favorite wife, or the wife with the greatest need or youngest children. In others, like the Butlers and the Simmons, the wives may have lived together part or all of the time out of economic necessity, but there was financial struggle.

Harmony within the polygamous families varied as wildly as their financial success.

Ezra T. Clark's families lived peaceably.

Daughter Laura later wrote: "Father lived at Aunt Mary's home, she being the first wife, and whenever he would come over to our home to eat the noon meal, often Mother would call over Aunt Mary to come over and eat too. Aunt Mary would admire a geranium on the windowsill and Mother would tell her to take it home with her. That is the kind of woman my Mother was."[162]

Alfred Randall's families seemed to get along very well, too.

His daughter Emily later wrote: "Father had five wives, mother being the second. He did not spend a great deal of his time at our house after I can remember, feeling that he was needed most with the younger children. There was always the best of feelings between Father and Mother and the rest of the family."[163]

First wives often attended their husband's subsequent weddings to show their support.

Edward Barrett Clark writes of the day he married Alice, "She [first-wife Wealthy] went to the Logan Temple with us, and on April 2, 1885 I was married to Alice Randall. . . . Wealthy was always true to me and to the principle. She never tried to persuade me from my duty to Alice."[164]

Some first wives were more challenged by the doctrine. Caroline Butler is not recorded as going with John to ceremonies for any plural wives other than second wife Charity (Caroline's sister). She expressed concerns about John's additional marriages to these mostly younger women.

John said:

---

[159] The Mormon Reformation will be discussed in greater detail later in this chapter.
[160] Hartley, p. 302.
[161] Hartley, pp. 302–305.
[162] Clark, Laura Blanche. "Autobiography of Laura Blanche Clark." *FamilySearch*, Intellectual Reserve, 7 December 2018, https://www.familysearch.org/tree/person/memories/KWCZ-YQH. Accessed 28 September 2020.
[163] Richards, Emily Randall. *Life Story of Emily Randall Richards. FamilySearch*, https://www.familysearch.org/tree/person/memories/KWCH-MFZ. Accessed 2 October 2020.
[164] Clark, Edward Barrett. "Incidents in the Life and Labors of Wealthy Richards Clark." *Autobiography of Edward B. Clark*, Ezra T. Clark Family Organization. *Ezra T. Clark: The Family Web Site of Ezra T. Clark*, http://ezratclark.org/familyfile_AEBC_IncidentsInLife.asp. Accessed 21 November 2020.

"She complained 'how she had always been with me in all my trials, had borne a large family of children to me' and then requested something 'that it was not her right to dictate, trying to rule the priesthood.'"[165]

To John, the practice of polygamy would have represented obedience. It became a topic he and Caroline disagreed over. Adding additional women to the family probably complicated the family's struggle to provide for themselves. The perspectives of both John and Caroline are understandable.

At the dedication of the Temple Square Tabernacle on 9 October 1875, Elder Wilford Woodruff preached, "We have many bishops and elders who have but one wife. They are abundantly qualified to enter the higher law . . . , but their wives will not let them."[166]

Sometime after hearing this speech, with the permission of his first wife, Thomas Tingey invited Thurza Randall (daughter of Margaret Harley Randall) to become his second wife. This marriage, and the plural marriages of most of Margaret's other daughters (including Alan's grandmother, Alice), followed the spirit of the religion they'd grown up with and the example of their parents, but led to challenging times for their generation, because the government's attitude toward polygamy was becoming increasingly hostile.

During the years 1882–1893, the Edmunds Act and the Edmund–Tucker Act created penalties for the Church and individuals who practiced polygamy and applied pressure toward ending the practice. A bounty of $20 for the identification of each "cohab" (polygamist) and other sanctions, including a prospect of jail time for polygamous men, drove many men, plural wives, and children into hiding.[167]

Plural wives on the run with children moved between homes of family, friends, and strangers who volunteered to host women "on the Underground," often while the women worked for the financial support of themselves and their children, sometimes with little access to emotional or financial support from husbands. Margaret had more than one daughter who was in the position of hiding or living quietly away from a husband, including her daughter Alice.

With persecution against polygamous marriages, some work-arounds were quietly devised to protect those who followed the practice, such as in the case of Annie Clark, who married her husband by proxy (someone else stood in for her groom). She came home alone on the train, and was met at the station only by her brother Wilford.[168]

"I remember being so glad that some member of the family was there at the station to meet me," she wrote. She dined on bread and milk at her father's home that night for her wedding supper, without her husband present.[169] This lack of fanfare made for a muted rendition of a major life event, but also helped to keep polygamous families away from attention.

---

[165] Hartley, p. 304.
[166] Tingey. "Thurza Amelia Randall - Life Sketch." *FamilySearch*, Intellectual Reserve, 4 August 2013, https://www.familysearch.org/tree/person/memories/KWNN-H4X. Accessed 28 September 2020.
[167] Clark, Antone. *Noble Pioneer: A Biography of Ezra Thompson Clark*. Ezra T. Clark Family Organization, 2002. *Ezra T. Clark: The Family Web Site of Ezra T. Clark*, http://ezratclark.org/Noble%20Pioneer%20A%20Biography%20of%20Ezra%20Thompson%20Clark.pdf. Accessed 21 November 2020.
[168] Despite never living as a polygamist himself, Wilford Woodruff Clark continually exhibited kindness toward women and children in the polygamous families of his relatives—including his sisters who lived as polygamous wives, his brothers' polygamous wives, and the children of his polygamous relatives. This was notable enough that multiple authors have recorded stories of his thoughtfulness. Our own ancestry later benefited greatly from his outgoing consideration, as we will see in a later chapter where Alice's children share how they considered him to be their father figure.
[169] Tanner, Annie Clark. *A Mormon Mother*, p. 66.

By 1890, the Church Manifesto ended Church approval for the practice of polygamy. In 1893, Congress approved the return of Church property. Men in the Church were instructed not to take additional wives, but were permitted to keep the wives that they had.

Many polygamous families attended mainstream Church together for the rest of their lives. Public perception among Church members took a long time to shift. Some splinter groups spun off to continue polygamy on their own. And some members of the mainstream Church entered new plural marriages even after a 1904 Second Manifesto by Joseph F. Smith reaffirmed the Church's position. The official stance was that these non-conforming individuals must be excommunicated.

The lifespans of those who practiced polygamy within our extended family extended well beyond the years of the early settler days in Utah. Laura Blanche Clark Cook Silver Cook, Ezra T. Clark's daughter and third wife of Joseph Askie Silver, lived until 1985.

So, what to do with this peculiar practice?

Many just didn't talk about it.

But the families, and their histories, remain. We have their stories.

Four families in Alan's ancestry, and three in Janet's, practiced polygamy.
Here are stories from these families.
Polygamy is not a current practice of the Church of Jesus Christ of Latter-day Saints.

Timeline of Polygamy

Boldface line entries indicate events in the Latter-day Saint Church and US political sphere.
Regular type indicates events in polygamous families in Alan and Janet's ancestry.
(Ancestral families not practicing polygamy are not included in this timeline.)[170]

Acronyms of the ancestral polygamous families are as follows; Clark/Ruppe ancestral mothers are in boldface font:
AR = The Randall family. Alfred Randall and wives Emmerette Louisa Davis Randall, **Margaret Harley Randall**, Mildred Elizabeth Johnson Randall, Hannah Severn Randall, and Elizabeth Elsie Elsey Anderson Randall.
DG = The Goulding family. Daniel Goulding and wives **Elizabeth Merrifield Pratten Goulding** and Fanny Pratten Goulding.
EBC = Edward Barrett Clark family. Edward Barret Clark and wives Wealthy Richards Clark and **Alice Randall Clark**.
ETC = The Ezra Thompson Clark family. Ezra Thompson Clark and wives **Mary Stevenson Clark**, Susan Leggett Clark, and Nancy Areta Porter Stevenson Clark.
JLB = The Butler family. John Lowe Butler and wives **Caroline Farozine Skeen Butler**, Charity Skeen Butler, Sarah Bryant Butler, Sarah Lancaster Butler, Ann Hughes Butler, Esther Emily Ogden Butler, Lovisa Hamilton Butler, and Henrietta Seaton Blyth Butler.

---

[170] Dates and ages for ancestors' personal events on these lists are taken from the FamilySearch timelines of the named individuals.

LSS = The Simmons family. Leven Simmons Sr. and wives **Harriet Bradford Simmons** and Lydia Rebecca Fisher Simmons.

MC = The Mads Christensen family. Mads Christensen and wives **Maren Johanne Jensen Christensen** and Johanne (Hannah) Christensen.

JLB 1831 January 29: John Lowe Butler (age 22) marries first wife Caroline Farozine Skeen (age 18) in Sumner, Tennessee. They will have 12 children together, 11 of whom will live to adulthood. Their eldest son, Kenion Taylor Butler, will be one of Janet's maternal great-great-grandfathers.

AR 1834 January 9: Alfred Randall (age 22) marries first wife Emmerette Louisa Davis (age 15). They will have 10 children together, 4 of whom will live to adulthood.

LSS 1836 February 27: Leven Simmons Sr. (age 23) marries first wife Harriet Bradford (age 14) in Carthage, Illinois. They will have 12 children together, 10 of whom will live to adulthood. Their seventh child, son Matthew Simmons, will be Janet's paternal great-grandfather.

1843: Joseph Smith announces baptisms for the dead, and polygamy. (PBS)

1844 June 7: First and only edition of Nauvoo Expositor is published, which is critical of the doctrines of polygamy and exaltation.[171]

1844 June 10: On the instruction of the Nauvoo city council, which has declared the press a nuisance, the Nauvoo marshal destroys the Nauvoo Expositor press. This leads to a charge of riot against Joseph Smith and he is subsequently arrested.[172]

1844 June 27: Joseph and Hyrum Smith are assassinated at Carthage, Illinois.[173]

Figure 94: Purported image of John Lowe Butler, one of the first men to enter the practice of polygamy in Nauvoo.
Public domain via FamilySearch.

JLB 1844 December 24: John Lowe Butler (age 36) is one of the first dozen or so men to take a second wife under the doctrine of plural marriage. He marries Charity Skeen (age 36), the deaf-mute sister of his first wife, Caroline Skeen. Charity communicates well through a version of signing. Charity and John will not have any children together.[174]

---

[171] Hartley, pp. 127–128.
[172] The Church of Jesus Christ of Latter-day Saints. "Nauvoo Expositor." *The Church of Jesus Christ of Latter-day Saints*, Intellectual Reserve, https://www.churchofjesuschrist.org/study/history/topics/nauvoo-expositor?lang=eng. Accessed 21 November 2020.
[173] The Church of Jesus Christ of Latter-day Saints. "Deaths of Joseph and Hyrum Smith." *The Church of Jesus Christ of Latter-day Saints*, Intellectual Reserve, https://www.churchofjesuschrist.org/study/history/topics/deaths-of-joseph-and-hyrum-smith?lang=eng. Accessed 21 November 2020.
[174] Hartley, pp. 136–137.

ETC 1845 May 18: Ezra Thompson Clark (age 21)[175] marries first wife Mary Stevenson (age 19) in Lee County Iowa across the river from Nauvoo, in a ceremony performed by Ezra's brother William O. Clark. They will have 11 children together, 9 of whom will live to adulthood. Their seventh child, son Edward Barrett Clark, will be Alan's paternal grandfather.[176]

JLB 1846 Winter: John Lowe Butler (age 37) marries his third and fourth wives: widow Sarah Bryant Lancaster[177] (age 74) and her daughter Sarah Lancaster (age 39). John's first two wives and his children are many miles away with the Emmett Expedition at Fort Vermillion and have no way of knowing of these marriages at the time, but Caroline knows the Lancasters because they were her backyard neighbors in Nauvoo. The younger Sarah will travel west with John; the elder Sarah will remain in the Midwest with her other children. Neither of the Sarahs will have children with John.[178]

JLB 1847–48 Winter: John Lowe Butler's brother-in-law visits the Butler family in Kanesville, Iowa, and returns Charity to Tennessee, where he leaves her.[179] Charity never returns to the Butler family and will die among her relatives.[180]

Figure 95: Alfred wed second wife Margaret in Winter Quarters. Public domain via FamilySearch.

AR 1848 January 29: Alfred Randall (age 36) marries second wife Margaret Harley (age 25) at Winter Quarters in a ceremony officiated by Brigham Young. They will have 7 children together, all of whom will live to adulthood. Their sixth child, daughter Alice, will be Alan's paternal grandmother.

DG 1851 February 19: Daniel Goulding (age 19) marries first wife Elizabeth Merrifield Pratten (age 18) in Wales. They will have 12 children together, 7 of whom will live to adulthood. Their sixth child, daughter Rosanna Susannah Goulding, born in Australia during her parents' long pathway from England to Zion, will be one of Janet's maternal great-grandmothers.

---

[175] "Ezra Thompson Clark by unknown author." *FamilySearch*, Intellectual Reserve, https://www.familysearch.org/photos/artifacts/111157637?cid=mem_copy. Accessed 21 November 2020.

[176] Clark, Antone. *Noble Pioneer: A Biography of Ezra Thompson Clark*. Ezra T. Clark Family Organization, 2002. *Ezra T. Clark: The Family Web Site of Ezra T. Clark*, http://ezratclark.org/Noble%20Pioneer%20A%20Biography%20of%20Ezra%20Thompson%20Clark.pdf. Accessed 21 November 2020.

[177] With the age gap, this likely would have been a sealing performed entirely to give the elder Sarah the benefit of temple blessings.

[178] Hartley, pp. 83–84.

[179] The motives for this action are unknown, though it is known that the Skeen family generally didn't like John Lowe Butler and the Church.

[180] Hartley, p. 253.

1852: The practice of polygamy is publicly announced to the Latter-day Saint Church at large in a sermon by Apostle Orson Pratt, and becomes available for broader practice.[181]

ETC Ezra's nieces (and Laura Clark Phelps' daughters) Paulina Clark Lyman and Mary Clark Rich are now openly acknowledged as plural wives and viewed as pioneers in the polygamous movement.[182]

MC 1854: Mads Christensen (age 29) marries first wife Maren Johanne Jensen (age 27) in Denmark. They will have 6 children together, all of whom will live to adulthood. Mads and Maren will convert to the Latter-day Saint faith and travel to Utah with Mads' mother, Karen. Their second child, son Joseph Mads, first of their children born in Utah, will be Alan's maternal grandfather.

1856–1857: During the Mormon Reformation years, devotion to polygamy among mainstream Church members reaches perhaps its greatest height. Leaders are especially encouraged to practice polygamy.[183]

Figure 96: Leven Simmons. Public domain via FamilySearch.

LSS 1856 February 21: In Spanish Fork, Leven Simmons Sr. (age 43) marries second wife Lydia Rebecca Fisher (age 18, who has one child by a previous marriage). They will have 8 children together, 7 of whom will live to adulthood.

1856: The US Republican Party labels slavery and polygamy "twin relics of barbarism" and embraces an anti-polygamy platform.[184]

JLB 1857 March 9: John Lowe Butler (age 48) marries fifth, sixth, and seventh wives Ann Hughes (age 63), Esther Emily Ogden (age 17), and Lovisa Hamilton (age 19) in Salt Lake City. Lovisa and John will have one child together, Lovisa Patience, who will live to adulthood. Ann Hughes is past childbearing age, and John and Esther Emily Ogden will not have children together.

JLB 1857 August: Esther Emily Ogden, unhappy with her living situation, is granted a divorce by John Lowe Butler.

JLB 1857 September 8: John Lowe Butler (age 49) marries eighth wife Henrietta Seaton Blyth (age 26). Henrietta and John will have 2 children together, the youngest of whom will be born four months after John Lowe Butler's death at the age of 52.

---

[181] Embry, Jessie L. "Polygamy." *Utah History Encyclopedia*, edited by Allen Kent Powell, University of Utah Press, 1994. *Utah Education Network*, https://www.uen.org/utah_history_encyclopedia/p/POLYGAMY.shtml. Accessed 20 November 2020.
[182] Tanner, Annie Clark. *A Mormon Mother*, p. 22.
[183] Hartley, pp. 297–305.
[184] Independence Hall Association in Philadelphia. "Republican Platform of 1856." *ushistory.org*, Independence Hall Association, https://www.ushistory.org/gop/convention_1856republicanplatform.htm. Accessed 21 November 2020.

AR 1860 May 30: Alfred Randall (age 48) marries third wife Mildred Elizabeth Johnson (age 32) at the Salt Lake Endowment House. Mildred and Alfred will have 2 children together, neither of whom will live longer than a few years. Mildred will accompany Alfred as his missionary companion to Laie, Hawaii.[185]

JLB 1860 June 1: Sarah Bryant (third wife of John Lowe Butler I) dies in Richmond, Indiana, at the age of 88.

JLB 1860 April 8: John Lowe Butler dies at the age of 52 in Spanish Fork, Utah. His last child, John William Butler, will be born on 11 August of that year.

Figure 97: Ezra T. Clark. Public domain via FamilySearch.

ETC 1861 November 8: Ezra Thompson Clark (age 37) marries second wife Susan Leggett (age 23) in Salt Lake City. Ezra stayed with Susan's family while he was on a proselytizing mission to England.[186] Susan is on good terms with Ezra's first wife, Mary.[187] For a time Mary and Susan live in the same house together; later Susan will move into a house that Ezra has built for her across the street from his first family.[188] Susan and Ezra T. will have 10 children together, 9 of whom will live to adulthood. Susan and Ezra's fifth child will be John Alexander Clark, who will be called on a mission to Palestine, pass away during his service, and be buried in the Holy Land.[189] Because the Church owns his grave site, this small property and one other grave will later prove the Church has historical presence in the area, paving the way for the BYU Jerusalem Center to be built.[190]

AR 1863 March 7: Alfred Randall (age 51) marries fourth wife Hannah Severn (age 21) in Salt Lake City. Alfred will spend most of his later years living with Hannah, who will have his youngest children and who will have frail health.[191] Hannah and Alfred will have 9 children together, 8 of whom will live to adulthood.[192]

---

[185] "Mildred Elizabeth Johnson." *Our Pioneer Heritage*, pp. 286–289. *FamilySearch*, https://www.familysearch.org/tree/person/memories/KWJB-JNM. Accessed 29 November 2020.
[186] "Ezra Thompson Clark by unknown author." *FamilySearch*, Intellectual Reserve, https://www.familysearch.org/photos/artifacts/111157637?cid=mem_copy. Accessed 21 November 2020.
[187] Clark, Laura Blanche.
[188] Clark, Antone. *Noble Pioneer: A Biography of Ezra Thompson Clark*. Ezra T. Clark Family Organization, 2002. *Ezra T. Clark: The Family Web Site of Ezra T. Clark*, http://ezratclark.org/Noble%20Pioneer%20A%20Biography%20of%20Ezra%20Thompson%20Clark.pdf. Accessed 21 November 2020.
[189] Clark, Mary Stevenson. "Autobiography of Mary Stevenson Clark." *FamilySearch*, Intellectual Reserve, https://www.familysearch.org/photos/artifacts/1542747?cid=mem_copy. Accessed 21 November 2020.
[190] "Jerusalem Center Miracle." *FamilySearch*, Intellectual Reserve, https://www.familysearch.org/photos/artifacts/37149489?cid=mem_copy. Accessed 21 November 2020.
[191] Kofoed, Lucy Randall. *The True Life Story of Alfred Randall*, p. 24. Lucy Kofoed. *FamilySearch*, https://www.familysearch.org/photos/artifacts/19244627?cid=mem_copy. Accessed 20 November 2020.
[192] Kofoed, Lucy Randall. "A Life Sketch of Hannah Severn Randall." *FamilySearch*, Intellectual Reserve, https://www.familysearch.org/photos/artifacts/11461919?cid=mem_copy. Accessed 21 November 2020.

1863 October 10: Alfred Randall's cousin Samuel J. Randall from Pennsylvania begins twenty-seven years of service in the US House of Representatives, including serving as House Speaker from 1876 to 1881. Samuel will be serving in the House during the passage of both the Edmunds Act and the Edmunds–Tucker Act.[193]

AR 1865 May 13: Alfred Randall (age 53) marries fifth wife Elsie Anderson (age 35) in the Salt Lake Endowment House. They will have 3 sons together, 2 of whom will live to adulthood.

JLB 1866 September 7: Ann Hughes (fifth wife of John Lowe Butler I) passes away in Spanish Fork at the age of 72.

DG 1870 May 16: Daniel Goulding (age 39) marries Fanny Pratten (age 27). Fanny is the sister of Daniel's first wife Elizabeth. Fanny, Elizabeth, and Daniel will live together in the same house for many years and divide the labor of running the household and providing for the family among the three of them.[194] Fanny and Daniel will have 6 children together, all of whom will live to adulthood.

Figure 98: Daniel Goulding and second wife Fanny Pratten Goulding. Public domain via FamilySearch.

1870 February 12: The Federal Government grants Utah women the right to vote in a belief that they will vote against polygamy.[195]

ETC 1870 July 11: Ezra Thompson Clark (age 46) marries third wife Nancy Areta Porter (age 44). Nancy was formerly the first wife of Ezra's brother-in-law Edward Stevenson. She had gone to Brigham Young and told him about her household difficulties. Brigham called Ezra to his office and asked Ezra to marry Nancy. Nancy lives for a time in Farmington, where she is active in the Church and in the broader Clark family, but eventually moves to live with her adult children and will die in Idaho. Nancy and Ezra do not have any children together.[196]

---

[193] "Samuel J. Randall." *Wikipedia*, Wikimedia, https://en.wikipedia.org/wiki/Samuel_J._Randall. Accessed 21 November 2020.

[194] Goulding, Zina E. "Fanny Pratten Goulding (written by her daughter Zina E. Goulding Johnson when Fanny was 81 years old." *FamilySearch*, Intellectual Reserve, https://www.familysearch.org/photos/artifacts/72131151?cid=mem_copy. Accessed 21 November 2020.

[195] National Park Service. "Utah and the 19th Amendment." *National Park Service*, National Park Service | US Department of the Interior, https://www.nps.gov/articles/utah-women-s-history.htm. Accessed 21 November 2020.

[196] "Biography of Nancy Areta Porter." *FamilySearch*, Intellectual Reserve, https://www.familysearch.org/photos/artifacts/76381754?cid=mem_copy. Accessed 21 November 2020.

Figure 99: The Young Family residence.
© marzolino/Depositphotos

JLB 1875 August 4: Caroline Farozine Skeen (first wife of John Lowe Butler I) passes away in Panguitch, Utah, at the age of 63. ("Caroline Farozine Skeen Timeline") At her funeral it was said: "Her faith was strong as the everlasting hills, and all these hardships only seemed to purify her soul until it was pure gold. Her very womanliness rested like a halo on her brow. She is one of the queens of the earth."[197]

LSS 1876 February 8: Leven Simmons Sr. dies at the age of 63, in Spanish Fork, Utah.

1879: Women in Utah lose the right to vote after it becomes apparent they are voting to maintain polygamy.[198]

EBC 1879 September 25: Edward Barrett Clark (age 20) marries first wife Wealthy Richards (age 18) in Salt Lake City. Wealthy struggles to get pregnant, and is told in a blessing that if she allows her husband to take a second wife that she will be able to have children.[199] Wealthy agrees to this course of action, saying she does not want to deprive Edward of having a family.[200]

---

[197] Geni. "John Lowe Butler." *Geni*, https://www.geni.com/people/John-Butler/6000000000697210472.
[198] National Park Service.
[199] Clark, Walter Edward. *Autobiography of Walter Edward Clark*, p. 2.
[200] Clark, Edward Barrett. "Incidents in the Life and Labors of Wealthy Richards Clark." *Autobiography of Edward B. Clark*, Ezra T. Clark Family Organization. Ezra T. Clark: The Family Web Site of Ezra T. Clark, http://ezratclark.org/familyfile_AEBC_IncidentsInLife.asp. Accessed 21 November 2020.

Figure 100: Mads in later life. Public domain via FamilySearch.

MC 1881: Mads Christensen (age 56) follows the council of the Church elders and takes a second wife, marrying Johanne (Hannah) Margarethe Christiansen (age 24) in Salt Lake City. His second son Joseph Mads will later marry Hannah's younger sister Emma. Hannah and Mads will have 10 children together, 8 of whom will live to adulthood.[201]

1882 March 23: The Edmunds Anti-Polygamy Act of 1882 is signed into law by US President Chester A. Arthur, making polygamy a felony in US states and territories.[202] A bounty of $20 is offered for each "cohab" (polygamist) brought to the attention of the authorities.[203] The Edmunds Act punished bigamous cohabitation by revoking the civil rights of polygamists. Anyone who practices or approves of polygamy is barred from serving in public office.[204]

MC 1883: With law enforcement officials making life uncomfortable for polygamists, Mads proposes moving his families to Arizona. Maren says she will not leave her home in Farmington. Mads and second wife Hannah go to Arizona.[205]

MC 1885: Mads and Hannah Christensen return to Utah.

1885 February 1: President John Taylor, in his last public address, advises brethren practicing polygamy to stop fighting and flee.[206]

---

[201] Ashby, Ruth C. "Life Sketch of Mads Christensen." *Short Life Sketches of Our Ancestors*, 2002, p. 79. *FamilySearch*, https://www.familysearch.org/photos/artifacts/39845217?cid=mem_copy. Accessed 21 November 2020.
[202] Washington County Historical Society, Washington County, Utah. "Edmunds Act (aka Edmunds Anti-Polygamy Act of 1882)." *Washington County Historical Society*, Washington County Historical Society. Accessed 21 November 2020.
[203] Clark, Antone, p. 178.
[204] Clark, Antone, p. 173.
[205] Christensen, Phillis. "Life History of Hannah (Johanne) 2nd wife of Mads Christensen." *Short Life Sketches of Our Ancestors*, edited by Ruth Card Ashby, pp. 93–97. *FamilySearch*, https://www.familysearch.org/photos/artifacts/39849976?cid=mem_copy. Accessed 22 November 2020.
[206] Clark, Antone, p. 178.

Figure 101: Edward Clark and Alice Randall Clark. Public domain via FamilySearch.

EBC 1885 April 2: Edward Barrett Clark (age 26) marries second wife Alice Randall (age 21) in Logan, Utah.

ETC 1886 September 1: Ezra T. Clark is arrested on a charge of polygamy.[207]

1887 March 3: The Edmunds–Tucker Act, enforced by US Marshals and deputies,[208] disincorporates the Church on grounds that the Church fosters polygamy. Church assets valued at over $50,000 are seized. Sanctions for polygamists are set at a fine of $500 to $800 and imprisonment for up to five years.[209]

1887–1890: All of Alan and Janet's ancestors alive and practicing polygamy during the enforcement of the Edmunds–Tucker Act are affected by it.

Figure 102: Ezra T. Clark. Public domain via FamilySearch.

Ezra T. Clark loses his position as Treasurer of Davis County.

After being put on trial and having several of his family members called to testify against him, Ezra is fined $300 and sentenced to six months in jail.

Ezra serves time at an adobe jail in Sugarhouse, where his beard and hair are shaved despite his offering the barber $300 to not remove his beard. Ezra is released in July 1887, after serving five months.

Ezra's daughter Annie Clark will later recall: "When father's term of imprisonment expired, his clothes were given him and replaced the striped prison garb, which he had been wearing. As he took his suit he said, 'I hope to prove to your officers of the law that I am not a criminal.'"[210]

His children find the appearance of their father much changed without his beard.

He is one of the rare men to pay his fine plus all of his jail expenses.

---

[207] Clark, Antone, p. 180.
[208] The Church of Jesus Christ of Latter-day Saints. "Antipolygamy Legislation." *The Church of Jesus Christ of Latter-day Saints*, Intellectual Reserve, https://www.churchofjesuschrist.org/study/history/topics/anti-polygamy-legislation?lang=eng. Accessed 21 November 2020.
[209] Ellsworth, S. George. "Utah's Road to Statehood: An Introduction." *Utah.gov*, State of Utah, 2002, https://archives.utah.gov/research/exhibits/Statehood/intronew.htm. Accessed 21 November 2020.
[210] Clark, Antone, pp. 184–186.

Edward Barrett Clark succeeds his father as Treasurer of Davis County, despite the fact that if it were known that he is also a polygamist he would not be eligible for the position.

In his autobiography, Edward writes: "I had been advised by proper authority to keep my wives in separate states. By so doing, I was left at liberty to look after the affairs of my father, Ezra T. Clark, as he was one who was incarcerated. I went often to visit him and when the time came to pay his fine, I went in Marshall Dyer's office and paid it, not knowing but what he had a warrant for my arrest but I was left alone, and Alice had her liberty, and it was not generally known to whom she belonged, as Joseph took her to Georgetown and I was there looking after the ranch and our cattle interests in Georgetown."[211]

Figure 103: Edward Barrett Clark. Public domain via FamilySearch.

Mads Christensen is arrested February 13, 1888, on a charge of unlawful cohabitation and is convicted. The grand jury sentences him to seven months in jail.[212] While there, he keeps an autograph book in which fellow prisoners record original poems, sometimes humorous and sometimes based on the history of their lives, as well as passionate thoughts on being jailed for living their religious beliefs.[213] After serving his term, Mads is released September 3, 1888, on condition of living with only one wife. He remains with Johanne (Hannah) Margarethe and they eventually move to Idaho. First wife Maren will live the rest of her life with her unmarried oldest daughter, Mary, in Farmington.[214]

Figure 104: Mads Christensen. Public domain via FamilySearch.

Figure 105: Alfred Randall. Public domain via FamilySearch.

Alfred Randall lives in Ogden with fourth wife Hannah. First wife Emmerette lives with an unmarried daughter, second wife Margaret lives on her own in Centerville where she keeps a large orchard and offers OB/GYN services, third wife Mildred lives alone in an apartment in Salt Lake City where she works as a teacher, and fifth wife Elsie lives in Ogden most of her married life and does janitorial work to help support her sons.[215]

---

[211] Clark, Edward Barrett. "Incidents in the Life and Labors of Alice Randall Clark." *Autobiography of Edward B. Clark*, Ezra T. Clark Family Organization. *Ezra T. Clark Family Organization*, http://ezratclark.org/familyfile_AEBC_IncidentsLifeLaborsAliceRandallClark.asp. Accessed 21 November 2020.

[212] Christensen, p. 95.

[213] Mulder, Dr. William. "Mads Christensen's Autograph Album." *FamilySearch*, Intellectual Reserve, 1963, https://www.familysearch.org/tree/person/memories/KWCT-YG1. Accessed 5 October 2020.

[214] Bunn, Celeste. "Mads Christensen." *FamilySearch*, Intellectual Reserve, https://www.familysearch.org/photos/artifacts/1497281?cid=mem_copy. Accessed 20 November 2020.

[215] Daughters of the Utah Pioneers. "A Few Facts and Stories About Emmerette Davis Randall." *FamilySearch*, Intellectual Reserve, https://www.familysearch.org/photos/artifacts/40508208?cid=mem_copy. Accessed 20 November 2020.

A sheriff shows up at Alfred's house in Ogden, but before he can produce the paperwork he has on hand to arrest Alfred, Alfred offers him a walk in his nearby orchard. Alfred gathers a box of fresh-picked peaches and offers it to the sheriff for his family. The sheriff takes the peaches and leaves, telling Alfred on another occasion that Alfred's good humor and fearlessness made him feel ashamed of his errand and unwilling to take him to prison for his religious convictions.

No one comes to arrest Alfred in the future.[216]

EBC 1888 May 31: Walter Edward Clark is born to Alice Randall and Edward B. Clark in Farmington, Utah. Alice and Edward will have 5 children together, all of whom will live to adulthood.

ETC 1888 September 30: Ezra's daughter Annie Clark Tanner, a plural wife to Joseph Marion Tanner, gives birth to her first child in hiding. She stays in Centerville with Mr. and Mrs. John Woolley, (Alice Randall Clark's sister's family). Alice Randall Clark (plural wife of Annie's brother Edward) serves as Annie's nurse during her recovery and Annie's half-sister Mary Elizabeth Clark Robinson assists in the birth. Here we see an interesting example of polygamous families in the Underground assisting each other.[217]

ETC 1889 August 11: Annie Clark Tanner dines at her father's home with Church leadership, and declines to tell even President Woodruff the identity of her husband.[218]

EBC 1890 September 14: Edward Franklin Clark is born to Wealthy Richards and Edward B. Clark in Farmington, Utah. Wealthy and Edward will have 7 children, 5 of whom will live to adulthood.[219] Walter Clark in his autobiography later calls his half-brother Edward Franklin Clark the "child of promise" within his family—the promised child who came to Wealthy and Edward because Father Edward B. Clark took a second wife.[220]

1890 September 25: The Manifesto ends officially Church-sanctioned polygamy.[221]

LSS 1891 March 16: Harriet Bradford (first wife of Leven Simmons) passes away in Spanish Fork at the age of 69. Those who knew her told her granddaughter "She was a wonderful woman and one of the best. You should be proud to have such a woman for your grandmother."[222]

AR 1891 March 21: Alfred Randall passes away at the age of 79, in North Ogden.

---

[216] Kofoed, Lucy Randall. *Life Story of Alfred Randall*, pp. 27–29.
[217] Tanner, Annie Clark. *A Mormon Mother*, p. 105.
[218] Ibid., p. 111.
[219] Clark, Edward B. "Wealthy."
[220] Clark, Walter E., p. 2.
[221] "The Manifesto and the End of Plural Marriage." *The Church of Jesus Christ of Latter-day Saints*, Intellectual Reserve, https://www.churchofjesuschrist.org/topics/the-manifesto-and-the-end-of-plural-marriage?lang=eng. Accessed 20 November 2020.
[222] Huff, Elizabeth F. "Harriet Bradford (1821-1890)." *FamilySearch*, Intellectual Reserve, https://www.familysearch.org/photos/artifacts/35018993?cid=mem_copy. Accessed 4 December 2020.

Daniel Goulding on 14 September 1892 is fined six cents by Judge Thomas J. Anderson at the Second District Court at Beaver for infraction of the Edmunds Act.[223]

Fanny is subpoenaed to testify in court that she is the plural wife of Daniel. She's willing but is notified before the trial that she doesn't have to appear. She tells her children the trial doesn't worry her, for Heavenly Father will bless and protect her family just as he always has.

Following his trial, Daniel builds identical side-by-side homes for his two families, who had previously lived together in one home.[224] Elizabeth, Daniel, and their youngest son Jim live in one house; Fanny and five of her children live in the other. The rest of the children are married by then.[225]

Figure 106: Daniel Goulding. Public domain via FamilySearch.

1893 January: President Benjamin Harrison grants amnesty and pardon to Mormons in polygamous marriages on the condition Church members stick to monogamy from then on. This leads some plural wives who had lived in hiding to be able to return to their husbands.[226]

1893 October 25: A congressional resolution grants the return of Church assets, on the grounds that the Church no longer allows for the practice of polygamy.[227]

1894 September 25: President Grover Cleveland restores civil rights and property rights to polygamists.[228]

ETC 1894: Ezra T. Clark offers a prayer at a Women's Suffrage Association meeting, where Ezra's daughter-in-law Lucy (married to Timothy Baldwin Clark) presides and Ezra's wife Mary is an honorary

---

[223] Goulding, James A., and Mint Farnsworth. "History of John Goulding Sr. & Daniel Goulding as Told to Mint Farnsworth by James A. Goulding." *FamilySearch*, Intellectual Reserve, https://www.familysearch.org/photos/artifacts/108653189?cid=mem_copy. Accessed 23 November 2020.

[224] Bunn, Celeste. "Daniel Goulding." *FamilySearch*, Intellectual Reserve, https://www.familysearch.org/photos/artifacts/1487281?cid=mem_copy. Accessed 20 November 2020.

[225] Johnson, Zina E. Goulding. "History of the Life of Fanny Pratten Goulding." *FamilySearch*, Intellectual Reserve, https://www.familysearch.org/photos/artifacts/23104532?cid=mem_copy. Accessed 23 November 2020.

[226] Harrison, Benjamin. "Proclamation 346—Granting Amnesty and Pardon for the Offense of Engaging in Polygamous or Plural Marriage to Members of the Church of Latter-Day Saints." *The American Presidency Project*, UC Santa Barbara, https://www.presidency.ucsb.edu/documents/proclamation-346-granting-amnesty-and-pardon-for-the-offense-engaging-polygamous-or-plural. Accessed 20 November 2020.

[227] "Historical Chronology of The Church of Jesus Christ of Latter-day Saints." *Deseret News | Church News*, Deseret Management Corporation, https://www.thechurchnews.com/archives/2010-02-08/historical-chronology-of-the-church-of-jesus-christ-of-latter-day-saints-66884. Accessed 20 November 2020.

[228] Cleveland, Grover. "Proclamation 369—Granting Amnesty and Pardon for the Offenses of Polygamy, Bigamy, Adultery, or Unlawful Cohabitation to Members of the Church of Latter-Day Saints." *The American Presidency Project*, UC Santa Barbara, 25 September 1894, https://www.presidency.ucsb.edu/documents/proclamation-369-granting-amnesty-and-pardon-for-the-offenses-polygamy-bigamy-adultery-or. Accessed 5 October 2020.

member.[229] From this we can gather that the rights of women and the practice of polygamy were not seen by the Clark family to be in conflict.

MC 1896 November 3: Maren Johanne Jensen (first wife of Mads Christensen) passes away in Farmington at the age of 69.

ETC 1901 October 17: Ezra T. Clark passes away at the age of 77, in Farmington, Utah.

1904 April: Joseph F. Smith reads the "Second Manifesto" at General Conference, which affirms any who enter into new plural marriage will be excommunicated. (Some members had continued to quietly enter polygamous marriages after the first Manifesto.) Previously established polygamous families continue.[230]

DG 1905 August 1: Daniel Goulding passes away at the age of 74, in Henrieville, Utah.

ETC 1911 November 24: Mary Stevenson (first wife of Ezra T. Clark) passes away in Farmington, Utah, at the age of 86.

AR 1913 May 20: Mildred Elizabeth Johnson Randall (third wife of Alfred Randall and his missionary companion to Hawaii) passes away in Salt Lake City at age 85. Members of leading Utah families attend Mildred's memorial service, including President Joseph F. Smith, and several members of the Young, Whitney, Clawson, Wells, and Kimball families, many of whom had been Mildred's students.[231]

ETC 1913: On 20 September, Ezra T. Clark's daughter Laura Blanche Clark, then a widow with three children, becomes the third wife of Joseph Askie Silver, a silversmith whose company had made, among other things, the iconic door handles of the Salt Lake Temple. Joseph is a well-to-do businessman who also has business ties with the railroad. He takes good care of Laura but there are family tensions between Joseph's wives because Joseph had not gotten permission from his first two wives prior to marrying Laura.[232]

MC 1914 June 14: Mads Christensen passes away at the age of 89, in McCammon, Idaho.

ETC 1915: Joseph Askie Silver is excommunicated two years after his polygamous marriage to Laura Blanche Clark.

DG 1918 July 18: Elizabeth Merrifield Pratten (first wife of Daniel Goulding) passes away in Panguitch, Utah, at the age of 86.

---

[229] "Women's Suffrage Association Meeting (1894)." *Davis County Clipper* [Bountiful, Utah], 13 December 1894, https://www.familysearch.org/photos/artifacts/94995765?cid=mem_copy. Accessed 20 November 2020.
[230] Embry
[231] "Mildred Elizabeth Johnson," p. 289.
[232] Clark, Laura Blanche.

AR 1919 April 5: Margaret Harley Randall (second wife of Alfred Randall) passes away in Georgetown, Bear Lake, Idaho. She lived in the home of her daughter Alice Randall Clark the last two years of her life, where she encouraged her grandson Walter to read the General Authority sermon carried in each edition of the *Semi-Weekly Deseret News*.[233]

AR 1938 October 16: Alice Randall (second wife of Edward B. Clark) passes away in Salt Lake City, at the age of 74.

EBC 1955 September 16: Edward Barrett Clark passes away at the age of 96, in Farmington, Utah.

ETC 1985 November 21: Laura Blanche Clark passes away in Draper, Utah, at the age of 105; she was Ezra T. Clark's last living child and the last surviving Clark of her generation who practiced polygamy.

---

[233] Clark, Walter E., p. 9.

7. Ezra T. Clark Family Stories

Ezra T. Clark (head of family)
    Wives:
        1. **Mary Stevenson Clark (our ancestor)** [m. 18 May 1845]
        2. Susan Leggett [m. 8 November 1861]
        3. Nancy Areta Porter Stevenson Clark [m. 11 July 1870]

Figure 107: The Ezra and Mary Clark family. Back row: Edward, Hyrum Don Carlos, Amasa, and Wilford. Front row: Timothy, Mary (mother), Ezra, Mary Elizabeth (daughter), Charles, and Joseph. Public domain via FamilySearch.

"My Father and Aunt Mary, as we familiarly called the first wife, knew personally the Prophet Joseph Smith and were thoroughly converted to his teachings. The principle of Celestial Marriage was considered the capstone of Mormon religion. . . . According to the founders of the Mormon Church, the great purpose of this life is to prepare for the Celestial Kingdom in the world to come. The tremendous

efforts and sacrifices of the Mormon people can be understood only if one keeps in mind this basic otherworldly philosophy."[234]—*Annie Clark Tanner*

Ezra Thompson Clark was the only child of Timothy Baldwin Clark to settle in the West with the Saints.

Mary Stevenson Clark, married to Ezra, was accompanied by more family—her mother, Elizabeth Stevenson, her sister Elizabeth, and brothers James and Edward all came along, too.

Though Ezra was offered some property near his friends and Church leaders in Salt Lake City, eventually the Ezra and Mary Stevenson Clark family settled in Farmington, Utah, where they had the pick of the best farmland. They settled in "North Cottonwood" in 1849, two years after the first white settlers came to the area.

The settlement was called "North Cottonwood" after two tall cottonwood trees that stood on Ezra T. Clark's farm, "about 35 rods west of the Shortline Depot."

As Farmington historian Margaret Hess recorded of the trees: "They could be seen for many miles and stood like a sentinel. You could see them from the point of the mountain as you left Salt Lake City to travel north. In 1853 when the population totaled 413 the name of our town changed to 'Farmington' because of the rich farmland and also due to the fact that Wilford Woodruff had come from a town in Connecticut called Farmington."[235]

A Description of Ezra T. Clark

Thanks to the writings of Ezra's daughter Annie, who wrote a book about his life, we have the following description of his physical appearance:

"He was athletic in build. With the greatest of ease and grace he could mount his horse. He was six feet tall, weighed 174 pounds, and his complexion was fair. His eyes were blue and reminded one that nothing escaped his notice." Annie remembers him as appearing kindly and intelligent. "All his children remember him with a beard and mustache, and that he was particular about the way they were trimmed." He had reddish brown hair and a sandy beard as a young man, and was balding on the top of his head in later years—a fact he covered with a comb-over. "His habitual walk with his head erect, then bent forward, occasionally, indicated a meditative as well as an observing mind."[236]

When Ezra was displeased, he would grunt once or twice, and walk away. This was the only way his children could tell he was not happy, as he had strong self-control and did not tend to display emotions.[237]

He was a keen businessman who was well-known for some of his sayings, including: "Don't sign a paper of any kind until you have slept at least one night on the proposition" and "Don't walk over the dollar to pick up the dimes."[238]

---

[234] Tanner, Annie Clark. *A Mormon Mother*, pp. 1–2.
[235] Hess, Margaret Steed. *My Farmington*, pp. 3–5.
[236] Tanner, Annie Clark. *A Biography of Ezra T. Clark*, p. 37.
[237] Tanner. *A Biography*, p. 41.
[238] Tanner. *A Biography*, p. 51.

Figure 108: Farmington, Utah.
© aliceinwonderland2020/Depositphotos

The Clark Firm

The Clark family of Farmington was perhaps less like a typical polygamous family and more a dynasty that impacted a few generations—the family organized together and ran its farm and business operations communally for many years as parents, children, and grandchildren interacted and collaborated in multitudes of complex and interwoven ways.

This exploration of the Clark family will examine the role of Ezra, Mary, Susan, Nancy, and the primary family home in Farmington. These held the center around which all things Clark navigated until the time of Ezra T.'s death.

It will also examine some of the key personalities, events, and values that shaped and informed the Clark family culture.

Ezra T. Clark successfully set up a family version of the United Order, which he ran until nearly the end of his life. This chapter and the following chapter will explore this complex and unique family, and the generations of our ancestors who were participating members in the Clark Firm.

He had a room that functioned somewhat like an office room at the home he shared with Mary, which held a safe (as he was county treasurer), and where he held his business meetings. The womenfolk of the family were never invited to the business meetings and did not know the extent of the family's holdings.[239]

---

[239] Tanner. *Mormon Mother*, p. 29.

The family United Order was set up with the permission of Brigham Young, and served as grounds for the Clarks being excused from a planned Davis United Order.[240]

The Values of Ezra T. Clark

Ezra Thompson Clark took pride in his wives and large family. He was not a man of many words, nor did he have an extensive education. Despite this, Ezra was a very successful businessman and farmer, skillful in overseeing the management of the Clark family's temporal and spiritual care. He was very well connected in the spheres of both religion and of local business. His three wives, Mary, Susan, and Nancy, all had decorum and grace.

Ezra valued religion, community, and family business perhaps more than he valued education. Ezra himself had very little schooling and still managed to become a man of stature in religion, business, and community.

He did not value the judgment of a woman, a feeling that most men of his time shared, but despite this he sympathized with the women's suffrage movement, of which his daughter-in-law was a leader, and is on record as having attended at least one women's suffrage event. "At one time," one of his biographers recorded, "he remarked that it was quite as important to educate girls as boys."[241]

Figure 109: Ezra T. Clark. Public domain via FamilySearch.

Many of the Clark children came to value schooling at a higher level than what their father had obtained, and the later generations came to embrace education as a value, with many Clarks becoming teachers. This may have been due in part to Ezra's focus on encouraging his children to read Church materials and to learn the arts.

Ezra's values and strengths included:

Hospitality: "Father was recognized as one of the most hospitable men of his time. He had always lived on the frontier and knew the advantages of friends and the joy of entertaining them."[242]

Shrewd Judge of Character: "One of his daughters referred with reverence to the high position of two young men in the Church. Her father remarked, 'Position doesn't make the quality of the man.'"[243]

---

[240] Tanner. *Mormon Mother*, pp. 26–27.
[241] Tanner, Annie Clark. *A Biography*, p. 58.
[242] Tanner, Annie Clark. *Mormon Mother*, pp. 5–6.
[243] Tanner. *A Biography*, p. 55.

Church Oriented: "He was intimately acquainted with the presiding authorities and they had great confidence in his judgment. One of them asked him once if he preferred to send a man to help colonize or go himself. 'I'll send two men,' was his response."[244] When the Davis Stake was organized, Ezra was called to the high council, and Mary was called to the Stake Relief Society Presidency.[245]

Religious Education: When Ezra gave his children books, they were always Church books, and his children got $5 for reading the Book of Mormon.[246] Ezra and his wives expected their children to attend church and read church publications, including *The Voice of Warning, The Pearl of Great Price, The Key to Theology, The Juvenile Instructor,* and *The Women's Exponent.*

A Family Man: "Successful as Brother Clark was in business and as a missionary and farmer, his greatest success was in keeping the love of his family."[247]

Successful Businessman: "Because of his natural resources and his financial ability, [Ezra] was soon known as a man of wealth and influence."[248] Ezra T. Clark was a successful farmer and rancher. He also oversaw other business operations.

"The Farmington Commercial and Manufacturing Company [F. C. & M. Co.] was incorporated March 30, 1891, with Ezra T. Clark as president. . . . They sold shares of stock for $5.00 each and the store opened for business in December of the same year."[249]

Ezra saw the need for a bank in the area, and set about creating one:

"In 1891 the Davis County Bank was organized. It was chartered with a capital of $25,000 and opened for business April 2, 1892, with Ezra T. Clark as President and Amasa Lyman Clark as Cashier. This bank was located on the north side of State Street east of Main in one room of the F. C. & M. Co. Building."[250]

The Davis County Bank opened in 1891 or 92, depending on the source, and ran for nearly one hundred years. For a long time, it was the only bank in Farmington. The Davis County Bank's status became "inactive" as of 22 September 1989. At that time, the bank was merged into First Security Bank of Utah. After a series of subsequent actions, in 2018 it voluntarily relinquished FDIC insurance and changed its class to "noninsured commercial institutions." The site became Wells Fargo Trust Company, National Association (13718). As of the time of this writing, the location operates as a Wells Fargo location.[251]

Balanced Spirituality with Enjoying the World: "One of the family asked Brother Clark if the Lord really did not like us to have fine horses and carriages, nice clothes, etc. 'Surely he does,' was his prompt reply, 'only we should love the Lord most of all.'"[252]

Valuing the Arts: Ezra paid for his daughters to take classes in music, elocution, and art. "The second family's home became decorated with flowers made of wool, paper, and wax, and mottos worked

---

[244] Ibid., p. 54.
[245] Tanner. *Mormon Mother*, p. 30.
[246] Tanner. *A Biography*, p. 13.
[247] Ibid., p. 59.
[248] Knowlton, Clark S. and Ruth. Oral interview with Orson Clark. Biographies and autobiographies of the descendants of Ezra T. Clark, L. Tom Perry Special Collections, Harold B. Lee Library, Brigham Young University, Provo, Utah.
[249] Hess, Margaret Steed. *My Farmington*, p. 306.
[250] Ibid., p. 319.
[251] See https://www.usbanklocations.com/davis-county-bank-9200.shtml.
[252] Tanner. *A Biography*, p. 55.

on perforated cardboard and framed."[253] Most of his daughters were with Susan, his second wife, which is why Annie references the second family's home in this quote.

Personal Responsibility: "In his religious philosophy he seemed to be free from a superstitious fear of God's punishments. He was never heard to attribute the misfortunes of people to a displeased God. Rather it was mismanagement on their own part or lack of judgment."[254] "Every blessing is predicated upon the observance of law" was his favorite scripture.[255]

Ezra would rise to become one of the leading citizens and largest landowner of Davis County. His family operated as a small United Order in Davis County, Utah, and Bear Lake, Idaho, for many years.

But when things started out for Ezra and Mary in Farmington, there was little to begin with. The Clarks were one of the first families there.

After Ezra's family became established in Farmington, and Ezra had built the central portion of his home (the side wings would be added later), Ezra left to serve a mission to England in the company of Parley P. Pratt[256]. During the time he was away, Mary ran the household on her own. She donated one of their best cows to help support the Salt Lake Temple building effort, a gesture Ezra approved of. Ezra and Mary seemed to live together harmoniously, and were good managers. Others commented on a feeling of peace in their home.

After Ezra and Mary had been married for seven years, the doctrine of plural marriage was announced to the main body of the saints in 1852. As a leader in the community, Ezra would have had some level of pressure to participate. But, as in all things, Ezra was very careful in how he made his choices. He wouldn't choose a second wife until just the right woman came along.

Second Wife Susan Leggett Clark

"April 1st, 1861, we had a child born and named him Charles Rich. Shortly after this, a Sister Susan Leggett came from England and lived with us. She became my husband's wife. She had ten children. Three passed on the other side. One lovely son (John Alexander Clark) died near Jerusalem in Palestine while filling a mission."—Mary Stevenson Clark[257]

When Susan Leggett came to Utah, she was "A tall, healthy, beautiful young woman; her abundant dark hair, brown eyes and tall stately figure, with her smooth olive complexion were admired by all who knew her."[258]

When Susan was 18, she, her parents, and all her siblings had joined the Church. They walked five miles to church each week and often housed elders in their home.

A skillful seamstress and dressmaker, Susan helped her family earn money as they saved up to move to Utah. At age 22, Susan became the first to go to the United States. She went alone. It was not uncommon at that time for families to send one person ahead to help earn money to bring the others.

---

[253] Tanner. *Mormon Mother*, p. 44.
[254] Ibid., p. 55.
[255] Ibid., p. 66.
[256] *Hyrum Don Carlos Clark Biography*. Biographies and autobiographies of the descendants of Ezra T. Clark, Box 4 Folder 44, L. Tom Perry Special Collections, Harold B. Lee Library, Brigham Young University, Provo, Utah.
[257] Clark, Mary Stevenson. "Autobiography of Mary Stevenson Clark." *FamilySearch,* Intellectual Reserve. https://www.familysearch.org/tree/person/memories/KWJ6-HKP. Accessed 28 September 2020.
[258] "Susan Leggett Clark." *FamilySearch,* Intellectual Reserve, 18 June 2014. https://www.familysearch.org/tree/person/memories/KW83-LGX Accessed 28 September 2020.

The names of arriving emigrants were published in the Salt Lake paper. When Ezra T. Clark saw Susan's name, he came to meet her. He had stayed at her family's home five years previously and promised himself that if she ever came to Utah, he would win her for his wife.

On November 8, 1861, Susan became the second wife of Ezra T. Clark. She stayed in the Clark home for a time doing mending and sewing, and later moved to her own home across the street. Eventually Susan and Ezra had ten children.

Figure 110: Susan, Ezra, and Mary.
Public domain via FamilySearch.

Susan learned to make candles, soap, and molasses preserves, and how to dry fruit. Her needlework was beyond compare—she created tailored effects on pockets and sleeves and her little girls loved the ruffles and puffs on their dresses. A methodical housekeeper, her dresser drawers were always in order, with her veil folded and the fingers of her gloves pulled out every time she used them.[259]

---

[259] Tanner, Annie Clark. *Mormon Mother*, p. 32.

After Susan's family emigrated a few years after she did, her father became a gardener for President Young's grounds on South Temple, and later cared for the Young family farm on South State Street.[260]

Susan and Mary seem on the whole to have had a very good sisterly relationship and to have been great friends, frequently spending time in each other's company and sensitive to each other's feelings. One day while Mary was visiting Susan for a meal, she commented wistfully that Susan's flowers always turned out better than hers did. Susan sent Mary home with some of her flowers. At another occasion at a family gathering, someone told Mary of how her son had gotten to enjoy some ice cream on a train just before he passed away some time before. Mary reacted with emotion to hearing this story of him, and Susan comforted her.

Susan and her daughter Laura enjoyed coming over to read in Mary's library, and were welcome to stay for dinner and family prayer.[261]

A skillful seamstress, Susan dressed her daughters "very becomingly and quite out of the ordinary for those times . . . whether away, or at home with his friends, father seemed pleased to introduce us, which was much to the credit of mother's meticulous care with our manners and appearance," wrote Annie Clark Tanner, daughter of Ezra and Susan.[262]

As the Clark homes were near the railroad and in an area frequented by passers-by, "Many Indians with their little papooses strapped on their backs would come. Mother [Susan] would give them soap, sugar, and flour. Mother would never turn anyone away from her door." (Clark)

The relationship between Mary and Susan was amiable, though there was definitely a status difference between the two wives, as noted by Annie in her book *A Mormon Mother*.

"When it came to Orthodox Religion, Aunt Mary was an extremist. She never missed a church meeting and never failed to bear her testimony. That she was not more help to my father in making polygamy more endurable to my mother may have been due to religious teachings in the Church at that time. . . . [T]hat she wasn't more generous, may have been because people in pioneer times vigorously practiced economy and thought it a great virtue. 'Waste not; want not,' was an ideal of those times, so people carefully stored away what they had. They seemed to live more for the future than is done today."[263]

Specifically, the first family kept the chicken house locked and objected if the second family knocked apples off a tree in the first family's orchard.

The provisions for both families were unpacked, stored, and distributed from Mary's home, and what was doled out was sometimes meager.

"No one knew how tried my mother was with the penurious handing out of provisions which were bought in abundance by father," Annie wrote. "How glad we were when he was there to dip out the sugar, rice, and beans from the 100-pound sack, or give us a few dozen yards of cloth from the bolts bought for dresses, aprons, gowns, and underwear. On the other hand, it must have been a great trial for Aunt Mary to have us go to her home so often for things we needed."[264]

---

[260] "Susan Leggett Clark." *FamilySearch,* Intellectual Reserve, 18 June 2014. https://www.familysearch.org/tree/person/memories/KW83-LGX. Accessed 28 September 2020.
[261] Clark, Laura Blanche. "Autobiography of Laura Blanche Clark." *FamilySearch,* Intellectual Reserve, https://www.familysearch.org/tree/person/memories/KWCZ-YQH. Accessed 28 September 2020.
[262] Tanner, Annie Clark. *Mormon Mother*, p. 6.
[263] Ibid., p. 12.
[264] Ibid., p. 13.

Despite this, Ezra would hear no complaint by Susan, or complaints in general by either wife regarding the other. [265]

"Naturally, the first family was aware of its superior position, partly because they were older than we," Annie wrote.[266]

When Ezra and his two wives traveled together by carriage, Mary would always ride in the front, and Susan in the back.[267] A hired girl would generally be paid to help at Mary's house, but there was no paid help at Susan's house.[268]

Susan did have a way to make a little money, which she used to shop for herself and her children: Utah-dried peaches were popular back East, and Susan could dry her own peaches to sell and get cash for these.[269]

Third Wife Nancy Areta Porter Stevenson

In 1870, when Ezra was 46, Brigham Young called him into his office, and counseled him to marry Nancy Areta Porter Stevenson following her divorce from her husband. At the time there was a belief in the Church that the highest exaltation in the God's Kingdom could only be attained through a marriage-trinity.[270] (A polygamous family with three wives.)

Nancy had four surviving children with her first husband, Edward Stevenson, who was the brother of Ezra's first wife Mary.

Nancy had sent Edward many tender letters on his mission and seemed very fond of him. She was very adept at caring for their children in his absence. But something changed over the years. Perhaps she was troubled when Edward married additional wives. As of 1870, Edward had three wives, and Nancy went to Brigham Young concerned about her household troubles. She divorced Edward and on Brigham's advice, married Ezra.

Ezra and Nancy did not have any children together. During Ezra's polygamy trials, both Mary and Susan stated they did not know where Nancy lived. According to records, Nancy lived with her adult children, eventually passing away in Idaho. However, before she moved to Idaho, she lived for a time in Farmington, where she was among the first to help raise silkworms, and served in leadership for the Young Women's

Figure 111: Ezra's third wife Nancy Areta Porter Stevenson. Public domain via FamilySearch.

---

[265] Ibid., p. 8 and 10–11.
[266] Ibid., p. 12.
[267] Ibid., p. 10.
[268] Tanner, Annie Clark. *A Biography*, pp. 60–61.
[269] Ibid., p. 40.
[270] Tanner. *A Biography*, p. 33.

organization. She is remembered as having participated in the cattle drives to Georgetown and having lived on the Clark ranch in Georgetown for six summers.

She was called "Aunt Nancy" by members of the family and was devoutly religious and always interested in Church activities.

Ezra was very good friends with Nancy's first husband, Edward Stevenson. In fact, Edward and his second wife, Elizabeth, named a son Ezra Thompson Stevenson just six years before Ezra married Edward's former first wife, Nancy. It may have been awkward for Ezra to marry the former wife of one of his closest friends, but despite this he was able to maintain a positive relationship with Edward.

Ezra's Children Who Practiced Polygamy

Ezra led his polygamous family well. Eventually several of his children followed his example by entering the practice:

Laura Blanche Clark married a polygamous man on 20 September 1913.

Nathan George Clark married first wife Esther Lauretta Ford on 16 February 1898 and second wife Cleo Afton Call on 08 March 1913.

Susan Alice Bell Clark married Walter William Steed as the second of his three wives on 22 June 1897 in Mexico.

Sarah Lavina Clark's husband may have had two wives.

Annie Vilate Clark became the second of Joseph Marion Tanner's five wives on 27 December 1883, and struggled without support from her husband for much of her child-raising life.

Wilford Woodruff Clark had two wives, though he only had children with his first wife.

Charles Rich Clark had two wives.

Edward Barrett Clark had two wives.

Hyrum Don Carlos Clark had two wives.

Mary Elizabeth Clark married twice, both times to polygamous men. She was the first wife of her second husband, but the two of them split up after he was injured in a carriage accident. She became trained as a nurse and delivered many babies.

Biblical Stories as Roots

Ezra and Mary's family had a strong grounding in scripture, and often looked at stories in their life as having scriptural parallels from the Old Testament.

If we look at Ezra's life, it somewhat follows the pattern of the Old Testament patriarch Jacob. Like the patriarchs of old, he took multiple wives. He had nine sons who lived to adulthood and had children of their own. (He valued sons highly for the work they would be able to contribute to the farm and other family endeavors. At the birth of each son and grandson, he'd exclaim the child was "A thousand-dollar boy!")

Most of the sons worked on Ezra's agricultural interests, and many were active in civic leadership.

When Ezra's son **Edward Barrett Clark** couldn't have children with his first wife, Wealthy, she was promised in a blessing that if she let her husband take a second wife, she would be blessed with children. This blessing came true, and it paralleled the story of Abraham and Sarah, where Abraham took a second wife before Sarah had children.

And when Ezra's son Hyrum Don Carlos Clark lost his fortune and his wife later in life and had to work for a daily wage to take care of himself as an old man, his old age was compared by other Clarks to the biblical story of Job.

Figure 112: Ezra and Susan's family. Back row: Nathan, John, Sarah, Eugene. Front row: Susan Alice, Susan Leggett, Laura Blanche, Ezra, Horace, and Annie.
Public domain via FamilySearch.

The Clark Family Alphanumeric Code

Ezra had fifteen children total who married and became parents.

In the Ezra T. Clark Family Organization, after the time of Ezra, an alphanumeric code was devised to identify how people were related to Ezra.

The code showed which children and which wives each person descended from—a complicated affair to keep straight in this large, polygamous family.

The descendants of the Farmington Clarks could track their heritage based on which of Ezra's children they descended from, just as the Israelites tracked their heritage based on which of the tribes they descended from.

If the Ezra T. Clark Family Organization code for Brenda Clark Sederberg was extrapolated down from Ezra's generation, it might look like this:

M7A1V2J1

M7 = the seventh child of Mary = Edward Barrett Clark

A1 = the first child of Edward's wife Alice = Walter Edward Clark
V2 = the second child of Walter's wife Violet = Alan C Clark
J1 = the first child of Alan's wife Janet

However, if a man only had one wife, a letter code for the children of that generation might not be used.

So, since Alan had only one wife, his daughter Brenda's code might look like this, if it was constructed according to the Clark Family Alphanumeric Code form:

M7A1V2-1

*Figure 113: Views of the side of the Ezra T. Clark family home, as of 2021.
Image © R.S. Kellogg*

The Ezra T. Clark Home

Ezra lived with his first wife, Mary, in a home where family parties were held and where the provisions were stored for all: bolts of cloth, cheese stocked by the wagonload from Bear River Valley, frozen beeves (plural of beef), barrels of flour and molasses, dried peaches and probably other fruits, and corn.

Fruit was harvested and preserved in "Cuttings," which were communal events that could last a few days and ended with an evening's celebration that may include a candy pull, a bonfire, games, and doughnuts or perhaps pumpkin pie. Sometimes a post-harvest celebration could be a picnic, with wagons full of young people going to the Great Salt Lake's shores about three miles distant.

*Figure 114: Front of Ezra T. Clark home, 2021.
Image © R.S. Kellogg*

The Clark home was like a free inn, always open to family, Church leaders, and visitors to the town. The Clarks fed people and let them sleep at their home, over the short- or long-term. Often Church leaders would dine with the Clarks and spend the night when they were in town for conferences or other events.

The home was close to the train station, and the family would often feed strangers who needed a meal. Ezra was very sociable, if quiet, and enjoyed inviting a wide variety of people over for dinner. Scarcely a day passed by without a dinner guest.

Family members often stayed at the Clark home. Whenever William O. Clark traveled from California to the East Coast by train, he'd spend the night in Farmington at his brother's home.

The family worked hard but was fun-loving, and regularly attended city attractions—be it a circus, an opera matinee, a dance, or a fair; they loved to attend celebrations and events.

With Clark family bonds interwoven with church, business, and civic life, Ezra's rock house served as a popular visiting place and meeting place.

For a while, the safe for the Davis County Bank was located in his room at Mary's house.

Playing Host for Children and Grandchildren

Figure 115: Annie Waldron Clark lived on the "Underground" with Ezra and Mary for a time early in her marriage and gave birth to her first child at their home. She was the second wife of their son Charles Rich Clark. Pictured here with sons Myral and Carlos.
Public domain via FamilySearch.

When Ezra's descendants needed a place to live for a time, he and Mary would often host them.

When Joseph Smith Clark was called to serve a mission to the Southern States, he moved his wife and children into his parents' home, where they lived in two rooms of Ezra's home while Joseph preached the gospel in Mississippi.

Joseph Smith Clark, Jr., Ezra's grandson, recalls, "We had access to Grandfather's home the same as if it was our own home—and we ran back and forth in his house. Grandfather was in hiding during that time and was caught and sentenced to serve six months in the territorial prison, which he served out. At the same time, President Taylor was in hiding and he visited my grandfather several times. I remember once, sitting on his lap and listening to him tell of the martyrdom of the Prophet Joseph Smith and the Patriarch Hyrum Smith, his [Joseph's] brother. He himself, carried two or three bullets to his death in his flesh that were never extracted after that terrible afternoon of June 27, 1844. John Taylor's life was spared by a bullet striking his watch and knocking him down—which if the watch hadn't been there would have been fatal. [I heard the account of that day] from the mouth of the man that was with the Prophet when he was martyred."[271]

During the time that polygamists were hiding from the marshals, the Clarks' son Charles C. Rich Clark had his second wife, Ann, live in hiding under the assumed name of "Alice" at his parents' home for a number of years. Thus, their older children spent their early years living in the home of their Clark grandparents, who were a much bigger presence in their lives than their father could be at that time. "Alice" couldn't tell anybody her true name or even who her husband was—the risk was too great. But she did get to socialize with the greater Clark family and their neighbors, making her life less lonely than that of many polygamous wives of the time.

---

[271] "Experiences in the Life of Joseph Smith Clark Jr. 1878-1963." Biographies and autobiographies of the descendants of Ezra T. Clark, Box 1 Folder 12, L. Tom Perry Special Collections, Harold B. Lee Library, Brigham Young University, Provo, Utah.

In a unique twist, Ezra's son Wilford recognized "Alice"/Ann from a dance where he'd met her when she was still single. As she lived in a different city, this was a lucky connection.

She recorded: "I have learned by this time that Wilford saw me before in Richville at a party, had an introduction to me, and danced with me; so he knows where I live and from this he has good reason to suspect the truth, which he does, and he tells me all about it; so I can now associate with him with a mutual feeling and the privilege is very much enjoyed for we visited together very congenially. He sent to town and bought baby a little walking chair which is so nice for him."[272]

Mary Elizabeth Clark Robinson—A Longtime Presence in the Clark Home

A constant member of Ezra and Mary's household for many years was their daughter, curly-haired Mary Elizabeth Clark, and her children.

Mary Elizabeth, or "Mary Lizzie" as she was called, had been divorced against her will by her husband Joseph after he was badly hurt in a carriage accident when Mary, her husband, and his new 15-year-old second wife were going to get their photographs taken together.

He had almost died, and Mary became frustrated with the weight of running the household. Shortly before the birth of her fourth child, she went to stay with her father for a time. But Joseph saw this as abandonment and divorced her.

So, Mary Lizzie raised her children in her parents' home.

After a stay in Georgetown where she served as her brother Wilford's housekeeper before his marriage, Mary took a nursing course in Salt Lake City, graduating alongside her cousin Paulina "Pliny" Phelps Lyman.

Figure 116: Mary Elizabeth Clark Robinson.
Public domain via FamilySearch.

Mary helped with hundreds of births. The only patient she lost hit her hard—her brother Amasa Lyman Clark's wife, Alice, died of phlebitis, leaving three small sons.

Mary and her daughter, also named Mary, helped raise these small boys until their father remarried.

She stressed a healthy lifestyle and was known for her delicious whole wheat bread.

Losing Missionary Sons

One of the great tragedies in Ezra's family's lives was the loss of two sons and brothers while giving missionary service. Ezra James Clark passed away on his way home from his mission to England, while John Alexander Clark passed away on a mission to the Holy Land.

In one of the peculiarities of the large age spread that polygamy could create among the children of such large families, Ezra James, who was born in 1846 and died in 1868, passed away before the birth of the second son who would be lost while on his mission. John Alexander was born in 1871 and passed away in 1895.

---

[272] Clark, Annie Waldron (second wife of Charles R. Clark). "An Excerpt from a Diary and Life History of Mr. & Mrs. Charles R. Clark and Family While Living in or Near Farmington." Biographies and autobiographies of the descendants of Ezra T. Clark, L. Tom Perry Special Collections, Harold B. Lee Library, Brigham Young University, Provo, Utah.

Ezra James Clark

Figure 117: Ezra and Mary's oldest son, Ezra James Clark. Public domain via FamilySearch.

Ezra James Clark, oldest son of Ezra and Mary, had been summoned to military service just as he was slated to embark on a three-year mission to England. His brother Timothy Baldwin Clark took the military service on his behalf. (Ezra seems to have been fond of Timothy, calling him T.B.C. in his letters.)

Ezra James wrote letters to his family and community members detailing his service under President Franklin Richards as well as various cultural activities he enjoyed, including attending the theater, visiting the Crystal Palace, and attending church in a cathedral.

In a move that foreshadowed his own future, he also copied inscriptions on gravestones to share in his family letters, including the following epithet:

"Weep not for me it is in vain.

"Death was no loss to me but gain.

"Only sleep removed from pain till Christ raise up again."

Ezra James Clark overworked himself, lost weight, and became sickly. A man with a height of 6'1, at one point he dropped to 126 lb.

"This country does not agree with me as my mountain home used to," he wrote. "I have been gaining, though slowly since May and I hope to do so and stand it till honorably released to return home to the mountain of the Lord's House in the top of the mountains."[273]

Charles Penrose, later of the First Presidency and eventual publisher of the Deseret News, also served in England with Ezra James. Charles Penrose's Farmington cabin is today a museum housing pioneer relics, located on property near the rock chapel. A hymn-writer of such notable pieces as "God of Our Fathers" and "O Ye Mountains High," Charles' hymn with greatest significance to our family history is the one written on the occasion of a visit by Brigham Young to Charles and Ezra James' mission, the title of which also captures Ezra's sentiment: "Beautiful Zion for Me."

Ezra James passed away on a train during a heat wave in New York, after helping other passengers with their luggage, on the ride between Albany and Fonda. His fellow leaders raised funds from other train passengers, and left his body in the care of village officials, along with the money, to be used to purchase a casket. Ezra James was buried almost 3,000 miles from home. His father would later travel east to retrieve his body.

Brigham Young described Ezra James as dying "in the saddle with his boots on."[274]

Ezra James Clark's letters are preserved in a book called *The Forgotten Missionary*.

---

[273] "The Forgotten Missionary," p. 52, Ezra T. Clark Foundation, http://ezratclark.org/familyfile_forgottenMissionary.asp

[274] Clark, Antone. *Noble Pioneer: A Biography of Ezra Thompson Clark*, p. 135.

John Alexander Clark—Second Lost Missionary Son

"An incident is told that illustrates John's personality and his father's understanding of him. One of the older boys manifested a little impatience in John's delay when they were getting ready to round up cattle in Bear Lake.

"'Don't mind his careful preparation,' said the father. 'When John gets off on a trip he never comes back for something he should have taken.'"[275]

Born on Leap Day, 29 February 1871, John Alexander Clark was the fifth of ten children of Ezra T. Clark and Susan Leggett Clark in Farmington, Utah.

He was very close to one of his sisters, Susan. The two of them enjoyed reading together and Susan even taught school for a time as John's assistant. When John received a mission call to go and preach in Palestine, he was delighted. His brother Charles, recently returned from a mission, took over his teaching position.

But John's imminent departure brought great sadness to his close sister Susan.

He asked if she was sorry he was going, and she told him:

"No, I'll try not to be, as it is the Father's calling."

John preached in the Holy Land. While he was there he went into a house where he contracted smallpox. He soon died.

Due to the nature of the contagious disease, his body had to be removed via the window rather than the door. His father was not permitted to retrieve the body for burial. John's body was buried in a cemetery near the foot of Mt. Carmel.

Susan took the news of her brother's death hard:

"One day I returned from school in a despondent and listless mood. The following morning I experienced a very unusual manifestation. John's voice, as plainly as when he was alive, quoted the same words he had spoken just before he left saying, 'You said you were not sorry I was going on a mission, now why are you?'

"I replied, 'I'll try not to be anymore.'"

This experience helped both Susan and her mother to move through the grief.

Years after John's passing, the Church wanted to build a Learning Center in Jerusalem. Some people there argued that the Church did not have a prior presence in the Holy Land and should not be granted space to have a building. But two missionary graves were identified in Haifa, proving a Church presence dating back to the 1800s.

Figure 118: John Alexander Clark. Public domain via ezratclark.org.

John's grave was one of two which paved the way forward for the Jerusalem Center.[276]

---

[275] Larsen, Ora Steed. "A Brief Life History of John Alexander Clark." *Ezra T. Clark Family Organization Web Site.* http://ezratclark.org/index.asp
[276] Larsen, Ora Steed. "John Alexander Clark."

Ezra T. Clark's Sons as Managers

Ezra's oldest son, Ezra James, had died on his mission.

Second son Timothy was more interested in being a writer than in managing farm doings and business.

So third son Joseph Smith Clark was for a long while Ezra's right-hand man. "A place he held with honor and integrity through his father's long lifetime."[277]

Joseph's apprenticeship began young. At age 11, he was "sent with a hired man and two teams to Coalville for two loads of coal, a five-day trip at that time."

The spring following his marriage with Lucy Maria Robinson, Joseph Smith Clark moved with her to Georgetown, where they lived for fifteen years, except from June 1882 to June 1884, during which Joseph served a mission to the Southern States, and Lucy and children lived at the home of Ezra and Mary. Joseph served in the bishopric the entire time the family lived in the Georgetown area, along with filling other callings.

Figure 119: Joseph Smith Clark served as one of the primary Clark foremen for many years. Public domain via FamilySearch.

In 1891 the Joseph Smith Clark family moved from Georgetown to Farmington, where Joseph served several terms on the Farmington City Council, during which time the city installed a water system, electric lights, and telephones, as well as being active in business matters, including serving as president of the Davis County Bank, which the Clark family had founded.

When Joseph Smith Clark was in Georgetown, the need arose for another foreman in Farmington. Edward B. Clark (Walter's father) filled the role.

Figure 120: Edward B. Clark. Public domain via FamilySearch.

Edward had inherited his father's skill at farming and at management, and oversaw the Clark ventures profitably and with attention to detail.

Eventually, Wilford Woodruff Clark and Charles C. Rich Clark would also work and serve in the Georgetown, Idaho, area.

Charles C. Rich Clark had more of a reputation as a scholar than a businessman, but he was kindhearted and always made sure that those in need had enough to eat.

Amasa Lyman Clark was less of a farmer than the others, and he was in charge of the Davis County Bank for many years.

Ezra's son Hyrum Don Carlos Clark (also known as HyD) opted out of the Clark Family Firm entirely, and moved with his family to Idaho, and then after several years of unsuccessful taming of the desert, moved to Star Valley, Wyoming.

All of the above Clark sons were Ezra's children with first wife, Mary.

---

[277] *Biography of Joseph Smith Clark, Sr.* Biographies and autobiographies of the descendants of Ezra T. Clark, L. Tom Perry Special Collections, Harold B. Lee Library, Brigham Young University, Provo, Utah.

Growing Up Clark

Laura Clark Cook Silver Cook recorded extensively her memories of her childhood growing up as one of Ezra's daughters. Ezra hired a lot of men to help with the thrashing, and never allowed any swearing on his land. His daughter Laura once heard him tell a hired hand that he had dedicated his land to the Lord.

"I bless my farm, I do not curse it," his daughter Annie recorded him saying.[278]

Laura remembered that her mother (Susan) always cooked dinner for the hired men at noon, and the men ate in her home. One time a hired man as he left asked Laura for matches. Ezra forbade him to ask anything of his daughter.

"On Saturday night, my brothers would get the hayrack with a lot of hay on it and my sisters would make up a big lunch," Laura recalled. "Down to the lake we would go to have a swim and then eat lunch and sing songs going down and back—a highlight of my life. Sometimes we would be asleep by the time we got home."

Laura as a child did not know that her father was well off. "We had one new dress in the winter and perhaps two in the summer. We had to wear these things as long as we could. At one time, Father took me to the ZCMI. I would nearly always have the first new hat or coat in Farmington. In my early teens, I wanted more things. When Father was out fixing the fence or gate, I would hand him the nails and gently ask him for money. He was very thrifty and would want to know what I wanted it for before he would give it to me."

Ezra felt it was important to teach his children the value of money, and told them that if he could do that, he would be doing them a great service. He taught his children while they were young the principle of paying tithing.[279]

He also created wonderful outings for his own children and the young people of the area.

"Ezra T. Clark had a big bobsled with plenty of buffalo robes and several strings of sleigh bells he had obtained in the East. Peach cutting bees were held in his home, followed by games around a bonfire in his backyard where there were croquet sets and swings. On Saturday afternoons in the summertime a hayrack was loaded with boys and girls and driven to the shores of the Great Salt Lake, which was only three miles away. A fine team of horses was the pride of his farm. On celebrations of the 4th and 24th of July he usually provided the bandwagon and a four-horse team. It was his delight to decorate them and then drive them while the band serenaded the town."[280]

---

[278] Tanner. *A Biography*, p. 63.
[279] Laura Clark Autobiography.
[280] Hess, p. 353.

Clark Friendships with Church Leadership

Figure 121: Brigham Young, 1801–1877. © Everett Collection/Shutterstock.

Ezra respected Church leadership so much that he named many of his sons after prominent men in the Church. Additionally, he was friends with many of them.

Brigham Young and other Church leaders were regular guests at the Ezra T. Clark home, especially at the times of regional conferences.

"Often the President of the Church and the Apostles were at his home. His sons and daughters were always invited into the front room to meet them. The reminiscent discussions by these prominent visitors of their experiences preaching the Gospel, etc. made lasting impressions on the minds of his children."[281]

Brigham Young trusted Ezra as an excellent horseman, and in fact invited him to join him on a unique adventure.

Figure 122: John Taylor, third president and prophet of the Church of Jesus Christ of Latter-day Saints. Public domain via Wikicommons.

"In the 1860s, President Brigham Young invited some of the most noted horsemen in the territory to take part in the annual three-day roundups for the purpose of checking out and branding the wild horses on Antelope Island. Some of the men chosen for this great display of horsemanship were: Lot Smith, Judson Stoddard, Brigham Young, Jr., Len Rice, Stephen Taylor, Ezra Clark, Heber P. Kimball and the Ashby and Garr boys." All these men could ride a bucking horse bareback and lasso wild mustangs.[282]

John Taylor recounted his experience of being with Joseph Smith during the martyrdom as young Joseph Smith Clark, Jr. sat on his lap in Ezra's living room, while Joseph's father was serving a mission.[283] John Taylor was also a visitor to the Clark home during his period of hiding in the Underground.

Wilford Woodruff was also a frequent visitor, and a close friend of Ezra T. Clark. Wilford referred to Ezra as a "bosom friend."

On one occasion, Wilford sought shelter with Ezra on the night of a terrible storm. As Wilford recorded it:

---

[281] Tanner, Annie Clark. *Mormon Mother*, p. 30.
[282] Hess, p. 5
[283] "Experiences in the Life of Joseph Smith Clark Jr. 1878-1963."

Figure 123: Great Salt Lake State Park. The Great Salt Lake was a regular relaxation spot for Ezra and his family. .
Photo 11615213 © wirepec/Depositphotos.

"Nov. 16, 1864. Wednesday. We started early in the morning to return home. Soon after we left Kays Ward a snow storm accompanied by a strong canyon wind struck us and it was almost impossible for us to travel. It came near to blowing over our carriages. I was in the lightest carriage of the company and it was with great difficulty we could keep it right side up. It blew four windows out. We finally reached Farmington. President Young stopped with Bishop Hess. J. Tayor, G A Smith & myself went to Ezra Clarks & spent the night in the worst gale I ever experienced on land in my life."[284]

It was not at all uncommon for severe east winds to plague Farmington. In 1896, the east wind blew so hard that it took all the ripe fruit from the trees. On one occasion, Brigham Young rebuked the east wind when it blew his carriage over, and tradition says that the winds were calmer there for years afterwards.[285]

Edward B. Clark would later write in his autobiography: "I remember as a little boy getting up one morning during an east wind, and seeing barrels of molasses, grindstones, and large boulders hanging by ropes over the house to keep the east wind from blowing the roof off."[286]

Heber J. Grant was well acquainted with Ezra T. Clark's grandson Joseph Smith Clark, whom he had supervised in the mission field. He also hired Ezra's granddaughter, Mary Robertson, to be a secretary for Heber J. Grant Home and Fire Insurance Company, "where she was the secretary to the manager and also

Figure 124: Wilford Woodruff, circa 1849.
Public domain via Wikicommons.

---

[284] Clark, Antone. *Noble Pioneer*, p. 220.
[285] Hess, p. 47, 53, and 129.
[286] Clark, Edward B. *The Autobiography of Edward B. Clark*. Ezra T. Clark Family Organization. http://ezratclark.org/familyfile_AutobiographyOfEdwardBClark.asp

Figure 125: Antelope Island with clouds reflecting. Farmington is near the Great Salt Lake. Photo 156091910 © Sernovic/Depositphotos.

Figure 126: Portrait of Edward Stevenson.
Public domain via FamilySearch.

took dictation and typed letters for Heber J. Grant himself." He got to know her from his time spent around the Clark family, as she grew up in Ezra and Mary's home.[287]

David O. McKay was close friends with Ezra's grandson Obert Clark Tanner, better known as O.C. Tanner. In O.C. Tanner's autobiography, he recounts how President McKay hired him to write a teaching manual for the Sunday School of the Church. Obert was reluctant to take the assignment, telling President McKay that he felt what he wrote was likely to be disapproved by the reading committee. President McKay said in that case they would change the committee.[288] Obert wrote the book *Christ's Ideals for Living*, as well as *Understanding the New Testament*, a text for Seminary students.

Hyrum Don Carlos Clark served a mission with his Uncle Edward Stevenson to Tennessee, during which they stopped at the home of David Whitmer in Richmond, Missouri, and heard his

---

[287] "A Brief History of Mary Elizabeth Robinson Porter." Biographies and autobiographies of the descendants of Ezra T. Clark, Box 4 Folder 41, L. Tom Perry Special Collections, Harold B. Lee Library, Brigham Young University, Provo, Utah.

[288] Tanner, Obert Clark. *One Man's Journey in Search of Freedom*, p. 117.

testimony of the Book of Mormon. "Asked why he had left the Church, he replied that he had not but that it had left him."

Ezra made resources and carriages available to help support official Church business. He went in the company of Brigham Young to the dedication of the St. George Temple, and on the way back the group paused to dedicate the site of the future Manti Temple. He was also in the president's party when the Logan Temple site was dedicated. When it was announced that $20,000 would be required to complete the Salt Lake Temple, Ezra donated $1,000.[289]

Figure 127: Eliza R. Snow, second General President of the Relief Society. Public domain via Wikicommons.

"My father possessed many fine horses and could supply teams and carriages for transportation, which was a great advantage to the authorities of the church," Annie later wrote.[290]

Mary's friends included leading women of the Church. Eliza R. Snow, Zina D. Young, Emmeline B. Wells, and Elizabeth Stevenson were often guests in her home.

"She was a splendid hostess," wrote Ezra's daughter Annie. "Always mild as a summer's morning. Aunt Mary had the peaceful attitude of a Saint."[291]

Figure 128: Zina D. H. Young, third General President of the Relief Society. Public domain via Wikicommons.

---

[289] Tanner, Annie Clark. *A Biography*, p. 56.
[290] Tanner, Annie Clark. *Mormon Mother*, p. 30.
[291] Tanner, Annie Clark. *A Mormon Mother: An Autobiography*, pp. 11–12.

Ezra's Arrest and Imprisonment for Practicing Polygamy

As prosecutions for polygamy under the Edmunds Act occurred from 1884 until 1890, US marshals raided Utah settlements in search of co-habs (polygamists). Many families went into exile, including to Canada and Mexico. Most high-profile Church leaders went into hiding.

Despite the critical situation, the Saints were so convinced of their righteousness that punishment had no humiliation. Despite this, those following the practice did what they could to avoid capture.

Ezra had a secret trapdoor under the living room rug of his home, through which polygamists could escape pursuit from the marshals. The trapdoor led to a tunnel, which came up next to the stables. From there it was but a horse ride up to the top of the canyon and onward to freedom.

Despite his precautions, eventually Ezra was apprehended by the authorities.

His daughter Annie wrote: "Polygamists were warned or smuggled to safety. Mothers ran with their babies to the neighbors; old men took to the fields. My father was an early riser and just at daybreak on Sept. 1, 1886, he saw some men riding down the street. I saw my father run into the house and rush through the two rooms. He made a dash for the back door and ran through the orchard down the hill to the big creek where he expected to hide in the willows, but was overtaken by an officer and arrested."[292]

Ezra was charged with polygamy, and placed under bonds. At his trial on 17 February 1887, he was found guilty by a trial, and on 21 February he was sentenced to six months imprisonment and a $300 fine.[293]

In jail, Ezra tried to avoid further indignity by offering the barber $300 to not shave off his beard. The barber said he would not be bribed even for $500. And so, Ezra lost his beard, and appeared very strange to his children when they came to see him.[294]

"Moroni Clark"

Torlief Knaphus, a Scandinavian convert to the Church, was hired to create a sculpture of the Angel Moroni to be displayed on the Hill Cumorah.

He chose as a body model Ezra T. Clark's grandson Elwin Clark, a stone mason/bricklayer who was renting a small apartment from him and had paid rent in kind by building him a fireplace, according to Elwin's daughter, Sylvia.[295]

But Torlief felt that Elwin's face was too young to depict the face of Moroni. He wanted a different face to complete his project.

---

[292] Tanner, Annie Clark. *A Mormon Mother*, pp. 66–67.
[293] Tanner, Annie Clark. *A Biography*, p. 35.
[294] Clark, Antone, p. 185.
[295] Clark, A. Charles, personal correspondence.

*Figure 129: Moroni statue at the Hill Cumorah.
Photo 190714996 © Dallas Golden/Dreamstime.com*

Figure 130: Hyrum Don Carlos Clark, the model for the face of the Angel Moroni. Public domain via ezratclark.org

Torlief did not own a car and famously would pick people off the street and ask them to come pose in his studio for a sitting.

One day in Salt Lake City, he saw an older, bearded gentleman, whom he followed until he could corner him and plead with him to come pose for his work.

This man, a rancher, responded to the persuasive artist and agreed.

Elwin was already in the room when the older man entered.

It was a chance meeting, but the old rancher was Hyrum Don Carlos Clark, Elwin's father.

The finished statue is a likeness of the father/son combination, and it now sits atop the Hill Cumorah.

Descendants of Hyrum Don Carlos sometimes refer to the statue as "Moroni Clark."

The statue still stands today. Every year tourists come to visit the Hill Cumorah and they can see the statue of Moroni, which was modeled on Hyrum Don Carlos Clark and Elwin Clark.

Ezra and Mary's Golden Wedding Anniversary

When Ezra and Mary reached their Golden Wedding anniversary, Ezra's brother William came to visit.[296]

William had performed their original wedding ceremony and, when at their Golden Wedding anniversary Ezra and Mary recreated their original vows, William repeated that role again, reciting the same words. Fourteen other relatives had come with William from California to Farmington on 18 May 1895 to attend the Golden Wedding anniversary.

A cousin reported that William said "You mutually agree to be each other's companion, keeping yourselves wholly for each other, and from all others, during your lives."

"Uncle William looked amused," she said. "But Uncle Ezra looked confused." (FamilySearch)

Wilford Woodruff, who was among the guests, recorded in his journal: "In company with Emma I rode to Farmington to attend the 50 years golden wedding. A single thing took place. William O. Clark married his brother 50 years ago and for some cause he wanted to perform the same ceremony again out

---

[296] William had left the Church after the death of Joseph Smith and moved to California. He had become a world-class preacher for the cause of Temperance, or abstinence from alcohol. His friend Leland Stanford funded William in traveling around the world to preach Temperance.

of curiosity I suppose which was done. Speeches were made until midnight."²⁹⁷ (Wilford Woodruff's Journal)

Joseph Smith Clark, Jr. recalled of the event:

"I remember President Woodruff because he came up to Farmington in 1895 at the golden wedding celebration of Grandfather Ezra T. Clark and his wife, Mary Stevenson Clark. It was held in the Farmington Social Hall. President Woodruff was sitting in a big arm chair up on the stage while they were dancing and carrying on a program on the floor. I was a young boy about sixteen years of age." Joseph went on the stage and President Woodruff spoke to him directly and bore a testimony of Joseph Smith.²⁹⁸

Ezra and Mary's Golden Wedding anniversary was a festive occasion celebrated by many.

They were a leading couple in their community, and steered their family well over many decades.

Toward the end of Ezra's life, however, the structure of the Clark Firm shifted.

Figure 131: William O. Clark, brother of Ezra, performed Ezra and Mary's original wedding and came to Utah to officiate in the renewal of their vows for their Golden Anniversary. Public domain via FamilySearch.

Ezra's End of Life

Ezra T. Clark was a quiet man of conviction and an effective manager. His goals were to build material wealth, be of service to his community, and be of service to his Church.

Sometime before Ezra's death, he divided up the fortune and land of the Clark Firm among his descendants. He created something like a raffle system where his children could draw slips of paper to see who got what shares. Gifts included stock in the bank and plots of farmland. He had set his family up to thrive.

In January of 1901, Ezra was thrown from his carriage while driving home at night, when the wheels of his buggy ran off a bridge. He was pitched out and left badly bruised around his face. He did not rebound from this accident, and it was clear enough that something was wrong that his son Nathan came home early from his mission. His health was up and down, and almost bimonthly notices ran in the paper about the status of his health.

The death of Ezra Thompson Clark at 2:10 a.m. on 17 October 1901 made the front page of the Deseret News. His passing was not a surprise. He had suffered for nearly a year from an abdominal tumor.

His brother William O., and other relatives, had come from California to see him in his final days, but left a week before his passing.

Speakers at his funeral included Apostle A. O. Woodruff, John Henry Smith, and Elders Angus Cannon and Seymour B. Young. His pall-bearers included ten sons and the Davis County Stake High Council.

---

²⁹⁷ Wilford Woodruff's Journal, as quoted in Clark, Antone, *Noble Pioneer*, p. 218.
²⁹⁸ "Experiences in the Life of Joseph Smith Clark Jr."

Born in Illinois and raised in a time of persecution, Ezra had gone from rags to riches. He had become one of the wealthiest Utahns, and his land holdings were nearly double that of the next-largest landowner in Davis County.

When Ezra T. Clark died, you could walk from the Bamberger Railroad Station in Farmington to the Great Salt Lake and not get off Clark property.

Susan passed away the following year after a short illness in November 1902. The day she died, she remarked that she was satisfied with all of her children who were now grown to manhood and womanhood.[299]

Her last words were, "Ezra, you came for me. I knew you would."

Third wife Nancy had already passed away in 1888, but Mary lived until 1911. She died and was buried in Farmington, as was Ezra Thompson Clark.

Annual family reunions for both of Ezra's families were usually held on November 23—Ezra's birthday.[300] The Ezra T. Clark Family Organization was formed with Joseph, Eddie, and Amasa as the original board members. As of this writing, the organization still maintains a website at ezratclark.org.

Biographies of Ezra T. Clark

A few biographies have been written on the life of Ezra T. Clark. Most recently, *Noble Pioneer: A Biography of Ezra Thompson Clark* was written by Antone Clark, published in 2002. This excellent book goes into great detail on the life of Ezra Clark and his wives and families, and is well worth reading. It is available to download for free on the Clark Family Organization website at http://ezratclark.org/publications.asp on the bottom of the publications list. Annie Clark Tanner also wrote a short biography of Ezra T. Clark, which is worth reading.

The original biography on Ezra T. Clark is *A Biography of Ezra Thompson Clark*, written by Annie Clark Tanner some years after the death of her father, with the help of her siblings and the Church Historian's office to research his life.

Annie's brother Edward sent a copy of this book to President Heber J. Grant, who wrote the following letter, which Joseph Smith Clark felt was "the stamp of approval" for the family.

Figure 132: Annie Clark Tanner home, 2021. Photo © R.S. Kellogg

January 10, 1934

Elder Edward B. Clark,
Farmington,
Utah.

Dear Brother Clark:

---

[299] "Susan Leggett Clark."
[300] Tanner, Annie Clark. *A Mormon Mother*, p. 39.

Many thanks for the little book, "A Biography of Ezra T. Clark." I read it aloud to my wife last evening from start to finish and we enjoyed it immensely. I congratulate your sister upon having written such a fine account of your father's life.

I esteemed your father very highly indeed. I was one that partook of hospitality very often, almost without fail every time there was a quarterly conference at Farmington when I was appointed to attend. I read his testimony of the transfiguration, so to speak, of Brigham Young at the time that Sidney Rigdon tried to claim appointment as the guardian of the Church, representing the Prophet Joseph, and how Brigham Young spoke with the voice, and used the gestures, and had the personal appearance of Joseph Smith. I am grateful that my mother was present and had the same testimony which she often gave in public.

Ever praying for your welfare and that of your loved ones, and with best wishes for a happy and prosperous New Year, and hoping that you and yours had an enjoyable Christmas, I am
    Sincerely your friend and brother,
    Heber J. Grant[301]

---

[301] Tanner, Annie Clark. A *Biography*, p. xi.

8. Edward B. Clark Family Stories

Edward B. Clark (head of family)
Wives:
1. Wealthy Richardson Clark [m. 25 September 1879]
2. **Alice Randall Clark (our ancestor)** [m. 2 April 1885]

Interviewer: In later life as your mother looked back on her life, how did she feel? Did she feel that her decision to marry for a better husband, a better father for her children was justified?
Walter Edward Clark: I think she did, yes.
Interviewer: And she was glad that she had made that decision.
Walter Edward Clark: She never regretted it.[302]

An Unexpected Plural Marriage

Alice Randall Clark is the grandparent who arguably had the most direct influence on the life of Alan Clark. Both in terms of culture (as she was the grandparent who raised Alan's father) and direct involvement in his life (as she raised Alan himself for a few years after the death of his mother). Despite Alice's powerful impact on the Clark family, details of the story of Alice and her family have not in the past been as widely accessible as stories of some of our other ancestors. Stories about Alice have been limited to mentions in other works and stories primarily centered around other family members, and a tribute book in Alice's honor, which quoted from her writings and shared stories about her by family and friends. Many of the stories of Alice have been held in various far-flung books mostly held in private libraries. This chapter seeks to make the story of Alice and her family more widely available.

This is the story of Edward, Wealthy, and Alice, whose lives somewhat paralleled the biblical story of Abraham, Sarah, and Hagar.

This is the story of an unusual polygamous marriage that wouldn't have happened if it hadn't been for a blessing and an intense desire for children.

This is the story of how Alice Randall came to join the Clarks.

---

[302] Charles Redd Center for Western Studies. *Walter Clark Oral History Transcript, Interviewed by Leonard R. Grover.* LDS Polygamy Oral History Project, 1979 October 12, File-folder: MSS OH 398, Identifier: MSS 7752 Series 1 Sub-series 2. L. Tom Perry Special Collections, Harold B. Lee Library, Brigham Young University, Provo, Utah.

A Childless Marriage with an Extraordinary Promise

"I asked [Wealthy] to go to a dance with me and she said that she would let me know at recess— we were then attending school in the old Rock School House. Her answer was, 'yes' and then we started going together. I took her to parties and walked home with her after meetings."[303] —*Edward B. Clark*

Long before Edward met Alice, he began courting Wealthy. Wealthy and Edward grew up together in Farmington, and began courting when he was 16 and she was 14.

After several years, during which Edward had not thought of marriage, "One Sunday evening [Wealthy] suggested that we had better 'play quits.' She said she did not know whether she loved me enough and that she would not marry a man whom she did not love with all her heart. I had not told her how much she meant to me or how much I loved her."

Other young men stepped forward to court Wealthy, including some of Edward's best friends. However, several months later, Edward was approached by Aunt Nancy Clark, the YMMIA president who served with Wealthy as her secretary. Aunt Nancy, who was Edward's father's third wife, let Edward know that a certain young lady would like to see him up town, and cautioned him about sincerity.

If marriage had never crossed Edward's mind before, perhaps this was a way that Aunt Nancy was encouraging him to take the relationship more seriously.

"It was a happy day for me for I had always loved Wealthy," wrote Edward. "When I met her, she said that if I had anyone else in mind she would not interfere, but that if I did not, she would be glad to be my sweetheart. She was just that until the day she passed away. No woman could be truer to a man than she was to me; she was willing to give her life for me."[304]

Edward and Wealthy had a sweet love match. One has to imagine that Edward's Aunt Nancy must have had some satisfaction in counseling Edward on relationship matters.

The courtship progressed, and Edward and Wealthy eventually married. The young couple by all accounts lived very harmoniously together, but they faced challenges. Wealthy was beset with health difficulties that at times left her almost an invalid. She was well-regarded as a good influence and leader in the community, but her health made it difficult for her to serve.

---

[303] Clark, Edward B. "Incidents in the Life and Labors of Wealthy Richards Clark," *Autobiography of Edward B. Clark*. Ezra T. Clark Family Foundation.http://ezratclark.org/familyfile_AEBC_IncidentsInLife.asp
[304] Ibid.

Upon the release of Aurelia Rogers, first president of the Farmington Primary, Wealthy Richards Clark was sustained as the second Primary President of the ward. However, she could only hold the position for a year before being released due to her health.[305]

A secondary issue was that after six years of marriage, Wealthy and Edward were still without children, and they dearly longed for some.

In a blessing she received from a Church leader, Wealthy was told that if she allowed her husband to take a second wife, she and Edward would be able to have children.

It must have been sobering to face this matter: Wealthy and Edward were deeply in love and by all accounts continued to be so throughout their entire lives. They probably wouldn't have added a second wife into the family mix of their own accord. Even after Edward did marry Alice, she didn't try to insert herself into Edward and Wealthy's life very much, saying "Their courtship is beautiful and I'm not going to interfere with it."[306]

Additionally, at that time polygamists were facing

Figure 133: Edward and Wealthy. Public domain via FamilySearch.

progressively hotter water from the government. The Edmunds Anti-Polygamy Act had been signed in 1882, making polygamy a felony in US states and territories. Edward would marry Alice in 1885, a few years after the Edmunds Act had gone into effect, and a few years before Edward's own father, Ezra, served jail time in 1887 for practicing polygamy. Taking a second wife in Utah in the 1880s was a fraught matter.

Despite these factors, loyal Wealthy didn't want to deprive Edward of children. She told him: "If I am unable to raise a family, I won't deprive you."

---

[305] *My Farmington*.
[306] Charles Redd Center for Western Studies. *Walter Clark*, p. 6.

Second Wife Alice

"I was born the daughter of Alfred and Margaret Harley Randall. My father was born in New York and my mother in Pennsylvania. I was born in Centerville, Utah, Dec. 21, 1863. I had two brothers and five sisters, the boys being the older. Mother was very partial to boys and I being the fourth girl in succession, did not seem very welcome. My younger sister coming five years later, and being more attractive and aggressive, my mother bestowed the love on her that we both should have had." —Alice Randall Clark[307]

Figure 134: Young Alice Randall Clark. Public domain via FamilySearch.

Alice Randall was the sixth of Margaret Harley Randall's seven children.

Margaret is recalled as having some good skills in survival from her time on the pioneer trail, and also eventually trained in OB/GYN work. She brought skillfulness to the raising of her children, as all seven lived to adulthood in a time when it was not always common to have all the children from such a large family survive childhood.

Despite having her physical needs met, Alice's autobiographical sketch reveals that during her growing up years, her mother favored Alice's younger sister, Emily.

Alice was often the last to eat at the family table, and received the dresses that no one else wanted.

"She takes whatever we give her," she recalled her mother telling a neighbor of an unflattering dress that Alice was wearing.

Despite some difficulties at home, Alice had happiness in her childhood. Her oldest sister, Mary Elizabeth, looked out for her.

"My older sister always made a great deal over me," Alice recalled. "When she married and moved to Ogden [when Alice was ten years old] she kept me there a good deal of the time. Her husband was yard master. I would go to the depot and ride the train out two miles, which was the distance the train went out to turn around on the Y."

---

[307] Clark, Alice Randall. "A Sketch of the Life of Alice Randall Clark."

Alice also had a good time with athletics and parties.

"I could run faster or jump the rope faster than any boy or girl on the school ground," she later recalled.

Though not initially a natural student, she did take to her studies eventually, and in math was competitive against B.H. Roberts, a fellow classmate. When an opportunity came for Alice to attend college, she wanted to pursue it.

Her life sketch records: "When we had finished school I had the opportunity to go to the University of Utah to school. I asked my mother and she said she would have to ask my older brother. (His favorite among all the family was my sister just older than I.) So his reply was, 'How can she expect to go when her sister hasn't been?' There were still two older than she and they had not been, it looked so silly to me and so I just got mad and sulked and grieved instead of putting up a fight as I should have done. I could have been a school teacher, I taught the first Primary school in our town."

Alice's son Bryant, recalled of his mother:

"She would like to have gone to school, but, of course, [her father, Alfred Randall] a man with five wives wasn't putting much out on anybody. In fact, that wasn't the way of the time."[308]

Having missed out on the possibility of college, and having avoided a long-term commitment to her chief potential beau, Alice felt her "goose was cooked," and that she had no good prospects. Then one day, Edward B. Clark showed up in her mother's kitchen and asked her to become his second wife.

Edward had formerly been Alice's teacher. At the time, she had been a girl of 14 and he a young man of 19.

"We all liked him fine as a teacher," Alice later recorded. "One day he had visitors from Farmington, he called on me to read as a show off. I refused because I had on a dress that I did not like; it was just new that morning but it was a mile too long. That is how he got to know me was by teaching. He did not want another wife, Aunt Wealthy, his first wife, had been told or promised or something by someone that if he would take another wife she would have children. So he picked out someone he thought would be easy, he did not want—need to bother about."

It was not to be a romantic relationship, but Alice suited Edward's second-wife needs.

Alice was now an intelligent, self-reliant young lady in her twenties, and, perhaps most importantly, Wealthy had agreed with Edward's choice.

Of his thoughts regarding selecting Alice, Edward recorded: "Alice, as a girl in school, impressed me as a good student, of a meek and humble disposition, so that later, when I was impressed to take another wife she appealed to me. She was fully natured with a mind of her own, being about 24 years old,

---

[308] "Life Sketch of Bryant Randall Clark."

Figure 135: Logan Temple.
© *lgouldie/Depositphotos*

without, at that time, a steady boyfriend. While she received a shock, and was taken by surprise, she was willing for me to come to see her and visit her occasionally, while she was considering the matter of matrimony."[309]

According to Alice's children's writings, Alice recalled that the day Edward walked into her mother's Centerville home that "she knew at once and without question or doubt that this man was to be her husband."

Alice's son Bryant wrote the following: "Concerning mother's marriage, it was not a matter of polygamy or no marriage at all. She had other suitors and was urged by at least one of them to marry monogamously. But as stated elsewhere, to the oft repeated question, 'why polygamy?' she would reply, 'For you and your brothers and sisters. I felt your father would give you a better heritage.'"

Alice was thinking on a high plane, Bryant noted. "The romance was out. That was the thing that was played down."[310]

The account Alice left in her life sketch of the day Edward came to court her is less flowery and quite vivid: "One evening mother and I were drying peaches and in walked your father; you could not

---

[309] Clark, Edward B. "Incidents in the Life and Labors of Alice Randall Clark," *Autobiography of Edward B. Clark.* Ezra T. Clark Family Foundation. http://ezratclark.org/familyfile_AEBC_IncidentsLifeLaborsAliceRandallClark.asp

[310] "Life Sketch of Bryant Randall Clark." Biographies and autobiographies of the descendants of Ezra T. Clark, Box 5 Folder 56, L. Tom Perry Special Collections, Harold B. Lee Library, Brigham Young University, Provo, Utah.

have knocked me more senseless with a club. I had gone to school to him one year and thought he was extremely nice."

Though, according to Alice, Edward loved Wealthy too much to even care a little for another, Alice and Edward were married on 2 April 1885 in the Logan Temple.

Wealthy accompanied Edward and Alice to their wedding as a way to show her approval for the match.

Bryant commented: "I think if [Alice] hadn't have found someone she thought was worthy of her she wouldn't have gotten married."[311]

It is said that Wealthy began to grow a little impatient after the wedding of Alice and Edward, waiting for a pregnancy to come. Alice said she felt she would be the one to have the first baby. And sure enough, four years after her wedding to Edward, Alice finally did become pregnant.

Edward later wrote: "Alice lived with her widowed mother until prospects of a family were near, when I brought her to live with a trusted family in Farmington, where our first born, Walter, came to bless our lives."[312]

The following year, Wealthy finally had a child of her own, Edward Franklin Clark, born nearly eleven years after Wealthy had married Edward.

Depending on who was telling the story, Walter and Edward were both variously referred to as the child of promise, who came to fulfill the promise of children to the family after Edward B. Clark took a second wife.

Alice on the Underground

"I drove [Mother] to Utah one time.
"As we approached a house, she said, 'Stop here, I want to go in.'
I said, 'Who is here?'
She said, 'Oh, a woman we stayed with when you were a baby.'
She was indicating she had to keep out of the way.[313] —*Walter Edward Clark*

Just like the biblical Hagar, Alice was caused by forces beyond her control to live apart from the father of her son. For four years, Alice and little Walter lived on the Underground, a movement that kept polygamous people hidden from government authorities.

During her time on the Underground, Alice lived in a town called Three Mile, just north of Brigham City, and also for a time kept house in Nephi for her widowed Uncle Edwin, her mother's older brother.

For a time, Alice lived in a house shared with her younger sister, Emily, while Emily's husband Wilford Woodruff Richards was away on a mission. Wilford's mother, Mary Thompson Richards, a wife of Franklin D. Richards, had given Wilford some farmland for Emily to live on and to rent out to support Wilford on his mission. This farmland where Emily and Alice lived is now part of the property of Lagoon.

---

[311] Charles Redd Center for Western Studies. *Bryant R. Clark Interviewed by Christ Nelson.* LDS Polygamy Oral History Project, 1981 January 11, Biographies and autobiographies of the descendants of Ezra T. Clark, Box 5 Folder 56, L. Tom Perry Special Collections, Harold B. Lee Library, Brigham Young University, Provo, Utah.
[312] Clark, Edward B. "Alice."
[313] Charles Redd Center for Western Studies. *Walter Clark.*

At last, Alice was offered a home of her own in Georgetown, Idaho. Joseph Smith Clark's home had become available, as Joseph brought his family to live in Farmington. Alice would become part of the Clark family presence in the Bear Lake area, where she would raise her family far enough away from Farmington to keep Edward out of suspicion. She would also help to oversee the Clark farm and cattle interests in Idaho.

"Joseph [Clark] took Mother and I to Georgetown," recorded Walter Edward Clark, in an interview he gave later in life. "We arrived April 20, 1893. The following month May 8, 1893 Wilford was called to Montpelier to be bishop where he served twenty-two years. Mother moved into the Clark home and cooked for the hired men."

To be clear, Alice moved into Joseph's home, which was the original home that Ezra T. Clark had built when he'd first come up to help build a settlement in the area. Joseph Smith Clark had spent fifteen years developing the Clark property in Georgetown. Wilford's family continued to maintain their home in Georgetown.

Alice was pleased to finally have a home of her own.

Edward would eventually have a total of seven children with Wealthy, and five with Alice. He would know tragedy as a parent. Three of his children with Wealthy would not live long lives—Wealthy and Edward lost a set of twins as infants, and their daughter Wealthy died in a tragic flash flood with her new husband shortly after returning from her honeymoon.

All of Edward's children with Alice, however, lived long and full lives.

Because Alice and Edward lived largely separate lives, their stories will be told separately below.

Because Alice's children grew up with her as their primary parent, Alice's story is told first.

Stories of Alice Randall Clark

Alice Randall Clark's autobiographical life sketch is quoted in a tribute book called *That You May Know Her Better,* which her youngest son, Bryant, compiled in her honor. It proved elusive to locate a copy of Alice's own original life sketch. Much like Alice's life itself, it remained largely hidden, and as I researched the material for this book, I encountered here and there only clues that it existed. Despite a lengthy search and inquiries to historians within the family and a thorough search of the official Ezra T. Clark family archives, which are housed in BYU's L. Tom Perry Special Collections, I had found no first-hand records of Alice that she had left herself, until very shortly before this book went to press. But that didn't mean there wasn't other content to be found.

Figure 136: Quilt made by Alice Randall Clark for granddaughter Carol Clark Call.
Image used with permission.

Because the Clarks were excellent record keepers, many details and anecdotes of Alice's life were preserved in the writings of others; I was able to reconstruct Alice's life and gather many stories about her, collecting these details from the life stories of Alice's sister Emily, Alice's husband, Edward, the life stories of Alice's children, Bryant's tribute book to Alice, and anecdotes from the life stories from other extended Clark family members who knew Alice and interacted with her.

And then, as I was working to obtain permission to include in this book an image of Alice's quilt, which I found posted to FamilySearch, I lucked into connecting with someone who held a copy of Alice's autobiographical life sketch.

I reached out to the woman who had posted the image of Alice's quilt to FamilySearch. She was happy to give permission for me to include the image of this quilt in the book, which Alice had made for granddaughter Carol Clark Call.

On an impulse, and because I'd become used to asking anybody who might have heard of it, I asked whether this distant cousin knew of Alice's autobiography.

It turned out she did.

This piece, written or dictated by Alice and sometimes quoted elsewhere, is about four typewritten pages long. It reveals a strong-willed woman who fought to create a better life for her children than the one that she had. Glimpses of Alice's personality are apparent in the stories that I gathered from these other sources, but reading about Alice in her own words really presents the force of her character. This is the woman who instilled in her descendants a value on education so strong that later, when her great-grandchildren recounted to me the driving force behind Walter's children (Alice's grandchildren) all getting college degrees—and many of them getting advanced degrees—her grandchildren attributed this focus to Alice.

Largely on her own, until her children got old enough to help, Alice was the one who directed the Clark holdings in Farmington. She later remembered:

"In a few weeks [after Alice's arrival in Georgetown] Wilford W. Clark, Edward's brother, was called to be Bishop in Montpelier, so I had to hold the ranch down. I had from one to three hired boys and men all the time. But it was home and I was my own boss. I do not remember when they divided up, but Walter was a mere boy, but he took hold of things in earnest."

Alice's Values

"She would never run a store bill as was the custom and said, 'I will live on bread and water for a month if necessary, so as to get on a pay-as-you-go basis.'"—Melvin Clark

Alice hated debt like poison.

She taught her children to be frugal and to work hard, and to be prepared for a rainy day. She kept some wheat in the grain bin at all times.

She also role-modeled a life of service.

"On one occasion she went to help a neighbor family," Melvin wrote. "The mother and children were sick. One of the children was an invalid. The mother said she prayed very hard for help to be sent; that Alice Clark came in answer to that prayer."

She was always on call to help others, and believed it is better to give than to receive.

Bryant recalled Alice as a woman with exceptional sympathy, not particularly outgoing but well thought of in the community.

Alice's Yard and Home

"I remember one of my pleasant pastimes was to lie flat on my back under the trees and watch the clouds move across the sky."—Maurine Clark Wiberg[314]

During the years that she raised her children, Alice's yard was rimmed with poplar trees, giving both shade and beauty. The grass which carpeted the yard was highlighted with dandelions, some yellow and some white, and Alice's daughters enjoyed threading the yellow-headed dandelions together to make flower chains, and blowing the seeds of the white ones through the air to "tell their fortunes."

---

[314] Wiberg, Maurine Clark. "As I Remember," p. 4. Biographies and autobiographies of the descendants of Ezra T. Clark, Tom Perry Special Collections, Box 5 Folder 55, Harold B. Lee Library, Brigham Young University, Provo, Utah.

*Figure 137: Home of Alice Randall Clark in Georgetown.
Image used with permission.*

A creek meandered over a rocky creek bed on one side of the lot, behind a dense growth of willows, along with the dreaded stinging nettle, and beautiful wild rose bushes that scented the air with their mature flowers. When she was a girl, Maurine used to hide in a bower in the willows to read a good book and to enjoy a long summer afternoon, tucked out of sight from the cares of the world.[315]

Alice's home was a remodeled cabin, which Ezra T. Clark had originally built back in the founding days of Georgetown. It was made of logs from a nearby canyon. It originally had two rooms, but then two more were built on the east side. The southeast room was larger than the other and served as a kitchen. The walls were covered with cloth and then with wallpaper.

Every few years, a new layer of wallpaper was added, "Much to the delight of all of us who enjoyed the new designs and colors."[316]

Eventually, the home's original pantry became a clothes closet, and part of the new kitchen became a pantry. A second well was dug close to the kitchen door. Water was obtained with a bucket at the end of a rope and pulley.

A tool house and a milk separator room were created just to the east of the house, and this space was later rebuilt to provide a utility room and an extra bedroom.

The home's gable roof was topped with pine shingles, and the rooms were covered on the outside by lumber clapboard.

---

[315] Ibid., p. 4.
[316] Clark, Bryant. *That You May Know Her Better*, p. 50.

The house was light yellow, with a front porch six or eight feet by six feet. The porch had a roof and two pillar support.

Also on the property were a log barn, a wagon shed, a shop, a granary, an ice and coal and wood room, a frog corral formed from the pig pens and a hen house, the root cellar, and the garden.

Alice's home didn't have indoor plumbing. When an electric light plant was installed up Georgetown Canyon, the community got lights. The Clark family was very excited to get a 25-watt globe hanging down in the middle of the room, but power was intermittent as the light plant was not initially very consistent.

Alice's family had a gramophone, and maybe six dozen rolls to play with, which they used to play over and over.

"They were good music, too; they weren't bad. That's quite different than we have today," recalled Alice's daughter Rhoda.[317]

Life on Alice's Farm

"It was quite a normal life. It was nothing spectacular. We had to work to run the farm. The income on which we lived was mostly the extracurricular activity of a farm like chickens and cream."[318]
—Maurine Clark Wiberg

Alice's family lived on a big farm, which Bryant compared to a small ranch. Most of the income of the farm went to the head of the family, as the Clark Firm, a United-Order-based family organization created by Edward B.'s father Ezra T. Clark, operated as a financial unit. The father was the head of the unit, so the farm income went to Edward after Ezra dissolved the Clark Firm.

The boys milked quite a few cows and the family sold the cream, shipping it to Salt Lake every week in an eight- or ten-gallon can until local creameries were built and the cream could be sold there. It was hard to make a good living.

"We didn't realize we were poor," wrote Bryant. "After we got older and could look back on it, poverty stared us in the face almost belligerently."

His brother Melvin agreed:

"She and her children did not have much money or an easy life but they did have a good heritage."[319]

Since everyone in Georgetown was at about the same economic level, it didn't stand out to the family that they weren't well off.

"My brother tells a good story," Bryant recalled. "He says that he had bread and milk gravy for breakfast, milk and custard pudding for dinner and bread and milk for supper. Then he says, speaking of me, Bryant says when he grew up he did it better. On Sundays he used to have ice cream."

Alice led family prayers, but according to her youngest son she didn't need to do a great deal of discipline.

---

[317] "An Interview with Rhoda Clark Taylor," circa 1975. Biographies and autobiographies of the descendants of Ezra T. Clark, Box 4 Folder 54. L. Tom Perry Special Collections, Harold B. Lee Library, Brigham Young University, Provo, Utah.
[318] "Life Sketch of Bryant Randall Clark."
[319] Clark, Melvin J. "Some Impressions and Lessons my Mother Left Me, Written by Melvin J Clark about his Mother Alice Randall Clark." Biographies and autobiographies of the descendants of Ezra T. Clark, Box 4 Folder 53. L. Tom Perry Special Collections, Harold B. Lee Library, Brigham Young University, Provo, Utah.

"We had a great respect for her," he said. "She took charge of things. When the family would decide something, she had the final word. She and the two older boys were running the place, and they made the decisions."[320]

Alice had good hired help to support running the farm, but her boys still did a great deal of work.

"She must have spent many anxious hours when her small boys traveled to the meadow below town to haul hay, drive cattle and take machinery to run the farm to and from the fields and drive cows to pasture, as there was a river to cross in order to get there," Melvin wrote.[321]

The local boys worked hard during the week, but still found ways to have a good time. They would go swimming in Bear River on Sunday afternoons between meetings.[322]

The family's transportation was by horse and by foot for many years. When Rhoda was about 12 years old, they got word there was a car going from Montpelier through Georgetown, and they all went down to Main Street to see the car go through.

Raising Children on a Farm as a Lone Parent

Alice's sister-in-law Laura Clark, who also parented small children alone on a farm, left an account that paints a picture of the unique challenges presented to single-parent families in those times.

During these early settler times, some women ran a farm largely on their own, due to the death of a husband or due to being a plural wife. Ezra's daughter Laura's first husband unexpectedly passed away at a young age, and for a time she managed a farm plus her three young children on her own. In Laura's words:

"In the buggy, we rode with one child sitting on the seat, one on the floor, and one on my lap. In order to hitch up the horse, I went half a mile down through the field with the bit and rope in my hands and I would have to talk to the horse and hold his head down while I slipped the bit up between the horse's teeth. Then take him up to the buggy and back him up into the shafts of the buggy and in the meantime, keep the children from falling out of the buggy. Then I drove to Farmington—I had done this many times."[323]

Alice's experience of wrangling small children as a single parent on a farm may have involved similar experiences.

The Local Church

"One of my early memories is of Mother taking me to Primary to help set up chairs."[324]— Maurine Clark Wiberg

The meeting house the Clark family attended was a long one-room building with a stage at one end and a curtain at the other. All activities of the Church or community were held in this building.

---

[320] Charles Redd Center for Western Studies. "Bryant R. Clark Interviewed by Chris Nelson on January 11, 1981 CRC-K138, Copyright 1981 by the Charles Redd Center for Western Studies. Biographies and autobiographies of the descendants of Ezra T. Clark, Box 5 Folder 56, L. Tom Perry Special Collections, Harold B. Lee Library, Brigham Young University, Provo, Utah.

[321] Clark, Melvin J. Biographies and autobiographies of the descendants of Ezra T. Clark, Box 4 Folder 53. L. Tom Perry Special Collections, Harold B. Lee Library, Brigham Young University, Provo, Utah.

[322] "Life Sketch of Bryant Randall Clark."

[323] Clark, Laura Blanche. "Autobiography of Laura Blanche Clark." *FamilySearch*, Intellectual Reserve, 7 December 2018, https://www.familysearch.org/tree/person/memories/KWCZ-YQH. Accessed 28 September 2020.

[324] Wiberg. "Faith."

Curtains could be drawn both ways through the hall to divide the room into smaller classrooms. Chairs were set up for Church activities and taken down for recreational activities.

Alice was a great proponent of priesthood blessings. Her daughter Maurine credits the faith of her mother and the blessings of her bishop for helping her recover from a bad bout of rheumatic fever and a subsequent leak to her heart.[325]

"Mother was a quiet soft-spoken woman and a friend to everybody," Maurine wrote. "Her children were her first concern, but she was always willing to help others. She served in many church positions in Primary, MIA, and Relief Society."[326]

Soda Springs

Located about eighteen miles north of Georgetown, Soda Springs featured natural mineral springs, which were strongly carbonated and had quite a strong iron flavor. The Clark family would bottle it up, cork it, and bring it home. They'd mix it with lemon juice and sugar for a good drink.

Alice at Bear Lake

Bryant recalls his mother as usually being calm and collected, but there is one story he recalls where she did get flustered.

During a family outing to Bear Lake, her two daughters, Maurine and Rhoda, took a rowboat into the lake with a friend or two. While they were still a ways out, a sudden wind squall came up, and the placid lake surface churned into whitecaps.

"It was impossible to bring the boat into shore because of the receding water and impossible to launch a boat out to help the situation," Bryant recorded. "However, the girls were experienced enough to keep the boat at right angles to the waves which were tossing the front of the boat far above the girls' head, then letting it drop equally low into the next trough."

Alice grew quite agitated.

She stood at the water's edge, calling repeatedly, "Come in! Come in to the shore. Why do you stay out there? Come in!"

The girls couldn't hear her in the storm, and they did have things as under control as possible in the moment and were having the time of their lives.

Bryant recalls feeling great sympathy for his mother's anxiety.[327]

---

[325] Ibid., p. 16.
[326] Ibid., pp. 3–4.
[327] Clark, Bryant. *Know Her Better*, p. 55.

Figure 138: Bear Lake
Image © NataliGlado/Depositphotos

Holidays at Alice's Home

"At Christmas time we'd have some oranges, and that's about the only time I ever saw oranges, was at Christmas time. We didn't have a lot of fresh fruit."[328] —Rhoda Clark Taylor

Alice and her children celebrated some holidays together with their little Church community. The Fourth of July and Pioneer Day (on the twenty-fourth of July) were both big events. About 90 percent of the 500 citizens of the community were members of the Church. They would get together and have races and other fun for the holidays.

At Thanksgiving and Christmas after Alice's sister Emily had moved away from Georgetown to Paris, the three Clark families of Georgetown (the Wilford Woodruff Clark, Charles C. Rich Clark, and Alice Randall Clark families) would gather in one of the family homes and they would all have a nice celebration together.

Bryant reports that even at holidays, "We never give it any thought that there was another family [Edward and Wealthy's family]. We were just one family there."

One year, Edward did celebrate Christmas with Alice's family:

"The Christmas of 1907 Father spent with us in Georgetown. The following February he left for the Northern States Mission where he labored for thirty-two months leaving two families and five children in each, all under eighteen years of age," Walter recorded in his oral history.[329]

---

[328] Charles Redd Center for Western Studies. *Bryant R. Clark.*
[329] Charles Redd Center for Western Studies. *Walter Clark.*

Alice Maintained Her Relationship with Family of Origin

Wealthy and Edward's son Orson recalled in an oral interview that Edward used to bring Alice down to Utah occasionally. She had plenty of relatives in the state and would stay first with Wealthy as a stopping point, then go visit her relatives. She had grown up in Centerville, not far from Farmington.[330]

The Value of Education

"When [Walter] went to school he'd be several weeks late getting in because he had to work on the farm, and then he'd have to come home weekends to take care of things, . . . He really had a very good mind. He finally graduated from college; he was the last one of us . . . [h]e got the best grades, I think he was valedictorian, and he was a special debater in college. But he had kind of a hard life when he was younger, taking care of the rest of us."[331]—Rhoda Clark Taylor

Alice placed an unusually high value on education for her era, especially compared to other families in her region. Perhaps this may have been due in part to her competitive nature. As she wrote about herself:

"I liked to swing higher [than anyone else]. One large barn had a swing where some would pull ropes to swing us. I was never satisfied until I swang out far enough to see over the barn.

"Another sport, when I was a girl, was to climb a high hill east of our home. I would climb higher than anyone else to get to run down. I had done so much of that that one time I ran down a board where B. H. Roberts was shingling his house.[332] I knew no fear until I heard him sort of scream."[333]

Figure 139: B.H. Roberts. Public domain via Wikicommons.

Alice's firm belief in the value of a strong education may have been the single most lasting legacy she left for her children, and a way she single-handedly helped elevate her family lineage. Her strong value on education might in large part be attributed to some key friendships that she had as a young person, especially her friendships with prominent scholar B.H. Roberts and another boy who Bryant writes grew up to become a president of the University of Utah.

Alice bragged that by the time she was in the Third Reader, "It was always I . . . who was asked to show off the reading class."

She further recalls:

"Our family were all sharks in arithmetic as we called it then. Many times, unconsciously, I have made B. H. Roberts feel foolish in mathematics, but later I went to his school after he had taken a year at the U. of U. He didn't teach me arithmetic, but he did give me a course in Grammar, didn't he though; that was easy but English, that was worse than spelling. I was always at the foot of the spelling class. We stood in a line to spell; when a word was

---

[330] Knowlton, Clark S. and Ruth. Oral interview with Orson Clark. Biographies and autobiographies of the descendants of Ezra T. Clark, L. Tom Perry Special Collections, Harold B. Lee Library, Brigham Young University, Provo, Utah.
[331] "An Interview with Rhoda Clark Taylor."
[332] My understanding from this is that the board was leaning against the roof to be used as a ladder, and she ran down it rather than walked down it.
[333] Clark, Bryant. *Know Her Better*, p. 2.

missed the one below who spelled it correctly went above the one who missed. The one at the top started at the bottom the following day. I was never at the head, hence never at the foot."

Alice learned to spell later, after she became an adult and began to write letters to loved ones. One of her boarders, a teacher, gave her a spelling examination and was surprised to find that Alice made a near-perfect grade.

She turned her frustration over her own failure to get a greater education into fuel that she drew on to support her children's education. She went to extraordinary lengths to ensure that each of them finished high school.

"After I decided we would never be looked after, I cared not a rap what anyone said," she recorded in her life sketch. "We scrimped and I put the children through High School when it was discovered I would do as I pleased. They put themselves through college. All except Melvin, his eyes were so bad he could not go."[334]

Alice felt that Melvin should have received better support from his father, and might have completed college with proper care. Apparently, he never received glasses as a boy. That Edward's disparity in financially supporting his two families bothered Alice shows up in small details like this.

When Alice's children were old enough to have aged out of the limited schooling available in Georgetown, she would move to Paris, Idaho, for months on end, so that they could have a chance to attend Fielding Academy there, or else she'd send them to live with her sister, Emily Richards.

To help her children attend BYU, Alice rented a house in Provo for a few years and took in boarders so her children might study at the University.

"She was dedicated to her children and desirous for them to receive a higher education," recalled Bryant.[335]

Four of her children graduated from BYU, one each year for four years. Walter, the oldest child, graduated last. Alice's second son, Melvin, went to school in Logan then served in the army.

Alice's attitudes on education came through loud and clear as her children grew up.

As Rhoda recalled: "When we graduated from eighth grade, we had to take county examinations. So, we took the county examinations and were ready to be graduated, but we had to go to Paris, Idaho for the graduation. But Mother didn't take me. She said, 'It isn't anything to graduate from the eighth grade. But when you graduate from high school, then we'll see that you go to graduation.'"[336]

She continually held a bigger vision for her children. When a circus came to Montpelier, she didn't take her children, saying, "Well, when there gets to be a real circus, I want you to see it. But I'm not anxious for you to see one of those little things."[337]

---

[334] Clark, Alice Randall. "A Life Sketch of Alice Randall Clark."
[335] "Life Sketch of Bryant Randall Clark."
[336] "An Interview with Rhoda Clark Taylor."
[337] Ibid.

Similarly, she would purchase some foods that were considered luxuries, such as celery, sweet potatoes, bananas, cranberries, and oranges to share with her children on occasion.

She would tell her children:

"Someday you will be away from home and I want you to know what these items are and how they are used."[338]

When Walter graduated from high school, someone told him to frame his certificate. But Alice refused to frame it, telling him to wait until he got through college.

It was quite a few years before Walter got through college, but he finally did.

Alice wanted her children to read good things, do good things, see good things, and not just pick up something because it was fun for the minute.

Figure 140: Alice with grandson Roland. Public domain via FamilySearch.

Alice as a Helper in the Community

"[Alice] was very healthy. She never spent a day in bed in her life except when her children were born. Yet she was constantly in somebody's home helping the sick."[339] —Bryant Randall Clark

On some mornings when the Clark children arose, Alice would be gone. They'd learn later from one of the neighbors that Alice had been helping someone who was ill.

Her son Bryant wrote the following beautiful tribute about Alice: "It is often observed that hardships make us sympathetic and helpful to others when they run into rough going. . . . Mother was particularly and acutely friendly and understanding in a helpful way to women who had problems. This told me something of her inner feelings. Women on more than one occasion reminisced to me of trying episodes in their lives when they had been subjected to the not always charitable attitude and actions of their neighbors or even families have told me that Mother's understanding and extension of friendship and sympathy were outstanding and sometimes even singular in their lives."[340]

---

[338] Clark, Bryant. *Know Her Better*, p. 18.
[339] "Life Sketch of Bryant Randall Clark."
[340] Ibid.

The Influenza Epidemic

When the Influenza Epidemic hit, it was bad enough in Georgetown perhaps only six weeks of school were held.

One family was hit by the flu so badly they hired a nurse to take care of them. She was there a week, and they couldn't afford to have her stay longer, so they asked Alice to come.

However, Alice's mother Margaret was staying with her at that time and was then in her nineties. Margaret required intensive care. So Alice couldn't go.

She instead sent her daughter Rhoda, who was not yet trained as a nurse, but stayed with the family for a few days. After then staying with friends for a time in Paris, Idaho, Rhoda caught influenza and went home.

"I didn't ever have it very bad," Rhoda later wrote. "But I really didn't get over it for quite a while afterwards. I was just laying around until Grandmother died and then Mother took her down to Utah for burial. So I got up and had to take care of the house and garden and so on, after that. The next year I taught school again."[341]

The family took careful precautions to keep Margaret safe from the disease, so it is likely Margaret died of old age and not of influenza.

Father Figures for Alice's Children

"Wilford [Woodruff Clark] made frequent trips from Montpelier to Georgetown, a distance of twelve miles. He was a father to me. I have more conversations with him than with my father. From the above it is evident why no one but immediate associates knew where Alice fit into the Clark family."[342]
—*Walter Edward Clark*

Because of the strange times in which Edward and Alice raised their family, with US marshals hunting polygamists, it was in the best interests of the family's safety as well as Edward's freedom to have Edward's exact connection to Alice be largely unknown and unnoticed.

---

[341] "An Interview with Rhoda Clark Taylor,"
[342] Charles Redd Center for Western Studies. *Walter Clark*, p. 4.

Edward only spent time with his second family when he went north to Georgetown to bring or retrieve the cattle. So he was not the primary father figure in the lives of his children with Alice.

Alice, in her life sketch, recounts: "The children . . . recognize in [their father] a noble character and a fine man. . . . I am proud of the children's father, but sorry they have missed so much by not having a father in this life. Perhaps they will understand some day why it was all to be."[343]

The men who served as the father figures for Alice's children on a more regular basis were their uncles—Edward's brother Wilford Woodruff Clark, his brother Charles C. Rich Clark, and Alice's brother-in-law, Wilford Woodruff Richards, who was married to her sister Emily and whose family lived close to Alice for some years.

Wilford Woodruff Richards

"My mother's sister, Emily, and her husband, Wilford Richards, came to Georgetown to make their home in the early years. They had a large family and as children we became very close."[344]
—Maurine Clark Wiberg

Figure 141: Wilford Woodruff Richards and Emily Randall Richards' young family.
Public domain via FamilySearch.

Alice was something of a matchmaker for her younger sister Emily. Wilford Woodruff Richards was the little brother of Edward's first wife, Wealthy.

As Emily later wrote: "When . . . Alice went to get married she met him and afterwards jokingly remarked to me that she had found me a beau. . . . [While I was no bell[e], I had plenty of boyfriends; but as she said that, there seemed to be something say to me that this was to be my future husband."

A year later, Alice told Emily that the young man she had told her sister about was going to be married.

---

[343] Clark, Alice Randall. "A Sketch of the Life of Alice Randall Clark."
[344] Wiberg, Maurine. "Building My Faith." Biographies and autobiographies of the descendants of Ezra T. Clark, L. Tom Perry Special Collections, Harold B. Lee Library, Brigham Young University, Provo, Utah.

"I said nothing, but thought to myself, 'Have I got to be a second wife?' I had three sisters who had married into polygamy. . . . I had thought it would be much nicer to be a first wife of this young man whom I had never met."

After more time had passed, one evening "E. D. Clark" [probably Edward Barrett] brought Wilford to the house, and Emily met him. Then one summer after the holiday vacation, Emily was at Wealthy's house and Wilford was also there.

"I saw him in the morning at breakfast only. He left by train immediately after. A few weeks later he returned having been restless with something seeming to compel him to return. He stayed a few weeks and we began 'keeping company,' as it was called."[345]

It turned out that Wilford had not actually gotten married, and Emily did get to be his first wife. In fact, though the couple at one point contemplated entering into the practice of polygamy, Wilford counseled with leadership who cautioned him against it, as they no longer supported the practice. Emily had liked the woman they had chosen as a potential second wife, but she was relieved to be Wilford's only wife.

For a time when Alice and Emily's children were young, the sisters lived quite near each other in Georgetown.

The Richards family and Alice's family celebrated Christmas together during those years, with Wilford playing Santa for all the children.

When Wilford was called to be the Bear Lake Stake President, he moved his family to Paris. Alice's family was eager to attend Stake Conference as it meant an overnight visit and good play with their Richards cousins, whom they missed dearly. They also would get to meet the visiting general authorities, who stayed in the stake leaders' homes.

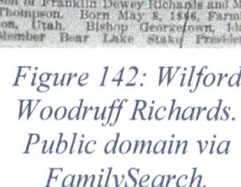

Figure 142: Wilford Woodruff Richards. Public domain via FamilySearch.

The stake building in Paris was built of rock, and Alice's daughter Maurine thought it beautiful and awe-inspiring.

"It was the finest and largest building in our experience," she recalled.[346]

With the Richards family in Paris, Alice sent her children to go stay with them sometimes. When Alice moved to Paris on a few occasions herself for a span of some months so her children could attend the Fielding Academy it must have been a joy to be living near her sister.

---

[345] Richards, Emily Randall. "Life Story of Emily Randall Richards," p. 4. https://www.familysearch.org/photos/artifacts/40633208?cid=mem_copy
[346] Wiberg. "Faith."

Wilford Woodruff Clark

"I had two uncles who lived in the town [this would be Wilford Woodruff Clark and Charles C. Rich Clark]. They used to take quite a bit of interest in us. As I was baptized and ordained, the one uncle appears on so many of my certificates of baptism and ordination that my wife says, 'I think that was your father.'"[347] —Bryant Randall Clark

Before Wilford was married, his sister Mary Elizabeth Clark (Mary Lizzie) took her children to Georgetown for a few years and served as housekeeper for Wilford W. When they left for the more civilized Farmington, Mary's son Albert, shouted "Goodbye, Pigtown."[348]

Though Mary's family was happy to leave, Wilford seemed content to spend much of his life raising not just his own family in the Bear River Valley, but also serving as a prominent local religious leader and helping to be a father figure to Alice's children as well.

Wilford Clark was the bishop for the area for many years, during which he and his family lived in Montpelier. Accounts of him paint a man who was generally thoughtful and

Figure 143: Wilford Woodruff Clark, on his favorite horse, Blaze. Public domain via FamilySearch.

---

[347] Charles Redd Center for Western Studies. *Bryant R. Clark.*
[348] *Mary Elizabeth Clark*. Biographies and autobiographies of the descendants of Ezra T. Clark, L. Tom Perry Special Collections, Harold B. Lee Library, Brigham Young University, Provo, Utah.

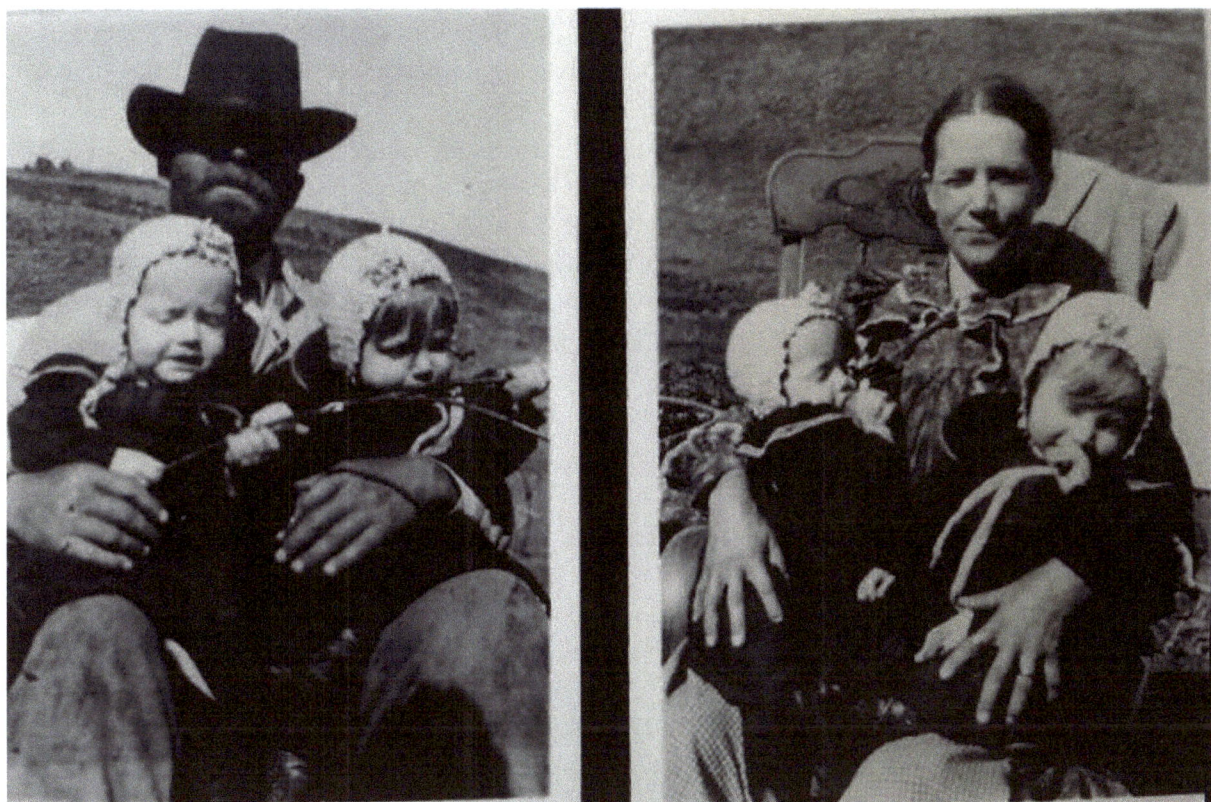

Figure 144: Wilford Woodruff Clark and his twins. Woman is probably first wife Pamelia Dunn Clark. Public domain via FamilySearch.

sensitive to the women around him, and also caring toward children. When his twins were small, he often conducted meetings with a twin hanging on to each leg.[349]

Wilford's family kept up their home in Georgetown,[350] which they called Springdale Farm, and Wilford oversaw the Clark Firm's business in the Georgetown area. For many years, he would drop off his oldest son, Wilford Woodruff Clark, Jr., with Alice to stay for the week, along with a work order for what tasks needed to be done on the farm. Wilford, Jr. was just three years older than Walter Edward Clark, and was a friend to him, along with some of the other local Clark cousins.

Together, Walter and his cousins would attend events and dances, which were held at a dance hall that his Uncle Wilford Clark had arranged to have built.

One of Wilford's own sons wrote of his father: "Wilford Woodruff Clark was a diplomat. . . . [T]here were two elements in Montpelier that were at odds with each other: Mormon and non-Mormon factions.

"He united the people by steady thoughtful efforts to bring them together in fun ways. He pitched the idea to the Church leadership of constructing a dance pavilion where the Church owned 51 percent. The prophet said it was a great idea, and it worked."[351]

---

[349] *Howard Nathan Clark*. Biographies and autobiographies of the descendants of Ezra T. Clark. Box 5 Folder 61, L. Tom Perry Special Collections, Harold B. Lee Library, Brigham Young University, Provo, Utah.
[350] Ibid.
[351] *Royal D. Clark*. Biographies and autobiographies of the descendants of Ezra T. Clark, Box 5 Folder 60. L. Tom Perry Special Collections, Harold B. Lee Library, Brigham Young University, Provo, Utah.

Figure 145: Wedding picture of Wilford Woodruff Clark and first wife Pamelia Dunn Clark. Public domain via FamilySearch.

Wilford and Pamelia's family held an early version of Family Home Evening for many years.[352]

Wilford Clark's Polygamy Story

Wilford believed in polygamy. In 1903 Wilford went ahead and married a second wife in a ceremony officiated by Mathias Cowley—without consulting his first wife.

When first wife Pamelia learned of this action, she told her husband to decide which he was to have: her for his wife or Perniecy—the second wife.

Pamelia and Wilford already had several children together, and he chose to stay with his first wife.

Perniecy went to Salt Lake, where she became a nurse.

In 1933, Pamelia died. A year after her passing, Wilford married Perniecy again, and the two of them lived together after that. She had waited for Wilford all those years and never married.[353]

Charles C. Rich Clark

"In Sacrament Meeting April 12, 1896, Charles [who was a polygamist] was called upon to read the manifesto signed by the First Presidency, ten of the Quorum of the Apostles, the Patriarch, and first seven Presidents of the Seventy."[354]

Yet another uncle who served as a father figure to Alice's young family was Charles C. Rich Clark, a man inclined to be bookish. He was a talkative sort who cared about other people.

The tale is told of him that on one occasion, Charles met a man at a watering hole and got into such a good conversation with him that the man invited Charles to continue along with him in his carriage. Charles did so, completely forgetting his horse until he passed by the same way the following year, and saw the skeleton of his horse tied to a tree.

It is unclear whether this story is apocryphal or not, but the Clarks agreed that it captured Charles' character.

Charles enjoyed teaching religion classes in Georgetown, served in the bishopric for a time (not at the same time his brother served), and also kept the tithing records for some period.

He was a compassionate man who looked out for the needs of families who were struggling.

Figure 146: Charles Rich Clark. Public domain via FamilySearch.

---

[352] *Elmer Ruel Clark*. Biographies and autobiographies of the descendants of Ezra T. Clark, L. Tom Perry Special Collections, Harold B. Lee Library, Brigham Young University, Provo, Utah.
[353] Ibid.
[354] *Charles Rich Clark*, p. 4. Biographies and autobiographies of the descendants of Ezra T. Clark, L. Tom Perry Special Collections, Harold B. Lee Library, Box 1 Folder 7, Brigham Young University, Provo, Utah.

His son Vernon recounts that, "Several families, widows and poor depended on the flour, potatoes and milk from the farm. Some families came daily for milk and vegetables from the milk house and cellar. Mother sometimes complained that he took better care of the poor than of his own family. He often plowed or weeded for the needy and then worked late that night to catch up on his own chores."

Some in Georgetown called the moon "Clark's lantern" because Charles would work late into the night. Accounts are split on whether he was working late to be industrious or because he'd get so caught up talking and proselytizing to people in his general store that he wouldn't get to the farm work until late in the day.

In any case, Charles set an example of industry for his boys and expected them to contribute to running the farm. A polygamist himself, he spent most of his time in Georgetown with his first family, then at General Conference time he would visit with and help his second family in Morgan for as long as his train ticket lasted.

Alice and Polygamy: A Summation

A popular question for Alice's children was how their mother felt about polygamy.

Alice's children recall that throughout Alice's life many people felt sorry for her, and the situation with her marriage. She didn't seem to find that helpful, and rarely complained about neglect. Overall, they recalled she seemed quite pleased to have a home of her own, which she managed well as she raised a successful and healthy family. After all, she had grown up as the daughter of Margaret Harley Randall, a polygamous wife who functioned largely as a single mother herself, so this was the world she had known all her life.[355]

The relationship between Wealthy and Alice was not close.

"Aunt Wealthy was rather a jealous woman and she was an invalid for a period of time," Walter Edward Clark said in an interview. "I have appreciated so much what [a man by the name of Steed who lived in Farmington] told me. He said 'Your Aunt Wealthy was sick, almost an invalid. Your father has had to wait upon her so much . . . he formed a habit of being with her and as a result your mother was sort of neglected.'"

Figure 147: Alice in old age with daughter Maurine and child.
Public domain via FamilySearch.

---

[355] "Life Sketch of Bryant Randall Clark."

Walter said he thought Alice didn't feel it until she was older, when others made it worse "by sympathizing with her and telling her that she wasn't getting what she was entitled to. So the relationship between the two wives was not congenial."[356]

For Alice's part, apart from her clear disappointment that her children did not get more time and care from their father, her life sketch seems to indicate ambivalent feelings toward the arrangement:

"I somehow think I was to marry him; it may come out alright in the future."[357]

Edward Barrett Clark

"The Clark family was quite a close-knit family . . . , and yet we didn't associate very much. The Clarks in general are not extremely outgoing, but in a sense they're very close; they're very loyal. One of my cousins said once that we were so loose in our relationships that you could have thrown a calf through anyplace but in any trouble, you wouldn't find a closer-knit family anywhere. That is about the way they were. That was the Clark characteristic."[358] —Bryant Randall Clark

At his full adult height, Edward Barrett Clark was maybe five foot ten or eleven, according to the estimation of his son Bryant.

Of his early years, Edward wrote: "I suppose that because of my red hair, freckled face and hot temper, and the fact that I was teased by so many; my father often sympathized with me, with kind words and gentle treatment. I have always felt a debt of gratitude to him for this. He frequently took me with him to Salt Lake City and elsewhere."

Edward thought it was marvelous to witness the evolution and inventions that came about in the world just during his lifetime.

"I remember as a youth of helping make wick candles from beef tallow rendered by the family. I remember crossing the road to get a start of a fire from a neighbor. Matches were scarcely known, and my mother in order to save them, kept a supply of folded paper for lighting candles and fires."

He was well-known as an excellent marble player:

"As a boy, I was quite an expert at playing marbles. This was especially true of 'knuckle Boston.' I had a strong thumb and could shoot very swiftly. I used to win the boy's marbles, trade and sell them back and then win them again. I accumulated many marbles."[359]

When Edward was an old man, he and his brothers used to gather in Georgetown on occasion to visit Wilford. They would get some marbles from the general store to have a game.

Even in old age, Edward could still beat the rest of them.[360]

Leadership in the Community

One of the roles Edward was proudest of was the service he gave to his Church and community.

He filled a mission to the Northern States Mission, serving for two years and eight months. During this time, married men could be called, and Edward left behind two wives and several children under the age of 18. While on his mission he was positively impacted by seeing a number of beautiful

---

[356] Charles Redd Center for Western Studies. *Walter Clark.*
[357] "Life Sketch of Alice Randall Clark."
[358] Charles Redd Center for Western Studies. *Bryant R. Clark.*
[359] Clark, Edward B. *Autobiography.*
[360] Knowlton, Clark S. and Ruth. Oral interview with Orson Clark.

cemeteries and decided to work for improvements for the Farmington cemetery, making it more attractive.

In the 1880s, when known polygamists were banned from holding public office, Ezra T. Clark stepped down from the office of County Treasurer, and Edward was voted to succeed him on 6 August 1883 and re-elected to the same office 2 August 1886.

He also served as president of Farmington's first Commercial Club, and served three terms as city councilman. While serving on the city council he, along with other council members, was successful in his strong desire to modernize the Farmington "City of the Dead."

"As I had secured the first lawn in our city of the living, so I did in our now beautiful cemetery."

He served two terms as Justice of the Peace, and was a four-year term County Commissioner.

"During that time I attended at Los Angeles a road convention where road machinery was being displayed. As a result and upon my return, I recommended the purchase of some improved road building machinery. At that time our county had only one grade of any value, and that was a horse drawn machine. It took about three men and three teams to operate it. We purchased a tractor, a scraper and a rooter. A little later we purchased two other motor graders. We immediately went to work and soon our poorer roads were greatly improved. We constructed the first and quite a number of hard surfaced roads in Davis County, other than the State Highway."

As chairman of the county commission, Edward oversaw the building of the Memorial Court House at Farmington, "or had it well along toward completion. We had quite a battle to put it over, as a faction in the north end of the county tried to enjoin us and as a result, a lawsuit followed, but the construction went right on."

He helped organize the North Cottonwood Irrigation Company and served on the board for many years. He was also a director in the Haight Bench Irrigation Company and the Spring Creek Irrigation Company, and served as one of the directors.

He helped found the Farmington Commercial and Manufacturing Company, and the Davis County Bank, and served as a director until departing for his mission 6 February 1908.

After Edward's mission, he served as a director of the Federal Land Bank Association of Farmington, and for more than twenty-one years served as chairman of the appraising committee.

"I was an honored guest at a convention held in Berkeley, California in 1927," he wrote in his autobiography. "The bank paid all of my expenses as I had been a director for over 20 years. I had a wonderful time visiting with bank officials, and also my daughter Mary and her husband Owen. I also greatly enjoyed seeing the sights in and around San Francisco."[361]

An associate, A.R. Cook, later wrote of Edward: "During the years that we served Davis County, there were several very serious problems confronting our county, which we had to decide. When these problems came up, Brother Clark would always say, 'We must think this matter over very thoroughly and determine the right course to pursue.' And when he had decided in his own mind the thing that would be best for the people he was elected to serve, he could not be bribed, coaxed, or frightened from that path. Brother Clark was very thoughtful and careful in all his dealings, and just as honest as the day is long."[362]

---

[361] Clark, Edward B. "Civic Service," *Autobiography*.
[362] Clark, Edward B. "Appendix," *Autobiography*.

Wealthy Also Served

Edward's first wife Wealthy was a good match for him in the realm of community service, as she also was sought after for community leadership when her health permitted it.

At the time Lagoon was built, parents were concerned about their young people wasting time at the amusement park. The bishop asked Wealthy Clark and a few other ladies to organize the young people into a supervised club. They kept minutes, had holiday parties, and really hit it off. Over sixty years later, the group continued to meet, and became the oldest "continuance" club in the nation, lasting even after all the members married and had children. Edward's half-sister Laura Clark was one of the original members.[363]

Losses as a Father

It was hard on Wealthy and Edward when they lost their twins. Then the next baby that they had was sickly and they worried he would not survive. But that baby, Orson, did survive and thrive—they counted this as a miracle.

As Orson later told it, he was born thirteen months to the day after his mother gave birth to and lost twins. His father took Orson and an attending woman into another room. He was uncertain whether the baby was living.

"Shall I go tell his mother that he has died?" Edward asked.

The woman replied "No."

Orson shares: "She paused for a moment, and in that moment of silence she offered a silent prayer telling the Lord that if he would spare this child, she would spend the rest of her life in doing temple work. She did, and she lived to the age of ninety years."[364]

Another hard loss was the death of Wealthy and Edward's daughter Wealthy, who trained as a nurse, married a sweetheart, and then passed away in a flash flood on 13 August 1923, shortly after her honeymoon.[365]

Wealthy and her new husband, Walter Wright, were camping up the canyon. Some scouts were also camping, not far away. Wealthy and Walter had been dropped off by her brother Edward Franklin Clark and his wife, Inez.

Ed Southworth "who was returning from a mine up the canyon talked with these people and had just reached the top of the ridge on the Rudd Creek trail when the rising flood tore down the canyon. He saw the people swept away and hurried to town and described what happened. The entire city was alerted."[366] Edward and Wealthy knew grief as parents.

---

[363] Laura Clark Autobiography.
[364] Knowlton, Clark S. and Ruth. Oral interview with Orson Clark.
[365] Hess, p. 377.
[366] *Edward Franklin Clark.* Biographies and autobiographies of the descendants of Ezra T. Clark, Box 4 Folder 51, L. Tom Perry Special Collections, Harold B. Lee Library, Brigham Young University, Provo, Utah.

Figure 148: Clark reunion. Edward, Wealthy, and most of Edward's children. Public domain via FamilySearch.

Edward B. Clark as a Father Figure

Interviewer: Did you ever think it funny that your father didn't live with your mother?

Bryant Randall Clark: No, not a great deal. I understood he was living down there with the first family. That didn't bother me. I can remember that I was always glad when he would come for a visit because I was glad to see him. Any kid likes to see his dad. We weren't close at all. There was no father and son relationship really. I already said it was just like I had grown up in a one parent family.[367] — Bryant Randall Clark

Though Edward did participate with his second family when he was in Georgetown, saying the prayer, helping on the farm, and engaging with the children, his character as a father figure was better known by the children of his first family, and by other young Clark relatives.

Most notably among the young nephews, Obert C. Tanner (founder of the O.C. Tanner Company) considered Edward (whom he called "Uncle Eddie") to be his own father figure and wrote compellingly in his autobiography about their relationship and the interactions he had with Edward when he was a young boy. His reminiscences are vivid and memorable.

Obert's own mother, Annie Clark Tanner, was a second wife who rarely saw her husband. She lived on the same street as Edward, and she sometimes had to be away for up to a week to help with a nursing case. During those times, Obert would live with Uncle Eddie's family. Obert was with them almost constantly during one five-year period during which Annie traveled extensively to work.[368]

---

[367] Charles Redd Center for Western Studies. *Bryant R. Clark.*
[368] Tanner, Annie Clark. *A Mormon Mother*, pp. 245–246.

When Obert was a boy, there were no child labor laws. The only question was whether a child was big enough to do a job.

Uncle Eddie was a truly hard worker and a man who believed in his sons (and Obert's) strength and capacity to grow and become great men. He taught the boys and young men who looked up to him to do hard work well, and all of the boys he helped raise (including Obert) became successful in the paths of their lives.

In his autobiography, Obert recalled a time when his teeth were horribly decayed. The dentist described them as being "just like chalk," and by the time Obert was 10 he already had two gold crowns. Eventually, the dentist asked Obert when and how he would be able to pay him for all the dental work he had done.

He told Obert that if he could send ten dollars the following day, he would count it as paid in full. Obert liked the dentist and wanted to pay him.

He didn't think of asking his mother, who was not well off, but instead went directly to his Uncle Eddie, offering to work for him all summer if Eddie would give him ten dollars to put in the mail to the dentist.

Uncle Eddie was hesitant about this arrangement.

"He called his three boys in and they cross-examined me to see if I really would keep my end of the bargain. Finally, my uncle gave me a check for ten dollars. I will never forget my great satisfaction as I handed the envelope containing that check to the clerk in the mail car."

Obert easily kept up his end of the agreement, and calls it his first experience with anything like a labor contract.[369]

Eddie trained his sons and Obert to work fast, hard, and long. By the time Obert got his first job with the railroad, he kept the pace he had learned from his Uncle Eddie and outpaced and outlasted all the other men.[370]

Eddie and Wealthy's own son Orson once tired of helping in Farmington and told his father he'd like a vacation. So Edward sent him to Georgetown to help for a month.

"Their procedure of harvesting was somewhat different than we have down here," Orson recalled. "[But] when I went there, I was treated just like one of [Alice's] children. You would never know the difference. We lived together and slept together. It was always just the same as though I was a part of their family."[371]

Driving the Cattle

"Grandfather [Ezra T. Clark] passed away in 1902 but before that he provided for the division of the estate among two large families. Three sons, Wilford, Charles and Edward my father received land. The cattle were divided equally between Wilford, Charles, Edward and the estate. The semiannual drive between Georgetown and Farmington ended."[372] —Walter Edward Clark

Every year prior to the division of Ezra T. Cark's property, the driving of the cattle would bring Edward to Georgetown, along with others from the Clark clan, some of whom would stay for part of the summer.

---

[369] Tanner, Obert C. *One Man's Journey in Search of Freedom*, pp. 34–35.
[370] Ibid., p. 49.
[371] Knowlton, Clark S. and Ruth. Oral interview with Orson Clark.
[372] Charles Redd Center for Western Studies. *Walter Clark*, p. 4.

Joseph Smith Clark, Jr. recalls of the big cattle drive events:

"Now I remember . . . President Snow who followed President Wilford Woodruff, because he lived in Brigham City. We drove cattle from Farmington to Georgetown in the spring to pasture them in the mountains between Soda Springs and Montpelier. In the fall we drove them back. We made trips by wagon and I remember one time stopping in Brigham City where President Snow was living and having dinner with him."[373]

Annie Clark Tanner wrote about the annual Clark cattle drives as well, in her biography of Ezra T. Clark:

"For five years Aunt Nancy spent her summers at the ranch in Georgetown. Each year, in the early spring, a large herd of cattle left the Farmington farm for the ranch in Georgetown, where some of his sons made their home.

"The cattle were often held on Bear River until the grass was more matured in the upper valleys of the Bear Lake. As each son of the family developed in years those camping trips were looked forward to as great adventures. The preparations for the journey were of interest to all the family, as cookies, bread, and biscuits were baked, beef roasted, etc."

Other provisions included cheese, honey, preserves, baked beans, chickens, pearmain apples, potatoes, and onions.

"Often a carriage of women and children from home joined the campers on Bear River and then preceded them to Georgetown, 150 miles north and east of Farmington. On these trips the girls learned to harness and unharness the teams and to feed them. . . . Then as fall approached, the boys, having explored all the hills in the Bear Lake Valley to round up the cattle, looked forward to the trip home and school."

Ezra T. Clark would often ride out and meet his family a few miles away from home, greeting them at the end of their trek back from Georgetown.[374]

For Edward and Alice, the trek marked the brief periods of time they spent as husband and wife. Edward does not appear to have spent the whole season in Georgetown; it appears he would come up for a brief period, and then return to his first family in Farmington.

Several of Edward's grandsons are very fond of pointing out that the close birthdays of Alice's four youngest children speak silent witness to the patterns of the cattle drives, with one child's birthday at the beginning of February and three at the end of January.

Driving a Car for the First Time

During Edward's lifetime, huge changes came to the world. He'd been born in a settler cabin, but before the end of his life he got to fly on an airplane.

Son Orson recalled Edward's experience with learning to drive a car: "There was a fence along there, and when he went to back up or something, he'd go, 'Whoa, whoa, whoa!' [The car] wouldn't stop, it wouldn't mind him!"[375]

---

[373] "Experiences in the Life of Joseph Smith Clark, Jr. 1878-1963." Biographies and autobiographies of the descendants of Ezra T. Clark, Box 4 Folder 43, L. Tom Perry Special Collections, Harold B. Lee Library, Brigham Young University, Provo, Utah.
[374] Tanner, Annie Clark. *A Biography of Ezra T. Clark*, p. 34.
[375] Knowlton, Clark S. and Ruth. Oral interview with Orson Clark.

Edward as a Father to Alice's Children

Walter Edward Clark was perhaps Alice's child who had the most to do with Edward, but even he considered Wilford Woodruff Clark to be more of a father figure in his life. Bryant recalled that Walter would go stay at Wealthy and Edward's house as if it were his own mother's house. But Bryant never felt so comfortable.

Bryant wrote of Edward, "When I was about fifteen, I lived with him and his first wife for about fifteen months I guess. But other than that I hardly knew him until I was grown and older . . . I would get him in the car and take him over the country where he had driven cattle and . . . [w]e visited. . . . I didn't know him very well."

Despite not knowing his father very well, Bryant had great respect for him because he knew Edward was a man of importance.[376]

When Bryant lived with Edward and Wealthy for a time to attend high school in Farmington, he had the impression that Aunt Wealthy was quite unhappy to have him around, as it was extra work to have him there. "There were little things that led me to believe that I was a kind of an unnecessary nuisance to have around the place."

But despite this, Wealthy was good to him, and the boys treated him like his other brothers and they were friends and had no difficulties. "That was the thing; that was the family unit. To go into polygamy was to look after the children of the other family just like your own brothers and sisters."

Bryant reflected of his experience of the two families: "My mother lived in Idaho and Aunt Wealthy lived in Farmington. They were not congenial but neither were they antagonistic towards each other at all."

Despite the more distant relationship that the Alice's children had with their father as compared to their mother, they all seem to have looked up to him.

Edward and Alice's daughter Rhoda got married later in life. She became the second wife of Harvey Taylor, a widower who had several children.

Edward officiated at Rhoda and Harvey's wedding in the Salt Lake Temple, which was closed at that time, but they were able to make special arrangements.

Walter and Lela oversaw a wedding breakfast, served at 2:00 p.m., after the wedding.

While in Salt Lake, Rhoda and Harvey stayed with Rhoda's half-brother Rulon, who was a respected judge.

These details illustrate how, even though Wealthy and Alice's children were not close when they were growing up, they looked out for each other as family and enjoyed a positive relationship as adults.

Edward was also a well-loved grandfather by his grandchildren. Grandson Alan Clark was honored to have Edward officiate at his wedding to Janet Ruppe Clark.

The Realities of Pioneer Farm Life as Impacting Children's Education

One of Alice's Clark neighbors would have rather have been a scholar than a farmer. Charles C. Rich Clark of Georgetown enjoyed school and had been encouraged by a teacher at BY Academy to get further schooling and teach, but he was needed on his father's farm, so he declined the invitation, though he always regretted doing so.

---

[376] Charles Redd Center for Western Studies. *Bryant R. Clark.*

In a similar pattern for the subsequent generation, when young Walter Edward Clark told his father Edward that he would like to go to college and become an engineer, Edward redirected him toward farm work.

Later, however, the pattern shifted. Perhaps due to the influence of Alice and her high priority on education, Walter would encourage all his children to go get college degrees and they all pursued professions other than farming.

This shift within the Clark family mirrored a shift that was also occurring in the broader landscape. Utah and Idaho were no longer pioneer states. Their communities and civilizations had grown up, and there was more space for diversity in careers and education and less need of committed farmers.

Edward's Thoughts on Polygamy

"My father [Edward] makes the comment that polygamy calls for sacrifice, but sacrifice brings blessings. Their motivation was not necessarily to get a work force, though that was conducive to it. They did it to get a greater experience in life so they would be more qualified for leadership and to be obedient to counsel."[377] —Walter Edward Clark

Edward, like Alice, had grown up in a happy and well-organized polygamous family. He had seen a system of balancing multiple wives in the life of his own father. Polygamy was the family structure that he had grown up with.

Of his first wife, Wealthy, Edward wrote: "She never tried to persuade me from my duty to Alice."

Perhaps tellingly, in his own autobiography, he refers to his children with Alice as "Alice's family," and writes about her with more distance than he does Wealthy, as if Alice is an independent woman:

"Although [Alice] was active in church affairs while living in Georgetown she never liked the place and was glad to move away and devote her time to her family. However, she raised a fine family, one any person might be proud of. . . . Her children are not afraid to work and all of them, with their companions are devoted to the church and to one another. I am proud of them."[378]

Alice's Later Years

"She was always worried about being a burden in her old age. She took care of her mother who was old and blind. She was granted that blessing; as she was active and able to care for herself until her death which came without warning."[379] —Melvin Clark

After her children were grown, Alice continued to be of service to her family.

She stayed with Maurine and her children for Maurine's husband's entire four-year mission to Tonga.[380]

Later she stayed with her son Walter for a few years to keep house for him and help him raise Wayne and Alan after the death of their mother, Violet.

In her last years, she lived with her daughter Rhoda in Salt Lake City. She passed away unexpectedly of a heart attack at the age of 74 on her way to a genealogical meeting.

---

[377] Charles Redd Center for Western Studies. *Walter Clark.*
[378] Clark, Edward B. *Autobiography.*
[379] Clark, Melvin.
[380] Wiberg, p. 12.

"She was walking down the street arm in arm with another lady, and she just slumped down on the sidewalk," her son Bryant recorded. "People in the nearest house called a physician. He came out and said she was dead before he ever got her in the house."[381]

Edward after Alice

Edward ended life alone, doubly widowed. Alice had passed away in 1938 at the age of 74, and Wealthy passed away in 1940 at the age of 79. Edward would live until 1955. Until late in life, he continued to enjoy serving as a temple worker.

In a move that was both kind, poetic, and probably deeply meaningful to him given his thoughtfulness around the care of burial grounds, he arranged to have the grave of his brother-in-law Wilford Woodruff Richards moved to the Farmington cemetery to a plot he owned. Wilford's new final resting place was near that of Edward's own two wives. Wilford had passed away young and unexpectedly after a brief illness, at age 46, when Emily was just 43 and pregnant with their last child. He had been buried in Idaho, and Emily had been devastated to have his grave so far away when life had necessitated her move to Utah.

Emily was deeply touched by Edward's kindness in relocating her husband to be near her, and this kindness may have also reflected thoughtfulness on Edward's part to Wealthy, who was Wilford's sister, to Alice, for whom Wilford had been a support and a father figure for her children, and to Edward's own ideals of looking out for his family in the ways he saw as significant.

Figure 149: Edward in old age. Public domain via FamilySearch.

Emily wrote of the event: "I had a small marker with both our names (husband and self) placed there. Then we covered the grave with flowers. He is buried in the lot belonging to Bro.-in-law E.B. Clark where his wife Wealthy and my sister Alice are buried. The place was so lovely with beautiful roses blooming at the head. So many of us were there it seemed almost like a home coming."[382]

Edward was a good man in unusual circumstances.

He and Wealthy and Alice raised industrious families shaped by their locations and time.

The story of Edward and Alice laid the ground for the stories of subsequent generations, and continue to impact their descendants over time.

When you focus on your education, know that value was elevated in the family by Alice.

When you work hard on a task, help build up your community, and take pride in a job well done, know those were values well-lived and well-taught by Edward.

And when you give love and thoughtful caring to the greater community of your family—to your cousins, to your nieces and nephews, to your more distant but still connected family—you are continuing the legacy and gifts of love offered to Alice Randall Clark's children by the families of Wilford Woodruff

---

[381] "Life Sketch of Bryant Randall Clark."
[382] Richards, Emily Randall. *Life of Emily Randall Richards*, p. 60. *FamilySearch.*

Richards and Emily Randall Richards, Wilford Woodruff Clark and Pamelia Dunn Clark, and Charles C. Rich Clark and Mary Emma Woolley Clark.

Their stories and legacy continue on with you.

Books on Edward and Alice

Alice wrote a life sketch, which is currently available in her profile on FamilySearch.

Alice's son Bryant Randall Clark created a tribute book in her honor, called *That You May Know Her Better*, which contains tributes from Alice's children. A copy of this book is also available on FamilySearch as of the time of this writing.

A few other resources on the lives of Edward and Alice are available:

Edward wrote a biography, which is available on the Ezra T. Clark Family Organization website.

The biographies of Edward and many Clark family members who lived and worked near Edward in Farmington and Alice in Georgetown are held in the Ezra T. Clark Family Organization Collection at the L. Tom Perry Special Collections Library at BYU. These are available from the librarians there via scanning and email for a fee.

All of these are great additional resources for Clark descendants to learn more about the unique family ecosystem that was the Clark Firm.

9. Randall Family Stories

Alfred Randall (head of family)
Wives:
1. Emmerette Louisa Davis [m. 9 January 1834]
2. **Margaret Harley (our ancestor)** [m. 29 January 1848]
3. Mildred Elizabeth Johnson [m. 30 May 1860]
4. Hannah Severn [m. 7 March 1863]
5. Elizabeth Elsie Elsey Anderson [m. 13 May 1865]

"Father had five wives. . . . He did not spend a great deal of his time at our house . . . feeling that he was needed most with the younger children. There was always the best of feelings between Father and Mother and the rest of the family. All of the wives and children often visited at our home, usually staying several days . . . especially at conference. . . . Those were happy times for me, even if I did have to sleep on a few quilts on the floor."
—Emily Randall Richards, daughter of Margaret Harley Randall[383]

The Randall family was a large and happy one. They created their own economy to some degree, but not to the level that the Clark families did. The Randall wives were self-reliant to a large degree, while supporting each other here and there with things. For example, Margaret hosted the extended family in her Centerville home at General Conference time, and Hannah made cream for all the wives.

Alfred was a prominent polygamist, a large man with a large posterity. He was devoutly committed to his families, and caring for them spanned his entire life.

He wed his first wife, Emmerette Louisa Davis, in 1834, when he was 22 years old, and their first child was born in 1835, when he was 23.

He wed his fifth and last wife, Elizabeth Elsie Elsey Anderson, in 1865, when he was 53 years old. His five wives bore him a total of 32 babies, 21 of whom lived past childhood.

---

[383] Richards, Emily Randall. *Life Story of Emily Randall Richards*. *FamilySearch*, https://www.familysearch.org/tree/person/memories/KWCH-MFZ. Accessed 2 October 2020.

The last child was born in 1881, at the time Alfred was 70.

Alfred loved his children, and his children looked up to him and were happy to be a part of the Randall family.

Figure 150: Alfred and wives. Back row: Mildred, Hannah, Elsey. Front row: Margaret, Emmerette, and Alfred.
Public domain via FamilySearch.

Alfred: An Attractive and Well-Mannered Man

Lucy, daughter of Alfred's fourth wife, Hannah, with whom he lived for most of his later years, wrote about how her mother met her father:

Hannah Severn, baptized in England, immigrated to Utah with friends, one of whom, Eliza, found work with the Randall family. Eliza invited Hannah to help her prepare dinner at the Randalls' for a gathering.

At the end of the night, Hannah asked Eliza who the man was who had preached that evening.

"'Why,' replied Eliza, 'That was Brother Randall, whose house we are at.'

"'My, but I do like him,' mused Hannah. 'I was struck by his appearance and manners.'

"'Why Hannah, he already has three wives!' said Eliza."

This did not discourage Hannah, for in time she met and married Alfred.[384]

---

[384] Kofoed, Lucy Randall. *A Life Sketch of Hannah Severn Randall*, p. 4. *FamilySearch*, https://www.familysearch.org/photos/artifacts/11461919?cid=mem_copy. Accessed 19 April 2021.

So who was this man who attracted five women to become his wives?

Alfred Randall "weighed about 200 pounds in his prime, and was about 6 feet in height, a well-built man with a heavy head of hair, rosy cheeks, and a merry twinkle in his eyes. He thoroughly enjoyed a clean, humorous story, and was always ready to either hear or tell one, many times laughing until the tears ran down his cheeks. This characteristic of humor was noted in many of his children."[385]

Alan Clark, the great-grandson of Alfred, was also known to laugh until tears ran down his cheeks.

Alfred was a skilled craftsman by trade. He was a carpenter and built many public and private buildings over his lifetime. He and his family also farmed.

Margaret Harley Randall: An Active Woman

Margaret Harley Randall was descended largely from the German Baptist Brethren, who fled religious persecution in Europe some generations before her time.

Her family's historical values included hard work, a neighborly attitude, and an attempt to live as a person of integrity while rejoicing in community.

Margaret was small, with dark eyes and hair. She was an energetic woman who had unusually good home management skills. She believed in helping others. Despite living apart from her husband for most of her married life, Margaret managed her farm, home, and children skillfully—with enough reserves left to contribute an outsized leadership role to her community.

She had good health and good humor, and was loved by both her extended family and the women of her ward and community. A believer in maintaining family ties, she kept up a correspondence with a brother she had left behind in Pennsylvania over the course of many years, even though the two of them had an amicable difference in their faiths. She even invited him to join her via train for Thanksgiving one year, though he was unfortunately unable to attend.

Her children all grew up to value family and community as well, and it is notable that all seven of her children survived to adulthood—a statistic not entirely common for pioneer families.

---

[385] Kofoed, Lucy Randall. *The True Life Story of Alfred Randall, Pioneer*, p. 7.

Figure 151: Alfred and Margaret Randall family. Back row: Thurza, Margaret Ellen, Melvin, Emily, Alice. Front row: Mary, Orrin, Alfred, Margaret.
Public domain via FamilySearch.

Margaret's Home in Centerville

"After Margaret Harley Randall moved to Centerville in 1862, there was not one of her husband's wives or children who did not like to visit Aunt Margaret, and they all did so whenever convenient, and often stayed several days at a time. Margaret was true, kind, and benevolent in all her family relations."[386]

Before Alfred bought Margaret a home and farm at Centerville, Utah, in about 1862 at about 400 South and 400 East, Margaret and her children had lived in an adobe dugout in Mill Creek Canyon, then later lived in Salt Lake City, Bountiful, "Over Jordan," and West Weber. Once she had moved to Centerville, Margaret lived there for the rest of her life, save for her last two years—when she stayed with her daughter Alice in Georgetown, Idaho, after she had gone mostly blind.[387]

Margaret had seven children: Orrin, Melvin, Mary Elizabeth, Margaret Ellen, Thurza, Alice, and Emily.

---

[386] "Margaret Harley Life Sketch."
[387] Emily Randall Life Story.

Prior to moving to Centerville, the family had gone through some hard times, including one year when the crops failed, and the family lived on roots and was without flour for three weeks.

Margaret recalled that during that trying time, the boys would lie on the floor for most of the time and not play. She wondered why, not realizing they were too weak. When they had bread again, she said the boys would play again.

During this hard time, one wash day, Margaret became so exhausted she could not go on. She found a single egg and ate it, receiving enough strength to finish the washing. The boys were asleep, and she felt so guilty for having something without sharing it with them that she remembered the incident for the rest of her life.

She would say, "That was the only time in my life that I ever ate anything when the children could not have some too."[388]

But when the family lived in Centerville, such hard times were behind them.

Emily, the youngest child, later wrote: "I had a happy childhood. We were quite poor and had few if any luxuries; but the worst of privations were over and I never had to go hungry as some of the older ones did when crops failed. Father was a wheelwright, a good carpenter and farmer."[389]

Margaret never owned a sewing machine and did all her sewing by hand. During the early years in Centerville, her family wore homemade canvas shoes and canvas coats. She lived with little help from her husband.

Margaret supported herself and her children by caring for cows, selling milk and butter, raising hay, grain, chickens and other animals, vegetable gardens, and more. She also carded wool and helped raise silkworms in the early days of Utah's silk industry. Margaret raised a small amount of cash by selling dried fruits, and used dried fruit and butter for bartering at the local store.

---

[388] "Margaret Harley Life Sketch."
[389] Emily Randall Life Story.

Figure 152: Centerville.
Image © aliceinwonderland2020/Depositphotos

Drying Fruit

Margaret and her children would dry their fruit for winter and for sale.

"The peaches and apricots were cut in halves, the pits removed, then placed one by one face up on scaffolds to dry, or even on the roof of the lower part of the house," daughter Emily later wrote. "What a scamper to cover up or carry in if rain threatened or came. A bushel of peaches would make seven or eight pounds of dried fruit and sold for from five to ten cents a pound. Peeled fruit was more. The usual price for the plain dried was from six to eight cents."

Emily and her siblings would sit under a great, large apple tree near the house and cut fruit, working several days a week for a number of weeks.

She could gather, cut, and spread up to seven bushels in a single day.

"Do you think you could do it?" she later wrote to her posterity. "Remember the spreading, carrying them through all the house upstairs, out a window, going across on the roof on to another and putting the fruit every one face up."[390]

---

[390] Richards, Emily Randall. *Life of Emily Randall Richards*, p. 2. *FamilySearch.*
https://www.familysearch.org/photos/artifacts/40633208?cid=mem_copy

Food at the Margaret Randall Farm

Margaret's family produced most of their food at home. They raised wheat, potatoes, corn, squash, vegetables, and orchard fruit. From their cows and chickens they got milk, cream, butter, and eggs. Meat was not plentiful but sometimes they had beef or pork. Money was tight. A dozen eggs or a pound of butter could be used to barter for other staples.

An entire meal could be made from what had come from the farm, with the addition of sugar, salt, and spices. They could even make vinegar on the farm, and had a few beehives from which they obtained honey.

Pioneer Life

Margaret's daughter Alice later recalled what she referred to as "one little item of Pioneer life—one evening I would not go to bed, I wanted to sit up until mother finished a pair of shoes she was making for me out of a piece of old pants, so she could take me to Salt Lake with her the next day. My earliest recollection of riding to Salt Lake was on a board, with a quilt on it across a wagon. Then later we had spring seats, then a topless carriage, then a covered carriage. My mother lived to ride in automobiles; she was about ninety years old when she came to Georgetown to live with me, where she died."[391]

Serving her Community

Margaret served from 1871 to 1901 as Centerville Ward's Relief Society President. She also studied obstetrics in Salt Lake City and delivered sixty babies.

On her sixtieth birthday, the ward Relief Society threw a surprise party in her honor with a large dinner and lovely presents.

She was always available to help the sick of the community, and often stayed for days at a time to help someone ill with any disease. She was called a ministering angel. She would prepare the dead for burial and often took food or other items to those in need, never mentioning it. If a daughter happened to see her leaving to take something of the family's to someone in need, she would say, "If we give it to them maybe we won't need it."

An excellent cook, Margaret loved to give small dinner parties for friends. Her married children often came home with their families, especially on Sundays.

Margaret in Old Age

Margaret lived in her Centerville home until the 1890s when one day, cleaning out her pantry, she found a paper containing what she believed were onion seeds. She threw them into the stove, but the "seeds" turned out to be gunpowder, which exploded. Her eyebrows were burned off and her hair got scorched.

Her son Melvin decreed she was now too old to live alone and said, "That is enough! You are coming to live with us."

Blindness had come to Margaret in her old age—at first partial blindness due to cataracts, and then total blindness later on. Though she missed reading scriptures and the Deseret News, she was grateful that she was still able to hear and to communicate with people.

---

[391] "A Life Sketch of Alice Randall Clark."

She was very independent and had never wanted to leave the farm that her husband had purchased and left in the care of his and Margaret's sons.

When her daughters would try to convince her to live with them, she'd say, "No, the farm has to keep me."

It wasn't until 1917, when Margaret was old and feeble, that she was taken by train to go live with Alice in Georgetown.

Alfred Randall, Wheelwright and Carpenter

Alfred helped build many structures in the Salt Lake area, including the Salt Lake Temple and the old Salt Lake County courthouse, which both still stand.

Alfred, a wheelwright and a carpenter by trade, soon after arriving in Utah built an adobe house for himself and his family on West Temple, north of the Tabernacle Square, on land he would have obtained from the Church. This land is now part of the plaza of the Conference Center.[392] When Alfred's biography was published in the early 1950s by his daughter Lucy Randall Kofoed, a large gas station stood on the site of this original Randall family home. Alfred set to work at his trade, helping to build the original Salt Lake County courthouse, mills, and many other public and private buildings.

He helped build a mill for Heber C. Kimball. Alfred's biography notes that this was a sawmill, but research into a Heber C. Kimball mill reveals only that he owned a gristmill. Perhaps this is the one that Alfred helped build. https://collections.lib.utah.edu/details?id=443798

Figure 153: A gristmill.
© lightscribe/Depositphotos

---

[392] Clark, Nolan. "My Convert Ancestors."

The Randall Family's Joseph F. Smith Story

Family stories say that Alfred Randall and Emmerette Davis' second child, Sarah Lavern, became engaged to be married to Joseph F. Smith. He was called away on a mission, and while he was away, Sarah died of consumption. When Joseph returned, the story goes, he had Sarah sealed to him in the Endowment House. Afterwards, Emmerette hosted a supper for the Randalls and the Smiths.[393] This story comes to us from Nora Randall Thomas, granddaughter of Emmerette and eldest child of Levi Randall.

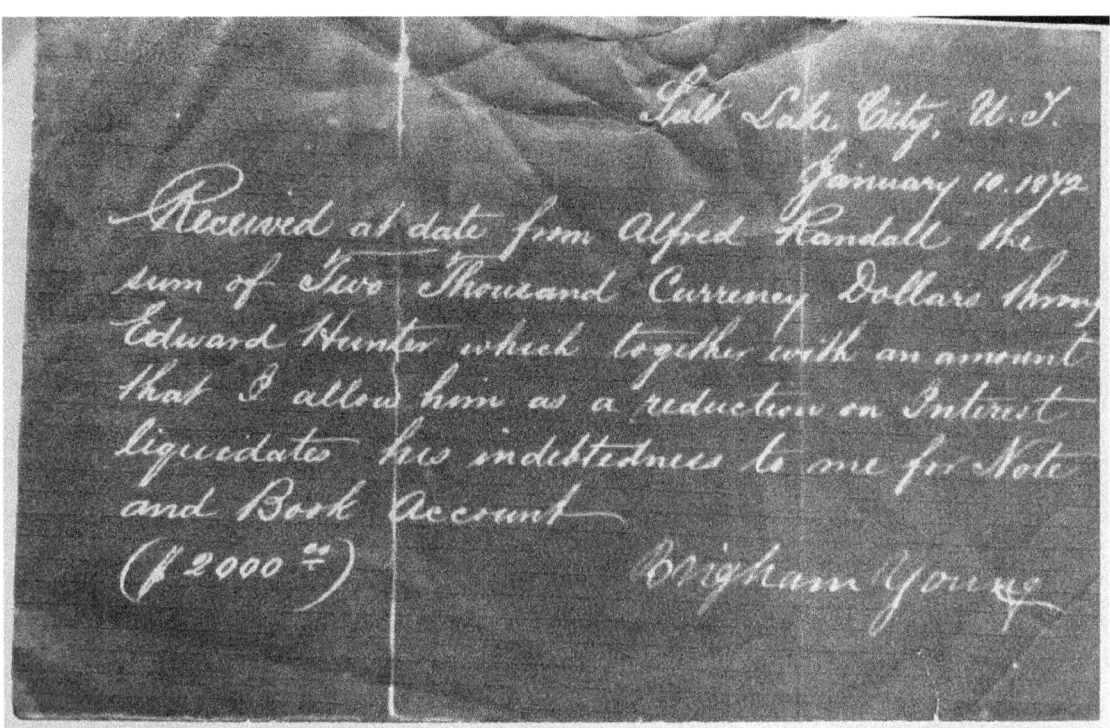

Figure 154: Note to Alfred Randall by Brigham Young. Public domain via FamilySearch.

Polygamy in the Alfred Randall Family

In his early years, Alfred lived with his first wife, Emmerette Davis Randall. For a time, second wife Margaret lived with the family, but eventually all of Alfred's wives had separate living places.

In his later years, Alfred lived with fourth wife Hannah. But when Alfred went for a carriage ride and Emmerette was around, Emmerette always sat next to Alfred.

One day Hannah took that seat, and Emmerette firmly told her, "No, Hannah, that is my place."[394]

The children of Margaret and Alfred had a favorable enough experience with polygamy that four of their five daughters became plural wives. Their son Melvin Randall, who was not a polygamist, hosted President John Taylor in his home during some of the days the prophet was hiding on the Underground. Melvin's home was safe because Melvin was not a polygamist.

---

[393] "Emmerette Louisa Davis." *FamilySearch*.
[394] "Emmerette Louisa Davis." *FamilySearch*.

A Healing Prayer in the Endowment House

Our ancestor Margaret Randall knew first wife Emmerette longer than any of the others. The two women lived together for a time and Margaret had helped her to care for her home and children. They maintained a positive relationship.

At one time, Emmerette was quite ill. She went to the Endowment House, where she was washed and anointed. Eliza R. Snow gave her this blessing: "Be of good cheer that you shall be healed and shall bear a daughter who will live to be a comfort to you in your old age."

Emmerette did return to health. On 2 December 1860, she gave birth to Martha Jane, the daughter Emmerette would live with during the later years of her life. Martha Jane and her husband Ed didn't have children, and Martha was a very devoted daughter.[395]

Figure 155: The Salt Lake Endowment House, circa 1855. An early building used to administer temple ordinances.
Public domain via Charles Roscoe Savage / Wikicommons.

Mildred Elizabeth Johnson

Alfred's most prominent wife was probably Mildred Elizabeth Johnson.

When Mildred reached the Salt Lake Valley, having crossed the plains as a single woman, she first worked in the home of John Taylor. In September 1859, she went to live with Alfred Randall's family at Bountiful. On 30 May 1860, she became his third wife.

Mildred eventually moved to Salt Lake City, where she worked as a school teacher in the 17th Ward and lived in a home her husband provided her on 1st North Street at the head of West Temple.

Mildred and Alfred had two sons together, Francis and Eli. Both boys died in early childhood.[396]

Mildred and Alfred served a mission together to the Sandwich Islands (Hawaiian Islands). This is written about in the "Missions" chapter. There, Mildred conducted two schools, one for the foreign children and one for native children.

After Mildred's first mission to Laie, she returned to Salt Lake and continued to teach school. Later she oversaw Brigham Young's private school at Eagle Gate.

In 1872, Mildred left on a second mission to the Sandwich Islands. She is honored as the first woman to be called on a mission without her husband.

After her second mission, Mildred taught throughout Salt Lake, including offering night school in her home. Fiercely independent, she refused help from anyone else as long as she was able to earn her own money. She lived to age 86.

Pony Express and the Telegraph

The Randall family had a personal connection to the Pony Express.

---

[395] "Emmerette Louisa Davis." *FamilySearch.*
[396] "Mildred Elizabeth Johnson," p. 288. *FamilySearch.*

With the invention of the telegraph and the forming of the Pony Express, the Church gained a stronger connection with the world beyond. Alfred Randall and Emmerette Louisa Davis' son Charles Franklin (Frank) was the rider who brought the first telegram from the United States to Salt Lake Valley, completing the ride between dark and daylight.[397]

Alfred Helps Immigrants and Supplies Cross to the Valley

Alfred traveled east multiple times on Church assignment, making four long, hard trips to help bring immigrants and supplies. They may have come across buffalo, deer, wolves, and sometimes hostile Native Americans.

Figure 156: Whip used by Charles Franklin Randall during his time with the Pony Express. Item in possession of descendant Aaron John McMurdie. Image used with permission.

---

[397] **Timeline of Western Settlement Mail and Telegraph**
1849 March. First post office established in the Great Salt Lake Valley. Prior to this, letters that reached the territory were typically distributed at the conclusion of church services.

1860 April 3. Pony Express established.

1861 October 18. First telegraphs sent to and from Utah, which read as follows:
Great Salt Lake City, Oct. 18, 1861.
Hon. J. H. Wade, President of the Pacific Telegraph Company, Cleveland, Ohio;
Sir: —permit me to congratulate you on the completion of the overland telegraph line west to this city; to comment the energy displayed by yourself and associates in the rapid and successful prosecution of a work so beneficial; and to express the wish that its use may ever tend to promote the true interest of the dwellers upon both the Atlantic and Pacific slopes of our continent. Utah has not seceded, but is firm for the Constitution and Laws of our once happy country, and is warmly interested in such useful enterprises as the one so far completed.
Brigham Young

The Civil War had begun just a few months prior, which is why Brigham Young's comment that Utah had not seceded and the affirmation of Utah's patriotism was of importance. The acting governor wrote a telegram on the same day with a similar message to the US President, and received the following telegram soon after in return:

Washington, D. C., October 20, 1861.
Hon. Frank Fuller, Acting Governor, Utah Territory;
Sir: —The completion of the telegraph to Great Salt Lake City is auspicious of the stability and union of the Republic. The Government reciprocated your congratulations.
Abraham Lincoln. (Genealogy Trails)
1961 October. Once the transcontinental telegraph was established, the Pony Express discontinued.

Mountain Meadow Massacre Jury Duty

One of the biggest trials the region had ever seen was for John D. Lee, accused of orchestrating the Mountain Meadow Massacre.

For this trial, Alfred Randall was called for jury duty.

A group traveling to California had been killed passing through Mountain Meadows in Utah.

John D. Lee was eventually put on trial for this, being held responsible for the event. His first trial ended in a hung jury. For Lee's second trial, Alfred Randall was selected as a juror.

Alfred always did his best to live honorably. He listened to the trial along with his fellow jurors.

This time the jury returned with a "guilty" verdict.

With the conviction of John D. Lee, the government dropped attempts to pursue additional targets.

Before being executed, John D. Lee wrote an autobiography, which became an instant bestseller after his lawyer sent it to a St. Louis publisher.

In Utah Territory, there was relief that the matter had been resolved to the satisfaction of the people and the law.

Years later, in 1998, President Gordon B. Hinckley would visit Mountain Meadows, committed the Church to building a proper memorial, and said "That land is sacred ground."

In 1999, he dedicated the new monument, saying, "[The past] cannot be recalled. It cannot be changed. It is time to leave the entire matter in the hands of God."

Alfred and the Woolen Mill

President Brigham Young, recognizing the value of wool production for the community, asked Alfred Randall to select some men and a good location and then to build and operate a woolen mill.

Figure 157: This handgun, which belonged to Alfred Randall, has been passed down through the generations. The gun went to Emmerette's oldest son Charles Franklin Randall, then to Charles' youngest son, Lester, and then to Lester's daughter Norma Randall. Currently in the possession of Aaron John McMurdie, grandson of Norma
Image used with permission.

Alfred selected the mouth of Ogden Canyon, a few miles from Ogden. Alfred and the other men who co-managed the mill imported machinery and erected a building.

The Deseret News on 19 August 1869 reported: "Ogden Woolen Mills is owned by Messors Randall, Puglsey and Company . . . In order to give President Young and company an opportunity of seeing the machinery work, Brother Randall put his hands together this morning and started the mill. The building is a substantial stone structure 90 feet long and 35 feet wide. It has two stories and an attic. The walls are 30 inches thick and all the woodwork is of the most solid character. Not the slightest tremors was perceptible in the building when the machinery was at work. There are 1200 panes of glass in the factory. The building cost about $51,000.

"There were two broad power looms for the manufacture of blankets and four narrow looms for the weaving of cloth of ordinary width."

The factory ran for some years, then something happened and the mill ceased operation. No record is left as to why. Alfred lost $14,000 on the venture—his life's savings.

Emily Randall recalls watching her father going over his books for hours, and of hearing her mother, Margaret, say, "Never mind. Let it go."

Alfred replied, "But it is mine, mine and I need it." He did need it for his large family.

Brigham Young told Alfred he would see justice done, but then President Young died, and the matter was ended.

Figure 158: The house Alfred shared with fourth wife Hannah in North Ogden. Public Domain via FamilySearch.

Alfred's End of Life

Alfred spent his last years mostly farming at his farm in North Ogden. There he had orchards of all kinds of fruits, and gardens that produced well.

"He was a large square built man, but not fleshy, had light hair and blue eyes. He was extra good-natured, never unkind, loved to tell clean stories and jokes, and never heard to profane."

He was a skillful craftsman and could make wagons, sleighs, cupboards, tables, and chairs well. He was very strong, and could work hard all day.

In his later years, he had rheumatism and kidney trouble.

He passed away 31 March 1891 after he had been looking over the farm and telling his boys what to plant. He went inside, sat on the sofa talking with the family, laid down, and went to sleep. He never woke again.[398]

Alfred left a very short autobiography behind; it is printed in full below.

The Autobiography of Alfred Randall

Born at Bridgewater New York, June 13 1811.

Removed to Kirkland Ohio February 1819.

Helped to clear off timber from the land where the temple was built. Father's family moved to Munson in the year 1830.

In 1831 I went to Mentor Geauga to labor for myself.

I was present at Joseph Smith's first appointment for meeting in Kirkland.

In 1832 I bought a farm in Munson Ohio.

In the year 1834, I married Emmerette L. Davis.

1838 sold my farm and removed my family to Chardon Geauga County.

1839, sold and moved to Quincey Illinois. Here I worked at the carpenter business.

While Orsen Hyde was on his way to Palestine, he baptized me on May 17, 1840.

John E. Page was with President Hyde. I was ordained a deacon by Jacob Crouse.

1841, moved into Nauvoo and labored on the Temple in 1842 and visited Ohio and was ordained an Elder by President F.G. Williams.

Went to Monmouth trial with Joseph Smith Jr. on the Missouri writ. Received patriarchal blessing under the hand of father John Smith and returned to Nauvoo in 1843.

1844 accompanied Joseph and Hyrum Smith to Carthage jail. June 26, returned to Nauvoo having to leave Carthage at the point of a bayonet in the hands of the mob. I heard Governor Ford informed of the plans to kill Joseph and Hyrum. Ford replied "hold your tongue if you know any such thing."

1845 I was ordained into the 15th quorum of seventy by H.C. Kimball. 1846. Sheriff called upon me in taking "Sharp and Deming."

1846, moved to winter quarters and was sent by President Kimball on business to Ohio.

1847, sick at winter quarters with fever and ague.

1848, married Margaret Harley January 29 and moved in H.C. Kimball's company to Salt Lake City.

---

[398] Kofoed, Lucy Randall. "My Grandfather Alfred Randall."

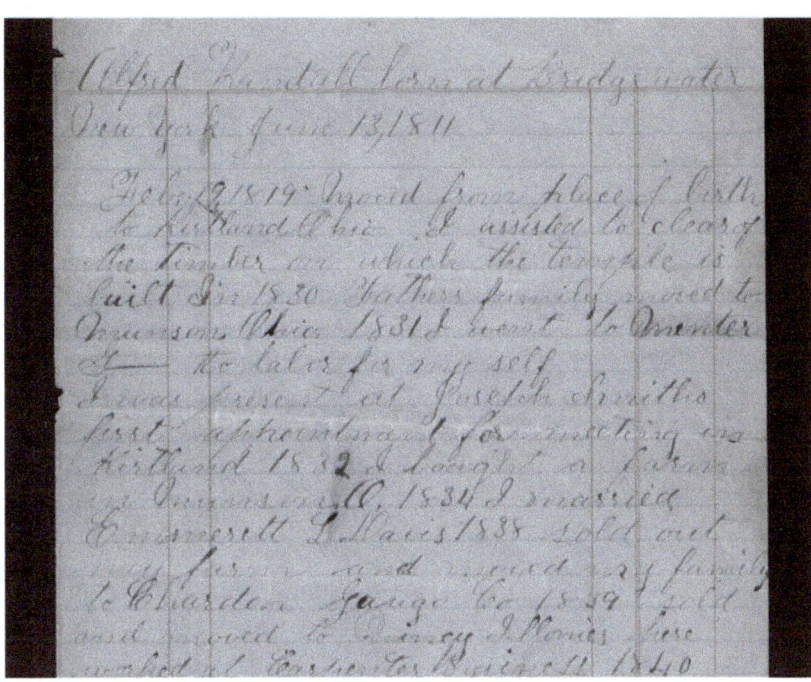

Figure 159: Autobiography of Alfred Randall in his own handwriting. Via FamilySearch.

10. Mads Christensen Family Stories

Mads Christensen (head of family)
Wives:
1. **Maren Johanne Jensen (our ancestor)** [m. 24 November 1854]
2. Johanne Margarethe Christiansen [m. 29 December 1881]

The story of the Christensen wives is a very different one than those of our other polygamous ancestors.

Rather than raising multiple families simultaneously and managing things with more than one wife at one time, Mads raised his families sequentially.

He married Maren, the sweetheart of his youth, in Denmark, where the two of them fell in love, married, and together made the life-changing decision to become baptized by the missionaries.

Together they raised six children, and eventually became established in the community of Farmington, Utah.

At some point, a Church authority advised Mads to take a second wife, during the era that polygamy was on its way out.

Mads wed Johanne Margarethe Christensen, the older sister of his son Joseph Mads' wife Emma.

Johanne was younger than Mads and Maren's oldest son, Rasmus. She would have been born the year Mads and Maren were immigrating to Utah. She already had a connection to the family—her younger sister, Emma, was the wife of Mads' son Joseph Mads.

Mads and Johanne married in 1881. By 1884, they had relocated to Arizona.

Maren said she would not leave her friends in Farmington, and so she remained there to continue living with her children and be near their families.

Mads moved Johanne around Arizona, then Utah, where despite keeping his families in separate areas he was eventually arrested and served jail time, and eventually he moved his second family up into Idaho, where he lived with them and helped raise the children. Johanne's family was very poor. They had ten children together, the last one who lived to adulthood was born when Mads was 72.

Maren died in 1896 at the age of 69. Mads passed away in 1914 at the age of 89. His second wife Johanne lived until 1934, when she died at the age of 76. Johanne and Mads' son Dr. Parley Alma Christensen eventually became the chair of the BYU English Department.

Here are some stories from the lives of Maren, Mads, and Johanne.

Maren's Health and Faith

After Mads and Maren arrived in Utah, they worked to get established. For a time they rented various houses, including, at one point, half a schoolhouse. At the schoolhouse, their second child was born, Joseph Mads Christensen.

After the birth of their third child, the family moved to Farmington. The family worked hard to fix up their own home and plant fruit trees and a garden.

When Mads went east to help a company of Saints one spring,

Figure 160: Maren Christensen. Public domain via FamilySearch.

Maren was left with the farm work and four small children, including a baby just a month old. She managed well.

Two more children joined the family, and Maren's health began to falter after the birth of her last child. She became sick for several months of each year for the rest of her life.

Figure 161: Mads Christensen in his later years. Public domain via FamilySearch.

Mads was called on a mission to Denmark, but his oldest sons were old enough to manage the farm work, and Maren was able to direct them. While Mads was on his mission, Maren became gravely ill. Her oldest son blessed her and all the children prayed.

Maren was healed.

Maren's greatest wish in life was to find the records of her ancestors and have their temple work completed, but she passed away before realizing this dream. Her children were left to do the research and temple work.[399]

Mads' Connection to the Primary

When the first Primary was organized in Farmington, the leadership wanted a helper to build supplies for the children and help them keep a community garden.

Mads Christensen was asked to fill this role.

As a carpenter and a farmer, he was well-suited for this task, and carefully worked to help make the first Primary a successful and happy experience for the children.

Some of his children with Maren participated in the program.

Mads in featured in the mural of the first Primary on the wall in Farmington's Rock Church.

---

[399] Bunn, Celeste. "Maren Johanne Jensen." *FamilySearch.* https://www.familysearch.org/photos/artifacts/1497291?cid=mem_copy

The Mads Christensen Polygamy Story

By the mid-1880s, plural families were going into the Underground. Anytime a stranger or casual acquaintance approached the home, extra women, babies, and small children were hidden. Friendly visiting between neighbors and associates was replaced by suspicion and outright distrust.

After Mads and Johanne (or "Hannah") returned from a mission to Arizona, the culture of the times meant it was prudent for Mads to keep his wives in separate areas of Utah. Hannah initially stayed in Kanesville, with her parents Jens and Trena Christensen.

Mads had a small farm in Farmington, but he had always relied on his carpentry skills to help meet the needs of his family. With the increasing danger to polygamous men, however, his carpentry occupation was hazardous as it gave him visibility. It also seemed risky to make the twenty-mile journey from Davis to Weber County—the two counties where his wives resided.

To help keep the space between his families and thus hopefully a measure of safety, Mads established a farm with a small frame house in Cache Valley for his second wife, Hannah, and her children to live on. Water had to be carried in and so did fuel. The cows and horses lived on hay for their winter food. With no garden the first year, the Farmington family was able to provide fruit and vegetables when someone made a visit between the two homes. The nearest community amenities of stores, church, and post office were at Newton and Trenton. But the area did have nearby a train service, with the Oregon Short Line going through Trenton. This provided mail service, as well as transportation if you could afford the ticket.

Figure 162: Hannah Christensen, second wife to Mads. Public domain via FamilySearch.

The train also provided transportation to federal marshals, however, and on 23 October 1887, Hannah's thirtieth birthday, Mads was arrested and taken to the penitentiary.

Hannah was required to testify against him before a grand jury on 25 November, or face imprisonment for contempt of court.

With a guilty verdict, Mads was sentenced to eight months of imprisonment. [400]

---

[400] jordananthonysmith1. "Mads Christensen and Family Story." *FamilySearch*, https://www.familysearch.org/photos/artifacts/118469412?cid=mem_copy

Mads' Autograph Book

Mads may have been a bit of a poet, or at least he encouraged that trait in others. While he was serving jail time, he passed around to his fellow prisoners what he called his autograph book. In it, he requested that his fellow inmates—all seemingly serving time for practicing polygamy—write poetry about their thoughts on the experience.

The resultant compilation of original writing by devout men, martyrs of a common cause, was the topic of a paper by a Dr. William Mulder, and is available to read on *FamilySearch*.[401]

It is unlikely that such a collection of such good men was often found together in prison, as many of the men there were leaders in the community—bishops, high councilors, and others. Mads renewed many old friendships with former fellow missionary companions and fellow emigrants.

Rather than reforming the prisoners to change their views on polygamy, as the laws apparently hoped to do, if anything the jail time seemed to make the men even more staunch in their beliefs. They certainly had no intention of abandoning their families.

"Bent Larsen, a fellow inmate of Mads, described the penitentiary as the 'Grand US Hotel where we are boarding with Uncle Sam.'"[402]

Mads' Families Band Together

The children of Maren were much older than the children of Hannah. They came to the comfort of Hannah and her children during this trying time that Mads was in jail. **Joseph Mads**, father of Violet and second son of Mads and Maren, was serving a colonizing mission in Arizona when his father was sent to jail, and sent moral support via his letters.

His brothers Peter and Hyrum looked out for not only their mother Maren's needs, but also went as frequently as possible to help at Hannah's Cache Valley farm. Hannah mostly stayed at the farm with her small children, though she did go to stay with her parents in Kanesville during the times of the births of some of her children.

Hannah's younger sister Lissie (Eliza) came to the farm and helped with chores and housework.

When Mads was released from jail, he returned to the Cache Valley farm to continue developing it. In order to avoid the appearance of flouting the law, Hannah went to stay with relatives for the next few seasons.

Mads invited Hannah's parents to take over the farm and leave their rental house in Kanesville. He offered that for the first year they could care for the farm and the animals in exchange for a percentage of the produce, and after that they could break new land or purchase the property, which would free Mads to go someplace else.

This offer was accepted. Jens and Trena moved to the farm. Meanwhile, Hannah went to a rental house in Logan. Here, her first daughter, Rhoda Margretta, entered the world on 2 April 1890.

The Christensen Family is Pulled Apart

Just a few months later, on 25 September 1890, President Wilford Woodruff's Manifesto declared an end to Church-sanctioned plural marriage, and called upon members to henceforth obey the laws of the land in every respect.

---

[401] "Mads Christensen's Autograph Album." *FamilySearch*. https://www.familysearch.org/photos/artifacts/109606612?cid=mem_copy
[402] jordananthonysmith1.

This new policy affected Mads' families directly: Existing plural households were to ascertain the father's greatest responsibility and then have him choose to live with that family.

Mads, Maren, and Hannah had worked to have a stable and successful expanded family for ten years, but now the family faced a tough choice.

Maren's children were grown, but she had poor health and could benefit from the presence of her husband.

But Hannah had five children, the oldest one just 8 years old. They needed their father.

Maren and her children had never had their status questioned, but Hannah and her children had faced scorn and ridicule by those who were unkind and unsympathetic to the dynamic of their family.

The family divided itself thus:

Maren received clear title to her Farmington home. Her children were all grown by now, and they could do well on their own.

Hannah and Mads went with their children and headed north.

Mads and Hannah in Idaho

In 1891, Mads, Hannah, and their children moved north to Idaho, eventually settling southwest of McCammon, where Mads built a frame house, with a long front porch and four rooms. He made it more sturdy by adding between the studdings on the outer walls adobe bricks, which he made himself. These held the walls anchored well against the occasional terrific west winds, and also helped insulate the house against the heat of summer and the chill of winter. Later he would add a new kitchen and an entrance hall.

The Christensens were fortunate in that the local irrigation ditch flowed through their land, giving them ready access to water.

They laid out a garden and planted currants, rhubarb, gooseberry bushes, apple trees, and vegetables.

They built a barn, corral, granary, calf and pig pens, chicken coops, and other farm buildings, and erected a tight picket fence to guard the boundaries of the dooryard. The cellar kept food cool, and operated as their version of a refrigerator.

His son Parley later wrote: "With all the strength that he still possessed, Father [then in his 60s] tackled his problem.[403] He trudged behind plow and harrow, and sowed by hand the wheat and barley. He swung the scythe, and the cradle. He hauled to the flour mill at McCammon his grist of wheat, and from the canyons the winter's wood."

The children helped out at the farm as soon as they were old enough and were given progressively more responsibilities as they grew up.

Upon the passing of his first wife, Mads wrote in his journal, "My beloved wife Maren Johanne Christensen died November 3, 1896 in her 70th year." After passing away at her home in Farmington, she was buried in the Farmington cemetery.

Even after Maren's death, Hannah and Mads' family continued to grow. They had another daughter, and then a son who died in infancy. Mads made him a little coffin and buried him next to another son who had passed away as an infant, setting the little burial place aside from the rest of the yard with a little fence.

In Idaho, Mads continued to practice his carpentry and cabinet work, for both his family and neighbors. In his 88th year he made a little stand or table for each of his daughters.

---

[403] Of establishing a productive farm.

He also looked out for friends and neighbors who were unwell. Parley wrote, "In his better days Father afoot, with cane in hand, was a familiar figure on the roads and in the lanes of the sprawling farm community, either on his way to church or to visit people in trouble. He administered to them and prayed for them when they were ill. He made their coffins when they died."

In 1898, he was set apart as the stake patriarch, and seemed pleased to bless and visit the people, coming home from his duties refreshed in spirit.

In 1906, when he was 81, Mads sold the farm, except his ten-acre homesite, to son Orson, for an agreed sum of $150 annually until the farm was paid for.

Learning English in America

Mads, Maren, and Hannah had all been born in Denmark, learned Danish but not English in school, and then immigrated to America, where they had to learn English to participate in their communities.

Mads worked industriously to learn to not just speak English well but also to read it. He wanted to read and study scripture and stay current on the newspaper, and these were only available in English. After diligently learning this new language in his thirties, he took great joy and satisfaction in leisure reading time throughout the rest of his life, especially during his declining years.

Maren had learned to speak English, but had not mastered writing or reading in it. Her daughter Annie in one letter to Mads asked him to write replies in Danish to Maren so she could read them herself and enjoy them more.

Mads, Maren, and Hannah did not teach their children Danish; some of the children served missions to Denmark and those learned the mother tongue of their parents.

Mads' Death

On 14 June 1914, Parley Christensen came to visit his parents, bringing the woman he hoped to marry. Hannah made a delicious dinner for those who gathered.

Later in the evening, Mads felt distress. Everyone thought at first it was a reaction to the hearty meal, however within a short time he passed away.

A train carried him to Farmington, where family and friends gathered to pay their respects.

He was buried in the Farmington cemetery, beside his beloved Maren.[404]

---

[404] jordananthonysmith1.

11. Butler Family Stories

John Lowe Butler (head of family)
Wives:
1. **Caroline Farozine Skeen (our ancestor)** [m. 3 February 1831]
2. Charity Skeen [m. 24 December 1844]
3. Sarah J. Bryant [m. 28 February 1846]
4. Sarah Lancaster [m. 28 February 1846]
5. Ann Hughs [m. 9 March 1857]
6. Esther Emily Ogden [m. 9 March 1857]
7. Lovisa Hamilton [m. 9 March 1857]
8. Henrietta Seaton Blythe [m. 8 September 1857]

Many stories of John Lowe Butler and family seem like Old West tales. But his life is one of the best-documented of our ancestors: it seems he was a true western frontiersman and also an educated man who wrote his own life story—a rare combo for that time. .

Two books focus on John's life: John's autobiography, which he wrote in his last years, and *My Best for the Kingdom*, by William G. Hartley, which includes backstory and context.

Multiple Parents to Run the Household

We are descended from John and his first wife, Caroline Farozine Skeen.

Since John had children with only three of his eight wives, multiple wives were child-free and able to help John, the family, and the community. This came in handy given that John was often away for Church assignments or efforts to provide for his family's temporal needs.

Here are a few stories of the Butler sister-wives. There are many more available; you may enjoy reading *My Best for the Kingdom* and the "Memory" pages for John, his wives, and their children on *FamilySearch* to explore the range of stories available for this fascinating family.

Charity's Conversion Story, and a Narrow Escape

Sometime after the Butlers converted and moved to Nauvoo, John served a mission to the Southern States and visited his in-laws. His sister-in-law, Charity, told John she wanted to be baptized and go with him back to Nauvoo. John agreed to take her with him.

Charity's father, Jesse, had passed away by then, but his sons were cut from the same cloth as he was, and the Skeen brothers pursued John and Charity after their departure. It was only luck or divine intervention that led John and Charity to take a different road than the one the Skeen pursuers followed.

Charity and John safely traveled to Nauvoo, and were reunited with Caroline.

When John became one of the first invited to practice plural marriage, Charity was a natural choice for a second wife.

She was deaf and mute but communicated using a form of sign language. She was a woman of courage and conviction.

Figure 163: Purported image of John Lowe Butler. Public domain via FamilySearch.

Charity and Caroline and the Emmett Expedition

Joseph Smith's death at the hands of a mob left no clear successor for Church leadership, which led to the formation of splinter groups. Many Saints left Nauvoo to follow various leaders.

One group followed James Emmett, the man who'd baptized John and Caroline some years earlier in Kentucky. Emmett had been tasked by Joseph before Joseph's death to take a group and chart the path west. After the Prophet's death, Emmett wanted to carry out Joseph's request, and left Nauvoo with a group of families, heading north. New Church leadership had a different vision and saw Emmett as just another splinter group leader.

After Emmett's group left Nauvoo, Brigham Young called John and his family on a very unusual mission: Join the Emmett group, win them over, and persuade them to return to the main body of Saints.

So John, Caroline, Charity, and the children went north, and joined the Emmett group, with whom they would remain for two and a half years.

The Butlers were welcomed, as James and John were friends. John soon had a position of leadership and trust in the group. The Emmett Expedition was ill-equipped to survive in the rugged terrain. John, with his frontiersman skills, would have been a big asset.

They traveled north through present-day Iowa, having many adventures.

Charity and Caroline and the Syrup Story

On one occasion, as part of the group's survival efforts, Charity and Caroline were among those tasked with boiling syrup to make sugar. They worked during the day to make sugar for the camp, then stayed up all night to make sugar for the family, taking turns to keep the pot boiling.

When finished, they put the sugar cakes for the group in a deep wooden box, and Caroline put the ones they'd made for the family in a different box.

When the company broke camp, Captain Emmett asked for the extra sugar they'd made on their night shift.

Charity shook her head "no," and when Emmett stooped over the box to get the sugar, Charity raised a big wooden paddle above his

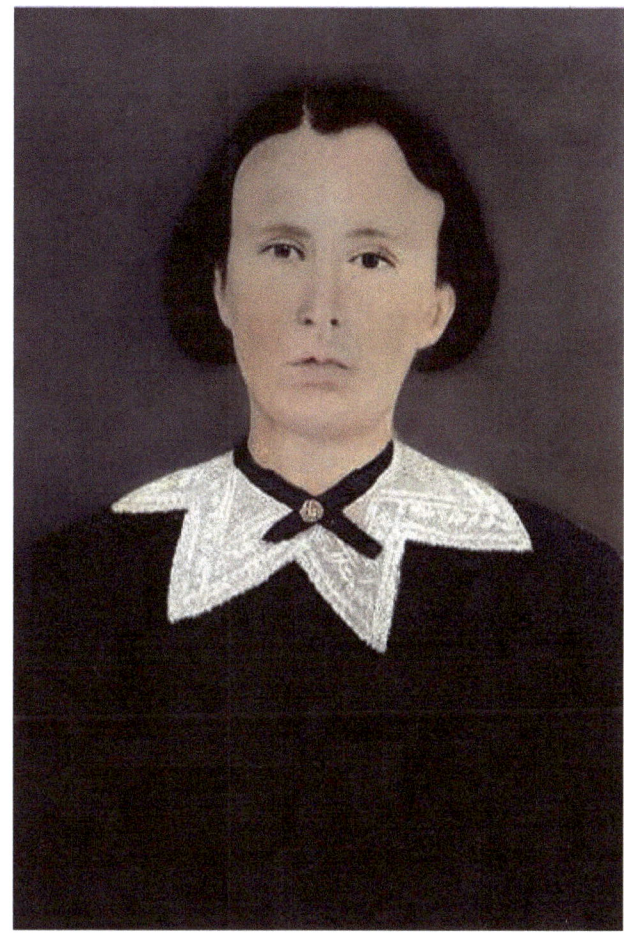

Figure 164: Portrait of Caroline Farozine Skeen. Public domain via FamilySearch.

backside. He stood, shouting, but each time he bent to reach for the sugar, she raised the paddle again. Curious onlookers gathered, and Emmett yelled at Caroline to give up the sugar.

The story goes that Caroline replied she could not, as the sugar had been made at night when no one else had worked.

The spectators laughed, and Emmett, seeing the crowd had been won over by the sisters, left without taking their sugar.

When the company used up its sugar later, the Butler women rationed their supply to the children, the elderly, and those who were struggling to walk.[405]

Eventually the Emmett group created a settlement.

In due time, they were visited by a pair of elders, and John was asked to return to Nauvoo in order to help sort things out, leaving his wives and children behind. This was bad news for the Butler wives and children, as it meant getting through the winter without John. Luckily, the sisters had each other to rely on.

James Emmett could be a challenging leader. Somewhat temperamental, he was accused by some in the group of feeding his own family better than many of the others. He could also be cruel to Caroline, possibly because she tended to stand up to him. One time while John was away, James left Caroline stranded across the river from the rest of the group for a few days, where she had to survive by foraging. When John returned to the group and saw that his wife had been kept across the river, it was lucky for Emmett that Emmett was not with the group at that time.

Figure 165: Caroline Farozine Skeen. Public domain via FamilySearch.

Charity and Caroline seemed to have worked well together and to have enjoyed one another's company. It must have been a sad day for Caroline later when the family, then living in Winter Quarters, was visited by one of the Skeen brothers, who took Charity home with him to Tennessee for a visit to their family and never let her return.

Grandmother Squaw and Chief Henry

During the difficult winter that Caroline and Charity spent with John away, they struggled sometimes to have enough food.

Most members of the camp had voted for John to return to Nauvoo, and had also voted that they would see that John's family would not want while he was away, but this had angered Emmett, who responded by not giving food to the Butler wives until others intervened.

The Emmett Expedition wintered in a fort at Vermillion near some Native Americans. Government Indian Agents didn't like that Emmett's group were there, but found that the Emmett group's animals were unfit for duty, and the natives didn't mind having the group stay until spring, and so they were allowed to stay for the winter.

---

[405] Hartley, William G. *My Best for the Kingdom*, p. 154.

The Saints followed Church recommendations to try and befriend the native people. The natives gave the company forty bales of dried buffalo meat to help them get through the winter.

But when Emmett distributed meat, he would not give any to Caroline and her family.

When a Brother Potter of the group learned of this, he challenged Emmett, who finally gave the Butler family some meat.

One old native woman visited Caroline that winter, and told her that she had just lost her only daughter. She asked if Caroline had a mother, and Caroline said her mother was not alive. The squaw asked Caroline to call her "grandmother" and all winter long kept the feet of the Butler children in warm buckskin moccasins. The family called her "Grandmother Squaw."

Caroline tried to survive that winter on meat alone, giving her other food to her children while also caring for them and nursing a sick native baby. She grew very ill.

Chief Henry, of the native group, noticed what was going on. One day he came to Caroline's door, and got her daughter Keziah.

"What is he going to do with my child?" asked Caroline from her sickbed.

Chief Henry took her to his home, and she returned after a while with a pan of flour on her head, a pint of sugar, and some tea. The chief told her she must not eat meat for now but must every day have a cake of bread made of the flour.

Caroline soon was well.[406]

When Latter-day Saint artist Minerva Teichert learned of this story from the Butler family history, she was so moved by it that she painted an original work of art based on the story, featuring young Keziah carrying food home from Chief Henry to her mother.

The Butler Family Succeeds with the Emmett Expedition

In the end, the Butler family succeeded with the unique mission that Brigham Young had called them to perform. They were successful in retrieving Emmett's group and reuniting them with the Saints, after many adventures, possibly preventing the formation of an off-shoot splinter group. John also used quick thinking and diplomacy to prevent Emmett's group from being killed by Indians. The full scope of their adventures on this mission cannot be fully recounted here; to enjoy reading the rest of the stories from this mission, read *My Best for the Kingdom*, by William Hartley (pages 135–208).

Disagreement over "the Practice"

Caroline seems to have been supportive of John marrying her sister Charity, or at least the two sisters worked together well to care for the family on the Emmett Expedition, but it seems Caroline had a harder time with many of his additional marriages.

She was not alerted in advance that John had married again while on his return visit to Nauvoo while she was north with the Emmett Expedition, and perhaps not being included in that decision may have contributed to her dissatisfaction.

Possibly due to stress between wives, or possibly for other reasons, third wife Sarah complained of the family situation during the early years of being in the Butler family strongly enough that John went with Sarah to an entirely different city, where the two of them lived and worked for over a year, with John only returning to visit Caroline and the children for a time after Caroline gave birth to a daughter.

---

[406] Hartley, p. 176.

Sarah accompanied John without Caroline on a few other occasions: When the Butlers first arrived in Utah, John and Sarah were the ones to go set up the initial homestead, and when John spent his second summer at Fort Bridger, Sarah accompanied him with two of his daughters, leaving Caroline and the other children in Utah.

*Figure 166: Fort Bridger.
Image © Lecock Freddy/Dreamstime.com*

The family record details that Caroline was certainly troubled by polygamy during the Mormon Reformation period of 1856–1857. Top Church leaders highly encouraged plural marriage then, especially for leaders. John, a bishop, took four new wives in 1857, the last of whom was recommended to him by the Presiding Bishop of the Church.[407]

Caroline had words to say to John about all of this.

In the Hartley book, we read, "Usually the first wife was the adult hardest hit emotionally when a new wife entered the family circle. This was particularly true of women in their middle years, like Caroline, whose husbands courted and married women young enough to be their own daughters."

John recounts that Caroline's feelings against plurality gave him "trouble in my domestic circle," and that she "would oppose me most vehemently sometimes." Caroline spoke with John about "how she had always been with me in all my trials, had borne a large family of children to me" and then, as John frames it, asked for something "that it was not her right to dictate, trying to rule the priesthood."[408]

Their disagreement seems to have centered around their approaches to the practice:

---

[407] Hartley, p. 303.
[408] Hartley, p. 304.

John saw polygamy as a matter of faith and a high level of obedience, whereas Caroline weighed it in terms of practicality and a matter of relationship loyalty.

Both of their perspectives are understandable.

Caroline was dissatisfied with the practice of plural marriage. Another wife became the connector who built bridges among plural wives and children in the Butler family.

That woman was Sarah Lancaster, third wife, a remarkable woman in her own right.

Sarah Lancaster, Frontierswoman and Sister-Wife

While Caroline, Charity, and the children were away with the Emmett Expedition, John returned to Nauvoo on the vote of the camp to work things out with Church leaders.

While in Nauvoo for the winter, John served as a temple guard, fireman, and officiator in addition to receiving his temple ordinances and endowments. He also married Sarah Lancaster in the recently completed Nauvoo Temple, on 6 February 1846, at a ceremony officiated by Brigham Young.

Sarah's widowed mother, Sarah Bryant Lancaster, would also marry John about a month later, probably to benefit from priesthood ordinances rather than to create a husband-and-wife relationship. (Hartley 184)

The Lancasters, backyard neighbors of the Butlers in Nauvoo, are placed by family stories as being well connected, recounting that the younger Sarah was a friend of Emma, Hyrum, and Joseph.

At the time, Caroline and Charity had no way of hearing of John's third and fourth marriages; no communication passed between Nauvoo and Camp Vermillion until after the winter thaw.

When the exodus from Nauvoo got underway, the elder Sarah went to Indiana to stay with her children. John and the younger Sarah went west, leaving Nauvoo in March 1846 as part of an early wave of the mass exodus. They moved faster than others on the trail, catching up with Brigham Young, whom John knew would send him to retrieve Emmett's group. Sarah stayed with the Saints, probably at Council Bluffs, while John and James Cummings traveled on to Camp Vermillion.

(Cummings' chronicles of their journey are recounted in *My Best for the Kingdom*, in "a tale deserving its own place in the literature of survival in America's western wilderness." John was "the frontiersman, the hunter, the route finder, the survival expert." This story is a few pages long and worth reading in its entirety in the Hartley book.)[409]

The Butler family and the Emmett Expedition rejoined the Saints at Winter Quarters after many adventures (including wintering near the Ponca Indians and having to form a bucket brigade to save their fort from burning down the evening after Christmas).

Sarah would never have children of her own, but she was a strong helpmeet for John and beloved by many of the Butler children and wives. After John married four more women in Utah, Sarah became especially close to one of the younger wives.

Sarah and the Relief Society

The Butlers were a founding family of Spanish Fork, Utah, and John served as one of the area's first bishops.

In the mid-1850s, women in Spanish Fork and other Utah towns restarted the Latter-day Saint Relief Societies, initially to assist the Indians, but soon expanding their focus to help needy Saints, too.

---

[409] Hartley, p. 189.

The Spanish Fork ward consisted of three sub-wards, each of whom had their own Relief Society Presidency. Sarah was asked to be the first counselor to Relief Society President Rhoda Snell in the "First Ward."[410]

The Spanish Fork Relief Society had staying power. After the Utah War, it was one of only three or four Relief Societies that continued to meet during that time.[411]

Sarah the Bridge Builder

Sarah cared for the children of her sister-wives.

After John's death in 1860, Sarah lived for a few years with Henrietta Blythe Butler, John's eighth wife. The two women became best friends. Together they cared for Henrietta's two small children, and when Henrietta married John Powell in 1864 and went to live at Deseret, Meadow, and then Fillmore, she left her daughter Isabella with Sarah to raise in Spanish Fork, for Sarah had never had a child of her own.

Figure 168: Henrietta Blyth Butler. Eighth wife of John Lowe Butler. Public domain via FamilySearch.

Figure 167: Lovisa Hamilton. Seventh wife of John Lowe Butler. Public domain via FamilySearch.

Henrietta named her firstborn with John Powell "Sarah," after her sister-wife.

Sarah Lawrence Butler raised Isabella until Isabella's death in 1872.

Henrietta grieved for her child; she wasn't able to travel to attend the funeral. But she still considered Sarah to be her best friend.

When another Butler sister-wife, Lovisa, chose to be sealed to her second husband rather than to John, her daughter Lovisa Butler, wishing to keep her Butler connection, chose to be sealed to John and Sarah.

At Sarah's funeral, she was praised[412] for her goodness and integrity of character.[413]

---

[410] Hartley, p. 324.
[411] Hartley, p. 345.
[412] Hartley, p. 352.
[413] See Hartley for more stories on Sarah and John's other wives.

12. Simmons Family Stories

Leven Simmons (head of family)
Wives:
1. **Harriet Bradford (our ancestor)** [m. 27 February 1836]
2. Lydia Rebecca Fisher [m. 21 February 1856]

Figure 169: Leven Simmons. Public domain via FamilySearch.

The Simmons may have stood out in the town of Spanish Fork.

Harriet smoked a tobacco pipe, a habit she'd acquired from her tobacco-growing ancestors. She worked non-stop to help care for her family, even knitting socks while walking or riding in a wagon. An excellent cook, Harriet made biscuits and gravy so tasty that people wanted a second helping.

As a nurse and a midwife, Harriet was popular with both the settlers and Native Americans, who would bring their children to see her for help.[414]

Figure 170: Harriet Bradford Simmons. Public domain via FamilySearch.

Leven served as an early mayor of Spanish Fork. He was an excellent singer and had a pleasant temperament. But it was only due to the invitation of a friend that the family had come to settle in Spanish Fork at all . . .

---

[414] Huff, Elizabeth F. "Harriet Bradford (1821-1890)." *FamilySearch*, Intellectual Reserve, https://www.familysearch.org/photos/artifacts/35018993?cid=mem_copy. Accessed 4 December 2020.

The Springville Farm

Figure 171: Leven Simmons. Public domain via FamilySearch.

After Leven and Harriet's arrival in Salt Lake City with their family on 26 September 1852, they paused to rest and then moved on. They built a home in Springville, where they lived and farmed for four years. One day, a friendly Indian warned Leven that Indians were on the warpath. Leven and Harriet loaded the family into the wagon and left. The next morning, they returned home to find arrows scattered across the property and all their pigs and chickens killed. Their house had been burned down.

Clearly it was time to move on, but to where, exactly?

An Invitation to Spanish Fork

Stephen Markham, a dear friend and the man who had baptized Harriet and Leven, offered them the north quarter of his homestead in Spanish Fork, along the Spanish Fork River. They accepted his offer and built a home there in which they lived the rest of their lives. (Huff)

There, Leven farmed and worked as a cooper, and Harriet raised sheep, which she would shear, wash the wool, and spin yarn, which she'd weave into cloth. It was a lot of work to feed and clothe their twelve children.

Leven also eventually entered politics. He served as a Spanish Fork city councilman for a number of years and was mayor from 1863 to 1865.[415]

Harriet's Unique Attributes

Harriet was a descendant of tobacco growers and smoked a pipe. (Williams) (Huff)

One grandchild recorded: "Grandmother was an excellent cook. She could make the lightest cornbread. We children were served large pieces of it dripping with butter and molasses and flanked by little sausage cakes. There was nothing more to be desired unless it was another helping."[416]

Harriet was a trendsetter. She acquired the first stove to come to Spanish Fork, which she purchased for the sum of one dollar. She also owned one of the first oil lamps.

An industrious woman, Harriet would make a ten-mile, two-day trip with the ox team to the woolen mill once it opened in Provo in order to trade her wool for cloth. On the way there, she'd knit one stocking. On the way back she'd knit another to complete the pair. She'd knit as she walked the four miles through sage brush and greasewood to Lake Shore to visit her grown children. She took care of all her adult children's mending and sewing needs.

---

[415] Simmons, Jr., Benjamin Franklin. "Biography of Levan Simmons and wives Harriet Bradford and Lydia Rebecca Fisher." *FamilySearch*, Intellectual Reserve, https://www.familysearch.org/photos/artifacts/101996849?cid=mem_copy. Accessed 4 December 2020.

[416] Huff, Elizabeth F. "Harriet Bradford (1821-1890)." *FamilySearch*, Intellectual Reserve, https://www.familysearch.org/photos/artifacts/35018993?cid=mem_copy. Accessed 4 December 2020.

"Many times [Harriet] would weave the cloth for a pair of pants during the day and then cut them out and sew them by hand at night, by the light of a tallow candle of her own making."[417]

One of her grandchildren later wrote: "Many times I have seen her walking down the road that wandered through the sagebrush and greasewood from the river crossing on north past our house. She was always knitting as she walked and seemed to enjoy it as she didn't need to watch her hands as they worked. We children always ran to meet her coaxing her to stay. But after an hour's rest and, sometimes dinner, back home she would go satisfied that all was well. If Father was home, he always took her back in the wagon (that meant a ride for us). If not, she would walk."[418]

Harriet hired carpenters to make her a drop leaf table that had turned legs, as Leven was too busy making molasses barrels, and buckets and tubs. She bartered for it by washing wool and forming it into rolls ready for spinning. She was proud of the table and kept it for many years.[419]

A Visit from Grandmother Elizabeth Scott, and Simmons Family Changes

The Simmons family move to Spanish Fork happened right before two major family events.

Shortly after Leven and Harriet moved to Spanish Fork to a lot east of the Spanish Fork River, they were visited by Leven's mother, Grandma Elizabeth Scott Simmons, whom they'd left behind in the Midwest!

Grandma Simmons, age 70, had sold all she owned to go seek her fortune in the goldfields with her only unmarried son. The two of them stayed with Leven and Harriet for a few days before continuing on to California, never to be seen again by Leven and his descendants.

The gold rush, a big draw for American pioneers of that day, wasn't the only significant influence on the extended Simmons family at that time.

The two-year Mormon Reformation was just starting, a time when Church leaders encouraged plural marriage perhaps more than at any other point in their history. Polygamy was touted as a mark of obedience and devotion.

On 21 February 1856, the Simmons family was reshaped forever when Leven married second wife Lydia Rebecca Fisher (age 18), six days before Leven and Harriet's twentieth wedding anniversary.

---

[417] Olsen, Gary Lamar. "Life History of Harriet Bradford Simmons." *FamilySearch*, Intellectual Reserve, 7 January 2018, https://www.familysearch.org/photos/artifacts/46276814?cid=mem_copy. Accessed 4 December 2020.
[418] Huff, Elizabeth F.
[419] Bunn, Celeste. "Harriette Bradford." *FamilySearch*, Intellectual Reserve, 17 June 2013, https://www.familysearch.org/photos/artifacts/1388056?cid=mem_copy. Accessed 4 December 2020.

Leven's Second Marriage to Lydia

Figure 172: Lydia Rebecca Fisher Simmons. Public domain via FamilySearch.

Lydia, the teenaged divorced mother of a young daughter, seems to have been happy to join the family.

There are mixed accounts of Harriet's response to Lydia, with one writer recounting, "This 'second wife' situation was only tolerated (at best) by Harriet and caused her a lot of heartache. She was never able to accept the marriage. . . . There was a lot of jealousy over things that never seemed quite equitable."[420].

Though the addition of Lydia to the family doubtless brought complexity, other sources say the women got along well. One challenge in tracing historical accounts is that sometimes information is found that gives opposite or different accounts.

First wives of Utah's polygamous families had a few common concerns about plural wives. Large age gaps between the first and subsequent wives and financial strain brought on by additional wives and children were two common stressors; and the marriage of Leven to Lydia brought both.

Lydia was just a few years older than Harriet and Leven's oldest surviving child, and would have been born just seven months before the birth of Harriet and Leven's first baby. The Simmons family already had to work very hard to meet basic necessities prior to adding a second wife. A new wife and subsequent children presented a daunting challenge.

Despite this, however, all sources agree both women treated each other's children with as much love as they did their own, and the children of the two women grew up as siblings, working together on the farm.

Neighbors often said they never could tell which children belonged to which mother.

Sources vary on the family's living situation after Lydia joined the family. One source says Leven built Lydia a log cabin on the farm next to the one where Harriet and her children lived.[421] Other accounts say the two families shared lodging for several years, which would make sense given that at a later point Lydia and her sons made a dugout for their side of the family, as the cabin they'd been sharing with Harriet's family had grown too crowded. (Simmons, Jr.)[422]

Lydia's Story

Lydia's story is one of the most fraught with challenges in our ancestral family tree.

Lydia married for the first time at age 14, to George C. Parsons in about 1853 in Missouri. In 1854, when Lydia was 16, George and Lydia had a daughter together and named her Mary Jane.

Lydia and George traveled with Lydia's parents in a company of pioneers migrating to the Salt Lake Valley.

---

[420] Olsen, Gary Lamar.
[421] Olsen, Gary Lamar.
[422] Simmons, Jr., Benjamin Franklin.

Their heartbreaking trek included the disappearance and possible kidnapping of one of Lydia's twin sisters, whom the family never saw again, and the death of Lydia's mother to cholera. Following the deathbed request of Lydia's mother, Lydia and the other women of the wagon train put Lydia's five minor siblings in their own wagons and continued on their way toward Utah despite her 70-year-old father's attempt to turn his family wagon back toward the east. Lydia's father, Vardis, saw the determination of the women and agreed to continue on toward Zion.[423]

After arriving in Utah, the struggles of Lydia and her family continued.

Their first winter in the Utah Territory in 1855–56 was described as unusually severe. Grasshoppers had cleaned out most crops from the previous summer so there wasn't much to eat, and cattle were dying. Vardis froze his leg while out in the timber and had to have it taken off at the knee; it then became infected and he had to have it taken off at the hip. His children stayed with him as long as they could, but eventually scattered to other families.

Lydia, still nursing Mary Jane, worked at anything she could find to get food. One week she had only one loaf of bread plus roots she had foraged.

Lydia's husband, George, told her he could not stand to see her starve. He said he would leave to hunt for work, and if he could make it, he would return, but if he couldn't she could be free. He headed off to the goldfields of California, and Lydia was left with their baby.

Hardships continued for Lydia, who took in washing and did housework to provide a living for herself and Mary Jane. She took crumbs of food from the floor of the home where she worked so Mary Jane could have the food.[424]

Some sources say Lydia never heard from George after he left. Others say George wrote with an offer to send Lydia money to come join him in California, but she replied he must come for her if he wanted her.

Either way, George never returned.

After two years, Lydia divorced George and wed Leven Simmons. She was 18 years old at the time of her second marriage. Leven and Lydia would eventually have eight children together.[425]

The Simmons Family with Lydia

Lydia was a strong and determined woman. She was up for the work required to live a settler's life in Spanish Fork.

One of Leven's granddaughters wrote that when Leven went into polygamy, the family had to work very hard to feed and clothe both families. "Grandmother [Harriet], being an excellent seamstress, would weave or spin all day, then cut and sew by hand at night the clothes to be made. Her light was a tallow candle of her own making or 'greasy bitch.'"[426]

Leven served as mayor of Spanish Fork from 1863–1865 while also providing for and raising his two families.

---

[423] Daughters of Utah Pioneers. "Lydia Rebecca Fisher (from Daughters of Utah Pioneers)." *FamilySearch*, Intellectual Reserve, https://www.familysearch.org/photos/artifacts/32269519?cid=mem_copy. Accessed 28 December 2020.

[424] Hertzel, Anna Lenz. "Vardis Fisher: Marriage, children and adult life." *FamilySearch*, Intellectual Reserve, 13 June 2014, https://www.familysearch.org/photos/artifacts/7811206?cid=mem_copy. Accessed 4 December 2020.

[425] Daughters of Utah Pioneers. "Biography of Leven Simmons." *FamilySearch*, Intellectual Reserve, https://www.familysearch.org/photos/artifacts/32269379?cid=mem_copy. Accessed 3 December 2020.

[426] Huff, Elizabeth F.

Today, the Thurber School stands near the former site of the Simmons family home. The family had a house on the west side of the school's current lot.[427]

According to the Daughters of Utah Pioneers, all of Lydia's children were born in the shared home except Sarah Elizabeth and Fannie. These youngest two daughters were born in a dugout built by Lydia and her sons when she was expecting her second-to-last child.

Lydia's Dugout

As the families grew, the house eventually became a tight fit.

On one occasion, while Leven was away freighting fruit; Lydia took her sons to the east bank of the Spanish Fork River, and led them in building a dugout. Twenty feet square, logged on the inside, with a large fireplace at one end of the building, this home would be the birthplace of Lydia's last two children, Sarah Elizabeth and Fanny Melissa.

Lydia's family spent many memorable happy hours singing around the fireplace.

After Lydia and Leven had been married for twenty years and had eight children together, Leven passed away at the age of 64.

Leven's Passing

Leven died of "heart disease and dropsy" 8 February 1876, just about eighteen months after the birth of his last child, Fannie Melissa, born to Lydia in the dugout. Harriet, Lydia, and all the children were left to handle things the best they could.

According to one source, he left his families fairly well off for those times, despite being survived by two wives and sixteen of his twenty offspring.

The boys were skilled at farm work by that point, and the family farmland was good. So the family continued to work together for a time.[428]

Harriet after Leven's Passing

After Leven died, Harriet lived with her two unmarried children in an adobe house she had built on the farm.

One of Lydia's granddaughters recorded: "I remember going with my mother, Sarah Simmons Forsyth, to visit Aunt Harriet, Leven Simmons' first wife before she died. She was a lovely, darting little old lady and so happy to have my mother visit her. Mother said Aunt Harriet and Lydia always got along good together, each doing their fair share of the work such as spinning, weaving, sewing and the many other tasks required for their large families."[429]

In spite of her life's hardships, Harriet was loving and happy. She passed away at age 69 on 16 March 1890.

Harriet and Leven's son Matthew was 2 years old when the family crossed the plains and is one of Janet's maternal great-grandfathers.

---

[427] DUP. "Lydia Rebecca Fisher."
[428] Simmons, Jr.
[429] DUP. "Leven Simmons."

Lydia after Leven's Passing

About four years after Leven's death, Lydia married Nathanial Babcock and moved to Southern Utah; according to one source, this was to Harriet's relief.[430]

Lydia's boys were on their own after that time. The youngest two daughters (Sarah Elizabeth and Fanny Melissa) traveled with Lydia and Nathaniel, who was "of a roving disposition and always on the move." They lived in various places in Utah and Idaho, and were poor enough that on one occasion the daughters heard Nathanial complain after they'd gone to bed that they ate too much. They quietly ran away to their brother's home where they were always welcome, but their mother retrieved them the next morning.[431]

Lydia Fisher Simmons Babcock died at Castle Gate, Utah, on 25 May 1910 at the age of 72.

"Her life had been a hard one, but she always kept cheerful and full of faith in better things to come."[432]

---

[430] Olsen.
[431] DUP. "Lydia Rebecca Fisher."
[432] Simmons, Jr.

13. Goulding Family Stories

Daniel Goulding (head of family)
Wives:
1. **Elizabeth Merrifield Pratten (our ancestor)** [m. 19 February 1851]
2. Fanny Pratten [m. 16 May 1870]

Daniel and Elizabeth were married for nearly twenty years before Fanny joined their family as the second wife. Daniel and Elizabeth married on 19 February, 1851. We are descended from first wife Elizabeth Merrifield Pratten Goulding. Daniel and second wife Fanny married on 16 May 1870. On the date that Daniel married Fanny, he brought both his wives to the Endowment House and both of the sisters were sealed to him.

Between 1851 and 1870, all three of them immigrated to Australia, and then on to America via California. They were all devout in their faith and Daniel led congregations in England and later Australia.

Here are the stories of Daniel, Elizabeth, and Fanny Goulding's family that have been handed down via the family histories.

Fanny's Conversion Story

Fanny, eleven years younger than Elizabeth, had her own coming of age and conversion story. In the chapter on conversion stories, you can read the conversion stories of Elizabeth and Daniel, as they are our direct ancestors. Here is the conversion story of Elizabeth's sister and Daniel's second wife Fanny.

Fanny lost both parents at a young age. Her father died when she was 4, and her mother, Dinah, died when Fanny was 14 and still in school. Before she passed away, Dinah arranged for Fanny to live with friends and neighbors and finish school.

At Dinah's funeral, a minister preached that Dinah would forget she ever had a husband and children now that she was dead.

This idea bothered Fanny a great deal.

One day, Fanny heard a man preaching at a street meeting. The man was a missionary for The Church of Jesus Christ of Latter-day Saints, and he was speaking to those who would listen about the resurrection.

Fanny told her friends, "This is my church!"

She thought of it as her church from that time forward, even though she would not be baptized until years later.

Fanny became a teacher at a young age, and started saving money to purchase passage to America, which she called a land "choice among all others."

The Gouldings in Australia

A few years prior to Dinah's death, Daniel and Elizabeth had moved to Australia. They had heard that the gold mines in Australia were producing well. Daniel had experience as a coal miner in England, and hoped he could make enough money in the Australian mines to fund his family's immigration to America and give them some money to take with them to Zion. It would take them at least nine years in Australia before they would move on.

Elizabeth and Fanny had an older brother named Elijah who had also immigrated to Australia. Elizabeth and Daniel held Fanny and Elijah in high enough esteem that they honored them by naming a child after each of them. Their son Elijah was born 16 October 1855 in Sydney, Australia, and their daughter Fanny was born 2 July 1859, a year after Elizabeth's sister Fanny immigrated to Australia.

In Australia, Daniel and his oldest son, William, worked in the mines. Daniel's second son, Elijah, worked as an errand boy for the miners once he was old enough, bringing them lunches. There were no child labor laws in those days. Daniel himself had started working as a miner in the coal mines beside his father when he was just 6 years old. Working families of those times often had children work as well as adults to help meet the family's financial needs. There

Figure 173: Elizabeth Merrifield Pratten. Public domain via FamilySearch.

wasn't a requirement that children be in school; so some of them worked from very young ages.

The details of Fanny's immigration pathway are a little hard to track. Fanny's daughter Zina recounts that Fanny sailed from England to San Francisco, California, where she joined Elizabeth, Daniel, and their children, who had already gone to California.

But an immigration record places Fanny as immigrating to Australia at age 15 in 1858, the year after her mother's death. Fanny and Elizabeth's brother Elijah is listed as Fanny's family member in Australia on the record.

Perhaps Fanny lived with Daniel and Elizabeth in Australia. Or perhaps she lived with her brother Elijah or on her own. Maybe she worked as a teacher there, earning fare to California.

Family history places Daniel and Elizabeth's move to California in 1865. Fanny's immigration date to America is less clear. But her brother Elijah died 4 April 1870, shortly before Daniel and Fanny's 16 May 1870 wedding. At that point, Elizabeth may have been Fanny's sole living family member.

Family Changes

Daniel, Elizabeth, and Fanny lived for a time on the Big Muddy River in Nevada near St. Thomas, which was later covered by Lake Mead in the 1930s after the construction of the Hoover Dam. Today, St. Thomas is a ghost town located in the Lake Mead National Recreation Area, which re-emerged when the waterline of Lake Mead receded in the early 2000s.

Elizabeth was very happy when Fanny agreed to become Daniel's plural wife.

In May of 1870, Daniel, Elizabeth, and Fanny went away for a few days to the Salt Lake Endowment House for both women to be sealed to Daniel.

While they were away, oldest son William, then age 18, took sick, died, and was buried before his parents returned. The entire family was saddened by this. Daniel and Elizabeth had given birth to ten children, five of whom were still alive when Fanny returned to the home as the second mother.

After that point, Elizabeth would have two more children with Daniel, and Fanny would have six children with Daniel.

Figure 174: Daniel and Fanny. Public domain via FamilySearch.

Growing Up Goulding

We are fortunate that two of the Goulding daughters—Elizabeth's daughter Henrietta ("Retty") and Fanny's daughter Zina—recorded stories from their childhood, preserving Goulding family stories for future generations.

Figure 175: The Goulding family, circa 1886.
Front row: Fanny Adelia, left, and Phoebe Alzada, right. Youngest daughters of Daniel and Fanny. Next row, seated, L to R: John Goulding (brother of Daniel); Daniel Goulding; Daniel's two wives, Elizabeth Pratten Goulding and Fanny Pratten Goulding. Third row: Three young boys standing in the center; L to R: Samuel Even, son of Fanny; James Arthur, son of Elizabeth; and William Eelan, son of Fanny. Back row, standing, L to R: Lucy Beatrice, daughter of Elizabeth; Rosanna Susannah, daughter of Elizabeth; George Joseph, son of Elizabeth; and Clara Elizabeth, oldest child of Fanny. At the time of this photo, Elijah had left home and five of Elizabeth's children had died. All six of Fanny's children are pictured. Public domain via FamilySearch. A note as to the identity of those in this photograph was found among Janet Clark's papers.

Retty recounts that the family lived together harmoniously with no jealousy between the two wives as the years went by, and that the family was full of love and happiness.

In 1875, the Gouldings moved north to American Fork. Retty remembers walking behind the wagon with other children and being almost overtaken by Indians. "The children really made tracks catching up with the wagon," she wrote of the incident.

In 1876, the family moved to a farm near Battle Creek (today's Pleasant Grove). There, Retty was baptized in icy water on her eighth birthday, 20 November 1876.[433]

There were a few schools in the region, but when Elizabeth's older children had been growing up, the family had never lived close to one. Her children learned at home, with one slate to share. In order for

---

[433] Workman, Phyllis. "Henrietta Goulding." *FamilySearch*, Intellectual Reserve, https://www.familysearch.org/photos/artifacts/33343081?cid=mem_copy. Accessed 22 November 2020.

there to be space for everyone to practice making letters, the children often drew figures in the dirt with a stick. Sometimes the Bible was their only book.

When Fanny joined the family, she was her children's first teacher. She also taught school in Pleasant Grove, as she did in other towns where the family lived. Most larger schools at that time in the territory had just two teachers. Fanny taught the older students.

The Tithing Story

While the family lived in Pleasant Grove, Daniel and Elizabeth's older boys and some of the cousins were given the chore of filling a wagonload of farm produce and taking it to the bishop as the family's tithing offering. The boys added Retty to the top of the wagon and began the journey, holding her there and telling her that since she was the tenth child in her family, she would be offered as tithing as well. Retty wiggled loose, and jumped off kicking and screaming.

*Figure 176: Fanny and Elizabeth Pratten Goulding.
Public domain via FamilySearch.*

Who might these cousins have been?

The most likely candidates are the children of Daniel's older brother John Goulding III, who also immigrated to the US. Evidence suggests John was also a devout Latter-day Saint and close to Daniel. Among John's sons are the names "Joseph Hyrum Goulding" and "Brigham Lawrence Lorenzo Goulding." Another son is "Daniel," perhaps named after John's brother Daniel.

John was included in a formal portrait we have of Daniel, Elizabeth, and Fanny's family. John died in Henrieville, where Daniel served as bishop during his later years.

How the Wives Split the Work

The Goulding mothers were skillful hard workers. They split the labor of managing the needs of their family and serving their broader community, and collaborated well. From accounts we have of how they worked together, it would appear that the Goulding sisters lived together in a fruitful, loving, and mutually supportive sister-wife arrangement.

In one family story, Daniel called the sisters "you two mothers," and it does appear that the women took an equal interest in all the children, giving the children of the family each two mothers to parent them and care for their needs.

To make some items, such as candles, the mothers worked together. Their candle molds made

*Figure 177: The combined Goulding family.
Public domain via FamilySearch.*

several candles at a time.

"First a combination of tallow and beeswax would be melted together. A twine would then be put in the center of each mold to serve as a wick and the melted tallow and beeswax poured around it. Then it was allowed to stand until the candles were 'set.' These candles looked very much like the candles we buy today but would last much longer."[434]

Elizabeth served as Relief Society President in Henrieville for many years.

Fanny ran the post office. An Escalante man got her to manage a branch of his store in Henrieville, where she sold groceries and dry goods; this helped the family finances. While running the

---

[434] Johnson, Zina E. Goulding. "History of the Life of Franny Pratten Goulding." *FamilySearch*, Intellectual Reserve, https://www.familysearch.org/photos/artifacts/23104532?cid=mem_copy. Accessed 23 November 2020.

store and the post office, Fanny also taught school and served in Church callings. She knew the scriptures extremely well; she had gone to Bible school when she was young, and could talk on any subject.

Figure 178: Daniel and Fanny with daughter Phoebe and granddaughter. Public domain via FamilySearch

Stories of Baby Clara

When it came to parenting, the mothers worked together.
When Clara was a baby, she found the bucket of lye tucked behind the big copper wash boiler. Lye cleaned the wash water, and the mothers left a little water in the can between uses to keep the lye soft. Lye was commonly used in those days to help with the laundry, but it is something to be careful with, as lye can cause chemical burns, which is probably why the mothers had hidden the bucket out of sight.
Baby Clara, however, found the bucket and began eating the lye.
The mothers heard her screaming and found her with lye burning her fingers, face, and mouth.
Fearing for her life or disfigurement, they went to work on her with oil and other home remedies. Soon, their darling child was well again.[435]

---

[435] "Lye episode." *FamilySearch*, Intellectual Reserve, https://www.familysearch.org/photos/artifacts/43244780?cid=mem_copy. Accessed 22 November 2020.

The mothers were skilled and talented in the complex homemaking and household management arts of their day, and they also had a bit of a wry sense of humor.

When Clara got a little older, she had a taste for meat, which her mother Fanny wouldn't always indulge. One day after Clara cried for meat, Fanny set her down from the table, so Clara sought out Aunt Elizabeth.

"And what's the matter with you?" Elizabeth asked.

"I wants a piece of meat," Clara said.

Elizabeth reached for something, and handed Clara a bone. "Here's a bone, eat that."

Clara began to cry again. "But I can't eat a bone!"[436]

Summers on the East Fork Ranch

Retta remembers the Goulding family as working hard but very happy.

For a period of fifteen years while the family lived in Henrieville, the family would divide forces to work at home and keep a dairy ranch and shingle mill about twenty-five miles up East Fork.

Elizabeth, daughters Rose (Rosanna, future grandmother of Reva) and Retty (Henrietta), and brother John would go up East Fork from May 1st to November 1st. There, they'd milk several cows and make cheese and butter of a fine quality. They'd churn butter in a ten-gallon barrel sometimes operated on water power but usually on elbow grease.

Their work from one season would fill a sixty-gallon barrel solidly with butter, with each days' churning separated with a thin layer of salt. The butter stayed sweet and fresh.

Zina remembers going with her father and aunty on the East Fork: "I helped with the work in the house, sometimes I bunched shingles" (in the shingle mill Daniel owned up East Fork). "Pa would pay us so much a bunch, then in the fall I helped cut corn and cane."[437]

Figure 179: Elizabeth and Henrietta "Retty." Public domain via FamilySearch.

---

[436] "The Meat Story." *FamilySearch*, Intellectual Reserve, https://www.familysearch.org/photos/artifacts/41535995?cid=mem_copy. Accessed 22 November 2020.

[437] Johnson.

Figure 180: Janet's ancestor Rosanna Susannah Goulding spent summers on the ranch with her mother. Public domain via FamilySearch.

While Elizabeth ran the ranch, Fanny raised the garden back at home. When vegetables came on, Fanny sent the first ones to Elizabeth. Fanny would dry all the fruit, corn, and string beans she could, and also raised wheat for flour and wheat corn and oats for the hogs. Fanny filled the cellar with potatoes and grew sugar cane for sorghum. The boys helped water and cultivate the crops.

Fanny also made yeast for everyone in Henrieville. Children would be sent to her home with a cup containing flour or salt to exchange for yeast. When there was no sugar at the house, Fanny used honey to sweeten her yeast. Zina remembers this as making the best of breads. Fanny mixed dough at night and made hot biscuits for breakfast. She held family prayer every night and morning, always praying for blessings she knew the family would need.

When November came, Elizabeth reserved plenty of butter and cheese for the family, then sold their surplus to a merchant in Springville who would buy the entire lot.

"We made fifty or sixty cheeses each season," recalled Henrietta Goulding Johnson. "The cheeses were kept on shelves around the room. They were turned and wiped regularly so that no moisture collected. Mother knew just how to do it so that we never had any moldy cheese or butter.

"In the fall Mother loaded her butter and cheese into the wagon and took it to sell to the merchants in Springville. The first man turned her down. He had had bad luck with a previous seller, so he sent her to another storekeeper. She invited the second man to test her cheese by cutting into the center of one and tasting it for sweetness and quality.

"He said, 'Do you guarantee all these cheeses and butter to be of this same quality?'

"Mother replied, 'If they are not you don't have to pay for them.'

So he took them. Thereafter Mother had a sale for all her dairy products."[438]

How the Gouldings Made Shoes and Clothes

The Gouldings traded food with Native Americans in exchange for buckskin, which they used to make gloves and other things.

Shoes were hard to come by.

---

[438] Unknown author. "Daniel Goulding and His Wives, Elizabeth Pratten Goulding and Fanny Pratten Goulding," p. 5. From Janet Clark's family history papers, copy in possession of the author.

So Daniel, who was an enterprising man, learned to make them himself for his family.

At some point, Fanny got a sewing machine. She'd cut tops for the shoes from leather Daniel had traded for or tanned himself. Daniel added heels and soles. They made shoes for their own family and many others during their first few years in Henrieville.

An excellent seamstress, Fanny could measure a person and make a pattern for any garment. She'd cut a pattern and create coats, suits, and dresses for people of all ages and sizes. This work helped her get enough cloth for her own large family's clothing needs.

Fanny's daughter Clara and Elizabeth's daughter Lucy were close in age and appearance. They were called "Fanny's twins," and Fanny always made their dresses alike.

The girls of the family usually received a new dress for special occasions: May Day, the Fourth of July, Christmas, and birthdays. The dresses were usually light calico, and Zina remembered them as the most beautiful dresses she had ever seen.

Elizabeth and Fanny and the daughters carded wool, spun, and knit stockings for everybody in the family. Retty carded and spun wool day after day throughout winter, working at the speed of a pound of yarn a day on the spinning wheel her father made for her. Some yarn was then colored for girls' stockings.

Figure 181: First Henrieville Relief Society.
Public domain via FamilySearch.

One of the first things Fanny's daughter Zina remembers is Elizabeth and Fanny making dye from tree and brush roots, such as juniper and wild sage rabbit.

"They would add salt for one color, alum for another, and mix alum and salt Peter to add for darker shades. For water softener they burnt root ashes. From osse roots they made the nicest shampoo for the hair."

The Story of the Gouldings' Candy Pull Parties

Daniel owned a molasses mill and raised sugar cane, which his children helped get ready for the mill by stripping leaves from the cane. Molasses was almost the only sweetening available locally. After it had been milled, it was stored in barrels and sold. Part of the last batch of the season was cooked longer, then the Gouldings invited the whole town to join them for a candy pull—a fun time for everybody.

Zina remembers of the candy pulls: "Sometimes when the corn was hauled and ready to shuck we would pull the cobs from the corn stalks, put it in piles and invite all the kids our size to a shucking bee. Pa would make a batch of sorghum candy and it would be ready to pull about 9 o'clock and by that time we would have the corn shucked and were ready for the party. We played games and had a lot of fun. We would have several shucking bees to get the corn taken care of before winter. Most of our candy was made with sorghum or honey. We had to make everything for our parties as there were no stores to run to for nick-naks, [sic] no high classed Society, just a bunch of fine people in the Henrieville Ward."[439]

The Story of Elijah's Exodus

The story of Elijah's exodus is an extraordinary story demonstrating the Goulding siblings' care for each other that their parents had raised them to demonstrate.

Daniel is recalled in one family story as a stern father who had a cat o' nine tails—a whip usually having nine knotted cords attached to a handle, used for flogging.

In 1871, when the family lived in the Battle Creek / Pleasant Grove area, Daniel and Elizabeth were away on business, leaving the children and home in the care of Fanny. While they were away, Elizabeth's son Elijah (then about 16 years old) left home over a disagreement with his father. This would have been just a year following the death of his older brother William; we can imagine that Elijah had had significant recent challenges and grief in addition to the hard work he'd been expected to perform over his young life.

Not until forty years later, after the passing of his father, would Elijah see his mother again.

Elijah kept track of his parents for some years after he left, until his parents were assigned to colonize a new area and moved to Garfield County, Utah. During his early years away from home, Elijah worked around mining camps in Arizona and Nevada.

Figure 182: Elijah Goulding. Public domain via FamilySearch.

---

[439] "History of Zina E. Pratten Goulding."

Later, he traveled the West, working as a cowboy driving large herds of cattle to shipping points. He separated from the Church and never again became an active member.

His first wife, Margaret Van Dorn, died of pneumonia after an early spring fire in Dubois, Idaho, led to the family's evacuation from their home into the cold weather. Elijah was left raising five children alone.

He continued freighting and homesteaded a new farm outside of town.

Elijah's second marriage, to English widow Harriet Bowers, was unhappy. During a quarrel, Elijah shot and killed a man in self-defense, and was shot in the hand.

Notice of his upcoming trial ran in the St. Anthony, Idaho, paper.

Elijah's half-brothers William "Billy" and Samuel Evan "Ev," who farmed near St. Anthony, saw Elijah's name in the paper, investigated, and found the half-brother who'd left home before they'd been born. He looked quite a bit like their late father, Daniel!

Billy and Ev contacted Joe (George Joseph Goulding), a full brother to Elijah who worked as a lawyer in Panguitch, Utah. Joe came to the trial, ably defended his brother, and Elijah was acquitted. Joe would have been 9 years old the last time he'd seen his brother.

Elijah took his children to Henrieville, Utah, where he was reunited with his mother and Aunt Fanny.

It had been forty years and eight days since he'd left his family of origin.

*Figure 183: Sons of Daniel Goulding.
Public domain via FamilySearch.*

Giving Service to the End

Until the end of their lives, Daniel, Elizabeth, and Fanny were devoted in serving their Church and community, and also remained devoted to each other.

Daniel served as a bishop for many years. Apostle Francis M. Lyman visited the ward when Daniel was 69, and Daniel asked to be released. Elder Lyman told him he would be released after five more years of service. Bishops in those days could serve for longer than they do today.

Five years from that day, Daniel passed away at the age of 74 on 1 August 1905.

Fanny was in good health for most of her life, and often told her children she hoped she wouldn't have to burden her family at the end of her life. She took sick on 1 March 1912, and passed away five days later on 6 March 1912.

An hour before she passed, Fanny told her sister, "Good-bye Elizabeth, we shall meet across the river."[440]

Elizabeth lived until 18 July 1918, outliving six of her twelve children, her husband, her parents, and all of her siblings. When Elizabeth's daughter Rosanna Susannah Goulding had passed away on 21 December 1890, a few days after giving birth, Rosanna's daughter Rosa and new baby Mary Ann had come to live with Elizabeth and Daniel until the girls' father, William Bryce, remarried the following year.

At the time of Elizabeth's passing, her granddaughter Rosa had grown up and had five children of her own. Rosa's eldest daughter, Reva Marie Simmons, was then ten.

Eleven years after Elizabeth's passing, Reva's daughter and Elizabeth's great-great-granddaughter Janet Lee Ruppe would be born.

---

[440] Johnson.

14. Johnston's Army

"In 1856 (Feb. 13th), our sixth child was born. We named him Hyrum Don Carlos. When he was seven months old, his Father was called on a mission to England. He started September 10th in Parley P. Pratt's company. I felt the responsibility of the care of five children but they were obedient and we got along nicely. I had an invitation to go on a pleasant trip up a canyon. While we were there (July 24, 1957) enjoying ourselves, those who were carrying the mail came bounding up with the news that we were to be massacred for they had the ropes to hang us or we were to be driven again from our homes. My husband with others of the elders was called home. The counsel was to leave our homes clean and ready for the match in case Johnston's army should attempt to enter the city. President Brigham Young said that the enemy should never again inhabit our labors or homes. A young brother came to me and said: "Would you like me to help you and drive the team?" He took right hold and helped me out."

—Mary Stevenson Clark

To celebrate the tenth anniversary of the pioneers' arrival in the Salt Lake Valley, 2,000 Saints gathered on 23 July 1857 at Silver Lake, near the head of Cottonwood Canyon, for a large celebration to be held the following day.

"Large bowries for good old-fashioned dancing had been erected; the bands kept the music continuously flowing through the air, from the two high peaks above floated the Stars and Stripes, the beloved flag of the USA. Everything seemed in readiness for a good time. . . . [W]hen up whirled a carriage and out stepped Porter Rockwell, who in a few hurried words told [Heber C. Kimball who stood near the carriages] of the approaching army."

The decision was made among the men to fight to the last man. Alfred Randall is reported in his daughter's writing to have stood with his leader in this decision.

Brigham Young addressed the people and announced that the army would find "the same desolation we, the Mormon pioneers, found ten years ago."[441]

General Daniel Wells encouraged the people to continue as if no army were on the way.

So the celebration picked up and continued until dawn.

After the party, the people went back to their homes, fearful of what might come next.

---

[441] Kofoed, p. 13.

Brigham Young put the city under Martial Law, and nobody was allowed in or out of the city without a permit. Instructions were given to take no blood but allow no one to pass.

The army was large and slow-moving, and the Saints had a lot of advance notice during which they could worry, plan, and take preventive action.

Johnston's army was accompanying a new governor for Utah appointed by the US President. President James Buchanan had appointed Alfred Cumming to replace Brigham Young as governor of the territory. The President sent armed forces with Cumming because based on reports Buchanan had heard from his officials in the territory, he expected violence in response to the change.

Lot Smith of Farmington, who served with Ezra T. Clark in the 40th Quorum of the 70 in 1855, was asked to harass the army to slow it down with the help of Porter Rockwell and a few others while President Young and other leaders worked to bring about a diplomatic solution and forestall violence.

Smith and his guerillas burned army supply wagons and forts on the plains, and caused other mischief that slowed the army's progress greatly.

By the time the army reached the eastern side of the Rocky Mountains, it was nearly winter season. They decided to winter near Fort Bridger's ruins starting in November of 1857. Lot Smith and his men had burned the wooden structures of Fort Bridger as well as Fort Supply (both then owned by the Church) so the army could not use them. The army, then numbering 2,400 soldiers and supply personnel, would not cross the mountains until spring, giving the Saints in the Wasatch Front an additional period of safety.[442]

Among the men guarding the entrance to the valley against Johnston's Army was Leven Simmons, who stood guard in Echo Canyon when Johnston's army was on their way to Utah.[443] Another who stood guard was Frank Randall, son of Alfred Randall and his first wife Emmerette. It was a cold winter, and Emmerette wanted her son to be warm. Goods were hard to come by in those days, but Emmerette was inventive. She pulled up the carpet on her stairs, and made a warm suit from it to keep her son cozy while he served as a guard.

When the army did enter the Salt Lake Valley the following summer, Emmerette, her husband, and his other families ended up relocating south briefly.

Karen Marie Hansen Christensen and her family also briefly relocated to American Fork, but would soon return to the Salt Lake area.[444]

Missionaries were recalled back home to the Utah Territory.

Ezra T. Clark, who had been serving in England, received word of the army's invasion, and hurried home to be with his family.

Due to the slow-moving nature of the army, Ezra and the other returning elders had time to cross the entire Atlantic on a ship called the *Empire*, from there take a train to Chicago, and then to cross the plains, all before the army reached the Salt Lake Valley.

Ezra's return home must have been nerve-wracking. Not only was he concerned about his family and fellow Saints back in Utah, but the ship's passage was marked by storms, and at one point the ship struck an iceberg. Despite this, the voyage was completed safely and took only one month—departing 19 February 1858 and arriving 19 March 1858—they had arrived thirteen days early.

---

[442] Hartley, p. 327.
[443] (Simmons Jr.)
[444] Everybodysmom. "Compiled History." *Maren Marie Christensen. FamilySearch.* https://www.familysearch.org/photos/artifacts/45192703?cid=mem_copy

When their train arrived in Chicago, Ezra and the other elders found that the government was actively re-enlisting soldiers for military service, offering men $30 a month and a bounty of "beauty and booty on their arrival in Utah."

Noble Pioneer, a biography of the life of Ezra T. Clark, reports: "Government agents claimed if a soldier killed a Mormon they would not prosecute him."[445]

These grim tidings may have hurried Ezra and his companions on their way.

They made good time.

"Ezra T. Clark and a company of 18 returning elders from Europe passed Col. Johnston's army in June near Echo Canyon. The company arrived in Provo on June 23, 1858. Ezra reunited with his family on June 25. Mary and his five children were living in a wagon box and tent south of Provo."[446]

Church leadership had decided that if the US Army came through by force, all in the valley would be burned. But they were open and receptive to finding another way to navigate the tense situation.

A diplomat friend arrived, who proved to be most helpful.

Thomas Kane was a lawyer from Pennsylvania, who never joined the Church but who was sympathetic to their cause. He had assisted the Saints in the past—helping them with public relations with the US government, and assisting in the creation of the Mormon Battalion.

Kanesville, Iowa, across the river from Winter Quarters in Nebraska, had been named in his honor to memorialize his help. In this town, John Lowe Butler and his family had lived for a few years before crossing the plains.

When Thomas Kane heard of the "misunderstanding" between the US government and the Latter-day Saint people, he offered to mediate. There was no time to lose, but the heavy winter was not conducive to racing an army across the continent, and so he took an alternate route. Leaving the East Coast, he took a boat south to Panama. From there he traveled by the recently completed railroad to the Pacific, where he traveled by boat to California and then finally made it to Utah via the southern branch of the California Trail, which would later become I-15. Arriving in Salt Lake, he convinced Brigham Young to agree to a peaceful transfer of power.

Kane then crossed the mountains to find the incoming governor, Alfred Cumming, and negotiated for him to come into the valley ahead of the troops to seek a peaceful resolution.

These efforts were successful. A peaceful transfer of power was achieved.[447]

Conflict Forestalled

In preparation for potential violence, the Saints had moved south with everything that they could. When the army came through, however, it marched peacefully.

So Salt Lake City did not burn.

---

[445] Clark, Antone. *Noble Pioneer*, p. 115.
[446] Clark, Antone, p. 128.
[447] Thomas Kane has been honored at the Utah State Capitol with a statue to thank him for his role in helping the early settlers.

Figure 184: Mary Stevenson Clark. Public domain via FamilySearch.

Johnston's army, as the group was called, marched south in an orderly way, and took up long-term camp at Cedar City.

The weary Saints were returned to their homes.

Mary Stevenson Clark wrote: "My husband found me at Payson. The word was to move back to our homes. There were not many things to move and we were soon in our homes again. Of course, no gardens, no crops raised. But we gathered greens and there were some onions in the ground. The Saints were blessed and prospered after the sacrifice. Our homes looked beautiful. The grass had grown all over the place, even up to the doors. We had left our homes the 5th of May 1858. I had never expected to see our home again but I felt all right. It had always been so. I felt blessed in returning. This was the 9th of July 1858, over lively roads.

"April 7th, 1859, we had a child born. We named him Edward Barrett. Although we raised no crops in 1858, we were prospered having our health and strength. The basement of the Salt Lake Temple had been filled with earth. It was taken out and the work resumed building the Temple. While my husband was on his mission, I felt that I wanted to put in a donation for the Temple. My little boys drove one of the best of our three cows out of the yard. I said: 'Send that.' My brother, Edward, made a note of it as one of the first donations. I wrote my husband about it and he replied that it was all right."

Aftermath of the Army

The Utah War ended in July of 1958. But Johnston's army stayed in Utah, and would remain there until about 1861, with the outbreak of the Civil War.

The arrival of Johnston's army brought challenges for the people, but also blessings.

The army men came with camp followers. Soon there were saloons and other establishments to cater to the vices of these men. The Saints had a religious-minded style of living, but some of those who were less devout, or who were not of the Church but lived in the region, began to patronize the establishments.

"Bishop [John Lowe] Butler disliked the evil influences that the army, with its 'camp followers,' brought into his county," reports Hartley in *My Best for the Kingdom* of the seventeen saloons that opened near Camp Floyd to accommodate the soldiers.

John Lowe Butler wrote in his autobiography, "They made quite a fine place over there but it was like going into hell at once. . . . I never troubled them myself, but there were several went from this ward, which I was very sorry to see, for when they were here they seemed to be pretty good Saints, but when they went over there they drank in the spirit that was there and they soon went by the board."[448]

On the plus side, the arrival of the army brought a tremendous economic boon to the Saints. Opportunities for labor came, and the army men patronized the businesses of the Saints, paying good money for goods and services in a territory where money had not previously been readily available to many. In addition, the army sold off many goods as surplus for very affordable prices to the Saints, in part because they needed the money to pay the enlisted men.

Harriet Bradford Simmons "was very fortunate to get some wagon covers to make all the boys some pants and shirts and had enough left for a dress for the youngest girl."[449]

When Johnston's army located in Cedar City, Alfred Randall and his son Charles Franklin (Frank) went with others to build housing for the troops. These carpenters built over 100 homes for the soldiers, providing Alfred, Frank, and the others with good employment.[450]

Eventually, many men in the army began to defect. A steady stream of soldiers left, and the army atrophied.

Sometimes a number of men would leave as a group, deserting their service, and then another group of men would be sent after them to find the deserters. Often men in the retrieval party would also desert.

Utah Territory was not a very attractive place for the members of the army to stay.

Though Johnston's army brought stress to the Saints and an initial fear of conflict, in the long run, their presence in the territory was probably a net positive.

In 1961, General Johnston and Utah Governor Alfred Cumming both quietly left. The remaining members of Johnston's Army were called in to support the Civil War, and Governor Cumming, a southerner, returned to be in his home region during that conflict.

---

[448] Hartley, p. 339.
[449] Huff.
[450] Kofoed, p. 12.

15. Western Settlement and Homesteading Stories

An Ancestral Connection Point: Archibald Gardner

Archibald Gardner was an early Utah leader with many ties to our family history. He served as a bishop for thirty-two years, was a prominent businessman, a polygamist who eventually had eleven wives and fifty-one children, and an active man with many friends. Among his friends and associates, he counted several of our ancestors, on both the Clark and Ruppe sides.

Archibald Gardner was a friend and fellow Canadian Saint to the David Park and Ann Brooks Park family. The Parks traveled from Canada to the United States in Archibald's company. David and Ann's daughter Sarah Jane would eventually marry Archibald, becoming the eighth wife in his large family.

Ebenezer Bryce was a brother-in-law to Archibald Gardner, and Archibald had Ebenezer help him build a sawmill in Mill Creek.[451]

For Archibald Gardner, Alfred Randall built a woolen mill on the Jordan River.[452]

Figure 185: Archibald Gardner. Public domain via FamilySearch.

Archibald also went into business with John Lowe Butler after the move south associated with the Utah War. Gardner and his family had temporarily settled in Spanish Fork. He noticed that John Lowe Butler was putting in a sawmill, and offered to go into business with him on it, but said the original location was in a poor place and it would have to be put in higher. Gardner had been a leading miller in Northern Utah, and Butler took him up on both the offer of going into business together, and the suggestion that the mill be relocated. They moved the mill and finished it. This sawmill helped the saints get shingles and do other sawing they previously would have traveled to another town for. Gardner went on to also put in a gristmill for Spanish Fork, which Butler called "one of the best gristmills in the territory." Gardner and Butler ran a successful mill together, sawing lumber and producing shingles, for the last few years of John Lowe Butler's life.[453]

---

[451] "Ebenezer Bryce," p. 2.
[452] Kofoed, p. 12.
[453] Hartley, p. 337.

After John Lowe Butler took ill, his son Kenion Taylor Butler worked with Archibald on the mill.[454]

Archibald later moved to Star Valley, Wyoming, where Ezra T. Clark's son Hyrum Don Carlos Clark would become a major ranch owner. And one of Archibald's granddaughters would marry one of Hyrum's grandsons—Dean and Yvonne Clark.[455]

Early Settler Days in Utah

After the peaceful resolution of the conflict, the Saints were able to settle in more comfortably and begin to establish their families and homes in earnest.

Ezra's daughter Laura wrote of growing up as a settler in Farmington during the early days of Utah:

"I wore short dresses and long braids. Then the time came when I had long dresses down to my ankles and my hair was pinned up. I was about fifteen years old and Mother hated to put me in long dresses and see me grow up. But the dresses were beautiful with ruffles and bows."

Laura and her siblings were playful, and liked to slide down the banister at home because it was the easiest way to get downstairs. But the Clark children were also industrious. They helped their mothers make candles, churn butter, bake bread, fill kerosene lamps, shine up the lamp chimneys, and sew. Laura's mother, an accomplished seamstress, taught her embroidery and how to sew without making the stitches show.

"I remember an incident when I was very small, with our kerosene lamp," she wrote. "Mother and Father had gone out and I was left home with Eugene and Nathan. We were reading and studying our books by lamplight. All at once the lamp started to sputter and the flames started up out of the chimney. We could see it would explode. So Eugene picked it up and threw it out into the yard."

Slang was not allowed in the family's home, and they didn't work on Sunday. Their mother Susan would cook dinner on Saturday and save the dishes for Monday.

Laura looked forward to a white dress on May Day, and would go "may-walking" through Farmington's meadows, which would be covered with beautiful deep pink flowers.

"Also, the first thing each morning I would be outside climbing a tree and eating apples. I always took a pocketful to school."[456]

---

[454] Personal family history papers of Janet R. Clark, in possession of the author.
[455] Clark, A. Charles, personal note.
[456] Clark, Laura.

Joseph and Emma Christensen

In Farmington, where the Clark family was prominent, the Christensen family lived and were acquainted with the Clarks.

Figure 186: Emma Christensen. Public domain via FamilySearch.

Emma Christensen was 15 years old when she arrived in Utah in 1879. Two of her sisters and one of her brothers had already arrived ahead of her. The Christensen family was sending individual members over and working to bring the whole family over.

Not being a native English speaker, Emma tried her best to do her job as a housekeeper, but due to the language barrier, she frequently disappointed her employer, and was given scoldings and abuse. It broke her heart to be unable to master the language well enough to keep a position.

Friends helped her get a job in the home of Horace Eldridge in Woods Cross, where she learned English—though she always spoke it brokenly. Her next employer was a man who had left the Church and expressed dislike for Emma's religion.

Figure 187: Trein Bendtsen Christensen, Emma's mother. Public domain via FamilySearch.

By then her family had immigrated and moved to Farmington.

One day, a letter written in Danish arrived in Farmington addressed to "Christensens." It was delivered to a man named Mads Christensen. He could not read the Danish letter, so he took it to Emma's parents, who had just arrived from Denmark.

Figure 188: Joseph Mads Christensen. Public domain via FamilySearch.

Jens read the letter and realized it was meant for him. It was from his daughter, who had been sick with diphtheria in Salt Lake but was now well.

In spring, Emma and her sister had a three-day holiday from work. They started walking from Salt Lake City to Farmington, bringing clothing and gifts for their family.

James J. Steed stopped and offered them a ride in his hayrack. He took them as far as Mads Christensen's house, where Emma met his son, Joseph Mads, who would be her future husband.

Joseph described Emma as having beautifully styled hair, and as wearing a neatly pressed dress with a full skirt, which was ornamented with pleats and scallops.

After finishing his chores, Joseph took Emma and her sister to their parents' home, giving them a ride in his lumber wagon.

Emma found a new place to work in Farmington, and she and Joseph were able to see each other frequently.

They were very prayerful about their courtship, and they felt that they were right for each other. They married on 24 May 1883 in the Salt Lake City Endowment House, and made their first home in Farmington, where Joseph was helping to build a steamboat. Farmington is right next to the Great Salt Lake.

When Joseph was called on a mission to St. Johns, Arizona, pregnant Emma went to live in Kanesville, Utah, with her parents for a time. Sadly, their first child, Clara Amelia, lived only a few short hours.

After Joseph finished building a home for them in Arizona, he returned for his wife. The couple departed by train on 7 April 1885 for Arizona. She found that their new home was twelve feet by sixteen feet. It had one large room with two windows, and an eastward-facing door.

*Figure 189: Joseph Mads and Emma Christensen family.
Public domain via FamilySearch.*

Their second child was a stillborn son, but Emma and Joseph were very happy when in 1887, their daughter Selma was born healthy, coming to bless their home.

The family relocated to Salt Lake City after Joseph got sick with malaria fever and was advised to move to another climate. In Salt Lake City, Pearl was born in 1889. After Joseph's health improved, the family returned to Arizona, where on 12 March 1892 Violet Catherine was born.

Joseph was released from his mission on 24 January 1897, and he took his family to Farmington, where he fixed up part of his mother's home for his family to live in.

Emma had two more sons who died soon after birth: Joseph Mads born on 4 June 1894 and dying the same day, and James Moroni, born 27 May 1895, and dying ten days later.

Emma passed away soon after the birth of her last son, dying on 6 June 1895 at the age of 31. She died of what was known as "childbirth fever," and was buried in Farmington.

The three daughters were raised by their father and his unmarried sister, Mary.

Daughter Pearl would later write, "We loved and respected her. We felt thankful to be blessed with such a wonderful aunt to care for us. But, as we grew older, how much we would have liked to have known our own dear mother. . . . We will always honor her name as mother."[457]

*Figure 190: Joseph Mads Christensen, June 1916.
Public domain via FamilySearch.*

---

[457] Sederberg, Brenda Clark. "Emma Christensen Christensen," *Violet Catherine Clark*, p. 37.

Joseph after Emma

Alan Clark recalled as a young boy going with his father, Walter, and his brother Wayne to visit his grandfather Joseph Mads Christensen in Farmington from time to time.

"He had a garden and raised some livestock but earned his living by doing carpentry work. A table he made by inlaying pieces of wood—especially cherry—was a masterpiece.... I recall being out in the corral with him and his animals. He was proud of his cows and horses and liked to have them appear well. His funeral in Farmington was the first one I remember attending."[458]

Figure 191: Joseph Mads Christensen on steps of South Davis ward hall, circa 1830.
Public domain via FamilySearch.

---

[458] Clark, Alan C. *Line Upon Line*, p. 10.

Ancestors throughout the West

The following collection of Early American West ancestral short stories and vignettes does not fit neatly into the earlier themes established in this book, but are included below for your information and enjoyment.

The Goulding Family is Helped by Indians on the Way from California

As the pioneers settled into Utah, streaming across the country to get to Zion, not everybody arrived via the routes on the Great Plains. There were others who crossed the western desert from California.

The Goulding family came to Zion in one of these caravans.

When the Goulding family first arrived in the United States from England via Australia, they were extremely poor. They lived in California for a time, working and saving up. Eventually they earned enough from working various places to move on, heading across the desert toward Utah.

They ran into adventure along the way.

After they ran out of water, and their stock was beginning to suffer, they realized a group of Indians was following them.

The Goulding group set the women to driving the teams, while the men hid under the canvases, rifles ready.

But the Indians motioned for the pioneers to follow them.

Deciding to take a chance, the Goulding group followed the Indians, who led them to much-needed water.

In 1872, the family moved to American Fork. From there, they later moved on to Pleasant Grove. In 1878, they moved to New Clifton. But a severe drought cost the family their fruit trees.

They moved again, to Henrieville. Here, Daniel became the first bishop, and Elizabeth the first Relief Society President. Fanny served as the first school teacher and postmistress.[459]

Karen Marie Hansen Christensen and the St. George Temple

The completion of the St. George Temple was a great triumph for the Saints. Ebenezer Bryce had been among the men who helped build it. Ebenezer, a carpenter who served many service missions for the Church, helped saw lumber for the temple.

After a construction period of about five and a half years, the dedication of the St. George Temple on 6 April 1877 was presided over by Brigham Young, with Ezra T. Clark among those attending as part

---

[459] Monson, Harold. "Daniel Goulding - Stalwart Mormon Pioneer." *FamilySearch*, Intellectual Reserve, 4 November 2014, https://www.familysearch.org/tree/person/memories/KWN2-ZKM. Accessed 23 September 2020.

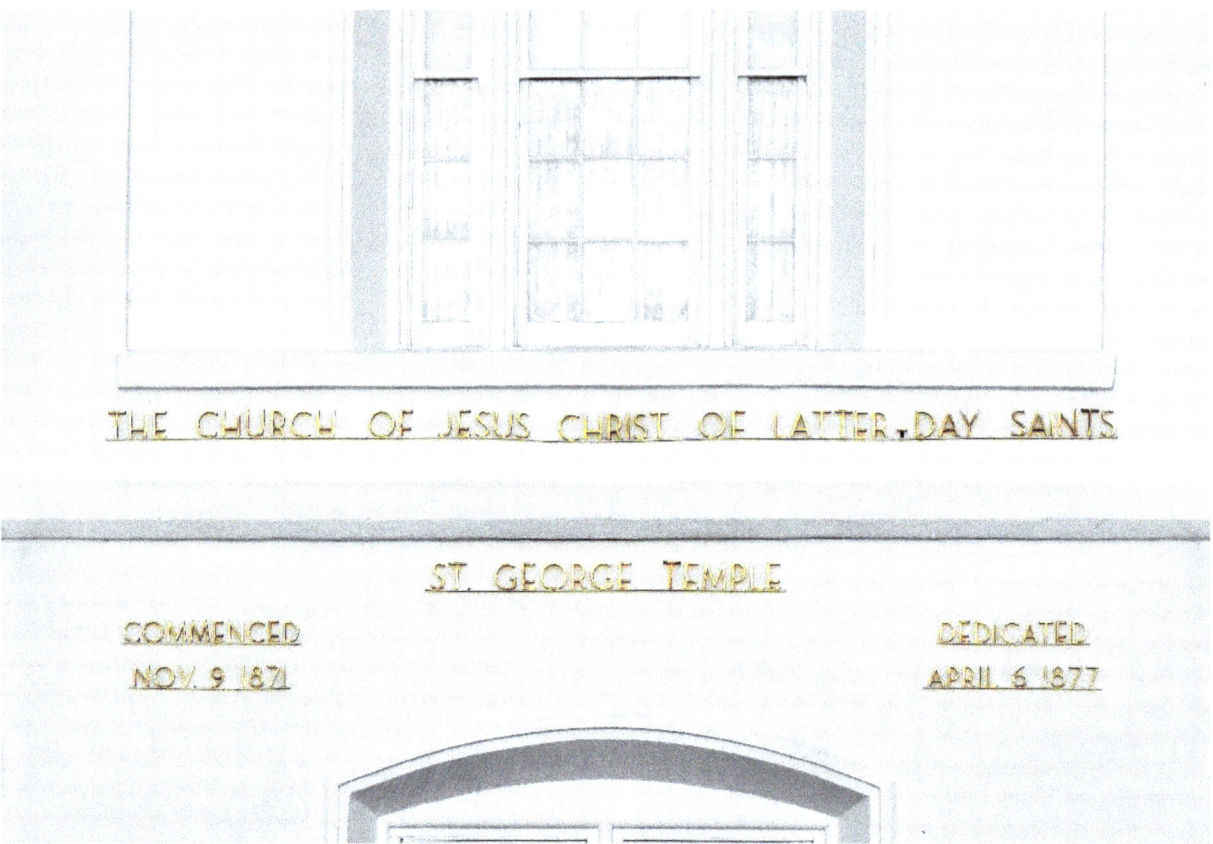

*Figure 192: St. George Temple.
Image © eric1513/Depositphotos*

of the president's party. This temple was the first one dedicated in Utah. It had been nearly thirty years since the Nauvoo Temple dedication, so the Saints had been looking forward to the temple's completion with great anticipation.

Karen Marie Hansen Christensen had waited years for the St. George Temple to be finished, anxious to do temple work for her ancestors. She and her son-in-law, Jens Jensen, had been among those called to settle Dixie country in Southern Utah, and Karen would live in Washington, Utah, for over twenty years. As soon as the temple was dedicated, Karen at age 80 was baptized for all relatives she had record of.

Once that work was complete, she was ready to go live with her daughter in Salina.

In 1875, Karen's son Andres had joined the Church and came to Utah, following his mother and a few of his siblings. He settled in Salina, near his sister and mother. This brought Karen great pleasure.

A granddaughter who visited Karen in 1884 in Salina later wrote: "She was a dear sweet woman; one could not help but love her. . . . Her husband never came to Utah. He died in 1860 [in Denmark], many years before she did. As she spoke of him, the tears rolled down her cheeks. She said, 'When I die, I want my husband, he is the father of my children and I know he will accept the gospel, for he was a good man.'"[460]

---

[460] Miller, Annie Christensen. "Karen Marie Hansen Life Sketch." *Family Search*, Intellectual Reserve, https://www.familysearch.org/tree/person/memories/L5D2-KFW. Accessed 2 October 2020.

Karen had seen many changes during her lifetime, making a massive transition to come to her new country. In America, Karen had learned to cook with new foods, adapted to new customs, and even mastered a new language. An eager learner, once Karen mastered English, she preferred it to speaking Danish.

In Utah, Karen lived in the home of her daughter Maren and Maren's husband Jens Jensen, who had been the Elder Jensen who had baptized Maren back in Denmark. Though Karen missed her husband and the father of her children, she enjoyed her family in Utah, and found great meaning in her rich spiritual life.

David Park and Walla Walla Jesus

Over the course of the history of the Church, a number of splinter groups and off-shoots have spun off over time.

The Clark/Ruppe ancestry does not have any direct ancestors who ended up with these groups over the long run.

But one man came close.

This is the story of David Park and the Walla Walla Jesus.

David and Ann Park, after arriving from their pioneer trek to Utah, moved on to settle in Nevada.

At some point, however, David became favorably impressed by the Kingdom of Heaven religion founded by former members of the Morrisites, a Latter-day Saint splinter group.

Figure 193: David Park. Public domain, via FamilySearch.

The Morrisites had become disillusioned with Church leadership following the Mountain Meadow Massacre, but then their own group began to atrophy when prophecies their leader made predicting a date for the Second Coming of Christ failed to materialize after multiple attempts.

Following the Morrisite War, in which the Morrisites were confronted with military force, William W. Davies and other disillusioned Morrisites relocated to Montana. While there, William said he received a revelation to relocate to Walla Walla, Washington, and there build the Kingdom of Heaven. The primary area where he differed from mainstream Church doctrine was in his teachings on reincarnation, specifically his teaching that he himself was the reincarnation of the Archangel Michael, and that his soon-to-be-born son would be the reincarnation of Christ—and therefore the Second Coming of Christ. William thus neatly sidestepped the issue the Morrisites had run into of Christ failing to show up when they looked for him.

Figure 194: William W. Davies and his two sons. Arthur was the Walla Walla Jesus. Public domain. F. Gilbert, 1882 via "William Davies and the Walla Walla Jesus History Website." https://ww2020.net/history-websites/william-davies-and-the-walla-walla-jesus/

The news of this reincarnated Christ child had a quickening effect on missionary work for the sect. Interest grew and new members gathered to be near the Walla Walla Jesus.[461]

David Park himself grew interested in the Kingdom of God sect, and spent a year in Washington among these people. After he returned to his family, he later visited the group two additional times.

---

[461] Hoehn, Jack. "Walla Walla Jesus." *AdventistToday.org*. https://atoday.org/the-walla-walla-jesus/

*Figure 195: The Davies Community's Main Compound.
Public domain via William Davies and the Walla Walla Jesus History Website.*

The Kingdom of Heaven group began to erode in 1880 when the Walla Walla Jesus and his brother (who according to their father was the reincarnation of God the Father) took sick of diphtheria and died.[462]

"After [David returned from his last visit to the Kingdom of God sect] he brooded a great deal over his religion until his health failed. He was taken into his son Joseph Park's home and given every care possible."[463]

David Park passed away in Mottsville, Nevada, on 22 July 1884.

His death was a great shock to his wife, Ann, who went to live with one of her sons until her own death five years later.[464]

Today, a roadside sign in Walla Walla, Washington, tells of W.W. Davies and the Walla Walla Jesus.

*Figure 196: David Park.
Public domain via FamilySearch.*

Kenion Taylor Butler and Olive Artemeshy Durfey Butler: Foster Parents and Early Settlers of Spanish Fork

On 5 December 1854, Kenion Taylor Butler (who went by "Taylor") wed Olive Artemeshy Durfey in Spanish Fork, Utah. The following year, the Endowment House opened in Salt Lake City,

---

[462] "William W. Davies." *Wikipedia*. https://en.wikipedia.org/wiki/William_W._Davies
[463] Egbert, Martin W. "Parks, David and Ann Brooks" *FamilySearch*. https://www.familysearch.org/photos/artifacts/3522451?cid=mem_copy
[464] "Ann Brooks Park." *FamilySearch*. https://www.familysearch.org/photos/artifacts/8737851?cid=mem_copy

where temple marriages could be performed. Kenion and Olive were sealed and received their endowments in 1858.

In a layout map of Fort St. Luke, where the early Spanish Fork settlers wintered to keep safe from the Indians one winter, the John Lowe Butler family had one room for themselves, next door to the Kenion Taylor Butler family, which had another room for themselves.[465]

Kenion and Olive eventually had three girls and six boys, plus a foster daughter.

While working on the railroad not far from Cheyenne, Wyoming, Mr. John Hogan asked that the Butlers care for his daughter, Myrtle Hogan, who had a birthdate of 5 November 1877. When the railroad camp moved, John asked the Butler family to keep her. He did return to see Myrtle when she was in her midtwenties.

Kenion served as an officer in Utah's 1866 Blackhawk War. He also served a few missions: one in September 1852, and a later mission to the Southern States in 1882, at the age of 51. On this second mission, Kenion developed brain fever. He returned home 16 October 1883. Taylor died at age 54 on 1 May 1886 in Spanish Fork, Utah. Olive died at age 65 on 6 May 1900 in Salem, Utah.[466]

Figure 197: Kenion Taylor Butler. Public domain via FamilySearch.

Figure 198: Olive Durfey Butler. Public domain via FamilySearch.

---

[465] Hartley, p. 271.
[466] "Biography of Kenion Taylor Butler." *FamilySearch*, https://www.familysearch.org/photos/artifacts/42968957?cid=mem_copy

Figure 199: Kenion Taylor Butler and siblings as adults. Public domain via FamilySearch.

The Bryce Family

Ebenezer Bryce and Mary Ann Park

When young Ebenezer Bryce arrived in Utah as part of a pioneer company, he made his home with George A. and Bathsheba Smith. Sister Smith would always call Ebenezer "my boy."

Working on the Smith farm, Ebenezer met Mary Ann Park, who was helping at the house with the cooking.

On 16 April 1854, Ebenezer and Mary Ann were married at the Smith home, in a ceremony presided over by George A. Smith. Mary Ann, who was an excellent seamstress, sewed her own wedding dress.

The Smith family gave the young couple a wedding gift of a pair of silver spoons—items then unavailable for purchase in the Utah area.[467]

The Bryce family would move around a lot during their marriage, and eventually grew to include twelve children.

Ebenezer seems to have had a large personality—or at least he was memorable enough that several things were named in his honor.

Figure 200: Ebenezer Bryce and Mary Ann Park Bryce. Public domain via FamilySearch.

Ebenezer Bryce and the Upside-Down Ship Church

Ebenezer Bryce was a carpenter by trade. With his previous experience as a shipbuilder, he was taken aback when the Church asked him to build a chapel in Pine Valley Utah in 1875.

The story goes that he worked with what he knew: He constructed the chapel's structure as if it were an upside-down boat.

If you go upstairs in the church, you can see the beams shaped like the bottom of a ship, upside-down.

Ebenezer Bryce and the Canyon

When the Bryce family moved to Paria Creek, near today's town of Tropic, Utah, Ebenezer settled his family at the mouth of a canyon, which had towering colored walls. Ebenezer dug ditches to bring water from the Paria Creek for irrigation, and built a road to obtain timber for a house, fences, and firewood.

People from Cannonville and from Paria used the road to get wood for themselves, as well, and called the canyon near Ebenezer's home Bryce Canyon.

---

[467] Bryce, Betty Jane. "Ebenezer Bryce," p. 2. *FamilySearch*, https://www.familysearch.org/photos/artifacts/123680918?cid=mem_copy

Figure 201: Janet Clark at Bryce Canyon. Ebenezer Bryce's mother's name was also Janet. Image used with permission.

Ebenezer found the main amphitheater of the canyon after heading off in search of a missing cow. His comment on the canyon was, "It's a hell of a place to lose a cow."

For many years, the Bryce family cabin was preserved as a museum not far from Bryce Canyon itself.[468]

Bryce Canyon, in Garfield County, Utah, became the twelfth US National Park in 1928. These days, the park is visited by 1.5 million people a year.

---

[468] "Bryce's Canyon." https://www.brycecanyoncountry.com/blog/post/bryces-canyon/

Figure 202: Bryce family cabin south of Tropic, Utah. Public domain via FamilySearch.

Ebenezer Bryce and Bryce, Arizona

After Ebenezer Bryce's wife Mary Ann Park Bryce got sick, he was advised to move to a warmer climate for her health. The family relocated to Arizona. After moving around a bit, in 1884 he moved his family to an area later called Bryce. Other families moved in nearby, and on 15 March 1890, Church leaders called a meeting at the Bryce home. They organized a ward and named the town Bryce.[469] Many years later, Bryce 3D rendering software was also named in his honor.[470]

---

[469] Bryce, Betty Jane. "Ebenezer Bryce," p. 4. *FamilySearch*, https://www.familysearch.org/photos/artifacts/123680918?cid=mem_copy

[470] "Ebenezer Bryce." https://www.familysearch.org/tree/person/details/KWJ8-YBB

*Figure 203: Bryce Canyon.
Photo © sugarek/Depositphotos*

William Henry Bryce, Rosanna Goulding, and Malinda "Aunt Lindy" Riggs

William Henry Bryce married Rosanna Susannah Goulding on 16 December 1885 in the St. George Temple. They had met when their families lived near each other in the Southern Utah area

At first the young couple lived in Bryce, Arizona, near William's family. But eventually they moved to Henrieville, Utah, near Rosanna's family. There, William had a herd of cattle.

The couple had four children, two boys and two girls. The two sons did not survive infancy, but the daughters grew up to have families of their own.

Rosa Jane "Janey" was born 14 October 1887. Her sister Mary Ann was born 19 December 1890 in Henrieville.

Rosanna died two days following the birth of Mary Ann. She was just 29 years old.

William took a second wife, Malinda Isabel Riggs, on 28 October 1891. They wed in the Manti Temple.

Living near an Indian Reservation, William would visit the Native people often. He learned their language and would serve as their doctor if any of them got sick.

Figure 204: Rosanna Susannah Goulding. Public domain via FamilySearch.

In October 1900, William and a friend made a plan to move their cattle to Canada. Upon reaching Price, Utah, however, they were tired of traveling. So they settled there instead.

William and Malinda had seven children together, and Malinda was the mother who raised Rosa and Mary Ann.

Malinda's two youngest sons were close enough in age to Rosa's eldest daughter, Reva, that Reva thought of these boys as being like older brothers to her.[471]

William died at the age of 70 on 1 October 1930 in Roosevelt, Utah. Malinda died at the age of 68 on 11 September 1942 in Roosevelt, Utah.[472]

Figure 205: William "Bill" Bryce and Malinda "Lindy" Riggs Bryce. Public domain via FamilySearch.

---

[471] Ruppe, Reva. *Side by Side.*
[472] "Biography of William Henry Bryce." *FamilySearch,* https://www.familysearch.org/photos/artifacts/105577417?cid=mem_copy

16. Organization of the Primary

"Our children are our jewels. We have counted well the cost. May the angels ever guard them, and not one be lost." —Aurelia S. Rogers' motto[473]

The Church organization of the Primary originated in Farmington. Bishop John W. Hess, who had seven wives and sixty-three children,[474] called a meeting of the mothers of the ward, and discussed the problem of how to find something to offer the younger members of the community. He urged the mothers to look after the children.

However, this was not enough for Sister Aurelia Spencer Rogers, a beloved figure in the community. "A fire seemed to burn within me," she later recalled. "I knew something had to be done to help these children."[475]

So she called a meeting at her home. The origins of the Primary would come to involve members of both the Clark and the Christensen families.

Mary Stevenson Clark and Ezra's third wife Nancy[476] were both present in a small group at Aurelia Spencer Rogers' home when Sister Rogers spoke with Eliza R. Snow "about the many children in Farmington who were allowed out late and were getting the name 'hoodlums.'

"'What will our little girls do for good husbands, if this sort of thing continues?' Sister Rogers asked Eliza R Snow.

"Sister Eliza said, 'I will speak to the First Presidency about this.'"

Figure 206: Eliza R. Snow. Public domain via Wikicommons.

---

[473] Hess, p. 297.
[474] Hess, Margaret. *My Farmington*, p. 83.
[475] Hess, Margaret. *My Farmington*, p. 130.
[476] Rogers, Aurelia S. *Life Sketches*, p. 207.

Figure 208: Mary Stevenson Clark. Public domain via FamilySearch.

President John Taylor presided over the Church at that time. Sister Eliza later wrote Farmington's Bishop Hess that it would be okay to organize something to keep the boys out of trouble.

Later, she agreed with Sister Rogers' follow-up request to include the girls also, writing:

"I feel sure that the inspiration of our Heavenly Father is directing you, and that a very important movement is being inaugurated for the future of Zion."

Sister Snow suggested the organization name of "Primary"—as it means first and original.

Sister Rogers and her counselors visited the ward and collected names of children ages 6 to 14 and asked if parents were willing to let them attend meetings. They gathered names of 112 girls and 112 boys, all of whom are listed in Sister Rogers' book.

"The bishopric also appointed a priesthood brother, **Mads Christensen**, to assist in the new movement. He was an ideal choice: a selfless man who had made a comfortable means as a carpenter in Denmark. Upon being converted to

Figure 207: The colorful sunset at the Great Salt Lake. Image 29563519 © gary718/Depositphotos.

the church in his native land, he had opened his purse to less fortunate saints emigrating to Utah. Then, with little left for himself, he pushed a handcart across the plains to Zion. Mads Christensen built bookcases and a table for the Farmington Primary."[477]

The first meeting was 25 August 1878, "to explain things to the Primary children."

After this, all meetings were held Saturdays at 2:00 p.m., in the meetinghouse built in 1862.[478] The Primary also became something of a lost-and-found bureau, as Sister Rogers taught her boys and girls always to seek the owner of all lost articles.

Amasa Lyman Clark as a child is depicted in the mural on the formation of the Primary, which is housed in the rock chapel in Farmington. So is **Mads Christensen**, who is shown as an old man with a beard, seated on the stand.

"In the spring they rented a lot and with Brother Mads Christensen in the lead would plant beans and corn. Some of the husbands and sons would plow the land in readiness for planting. Beans were stored in case of famine and corn was popped and made into popcorn for the children's party."[479]

Figure 209: Mads Christensen. Public domain via FamilySearch.

Figure 210: Ezra T. Clark. Public domain via FamilySearch.

"As children we would glean wheat and beans for the Primary and Relief Society. These Church organizations would store away such goods against a future day of need."[480]

As a small girl, Annie Clark Tanner was one of the original members of the Primary. Later, while a student at the University of Utah, Annie served as one of the counselors to Sister Rogers.[481]

Ezra T. Clark was among brethren present at a gathering honoring Amelia Rogers when she was ill, and assisted in administering to her.[482]

---

[477] Hess, p. 130.
[478] Hess, Margaret. *My Farmington*, pp. 292–293.
[479] Hess, p. 295.
[480] Tanner, Annie Clark. *Mormon Mother*, p. 12.
[481] Ibid., p. 39.
[482] Hess, p. 296.

Figure 211: The Salt Lake Railroad.
©Marzolino/Depositphotos|13297464

Figure 212: Aurelia S. Rogers, creator of the original Latter-day Saint Primary organization, beloved figure in Farmington, and friend of the Clarks and Mads Christensen.
Public domain, found in Life Sketches, by Aurelia S. Rogers.

Organization of the Primary

17. Missions

Here is a list of the missions we have on record for Alan and Janet's ancestry.

There have been multiple categories of missions the family has served over the years: most typically proselytizing missions, service missions, and colonizing missions, with a few exceptions.

Figure 213: Salt Lake City.
Photo © marzolino/Depositphotos

Six Generations Back from Janet

John Goulding, Sr.

John Goulding, Sr. was baptized by Parley P. Pratt in 1840 in England. John Sr. did not serve a mission, but he did provide a home to his grandson Daniel Goulding after Daniel's baptism in 1845 at the age of 14. Daniel's parents were not supportive of his religious choices. Daniel thrived living with his grandparents and within a few years became the branch leader while still a teenager. From there Daniel went on to preside over congregations in Australia and America.[483]

Five Generations Back from Janet

John Lowe Butler[484]

Figure 214: Purported image of John Lowe Butler. Public domain via FamilySearch.

John served a mission to Illinois, in 1839. While the Saints were centered in Illinois, John was called to be a Seventy, which was then a missionary calling. On June 1 he received a license to preach, and he served for about seven months in **Illinois**, with great enthusiasm though no converts.[485]

John served two missions among the **Sioux Native American Tribes**, in 1840 and 1840–1841. During the first one, he and James Emmett were called to serve, and Caroline and the children came along. For the second one, Caroline and the children stayed behind, but James Emmett was again John's companion.[486]

In 1843, John was called to the **Southern States Mission** and later that year there is also a record on the Church website of John being called to the **Northern States Mission**. The primary success of this mission was his retrieval of Charity Skeen, Caroline's sister. Charity had gained a testimony of the Church when James Emmett and his companion had originally preached in the South and converted John and Caroline. Charity asked to return to Nauvoo with John, and John successfully took her with him, despite the fierce opposition of Charity's brothers and their friends.[487]

Brigham Young called John on a unique mission: to retrieve the Emmett Expedition after John's friend James Emmett left Nauvoo with a body of Saints following the death of Joseph Smith (John was successful in retrieving the group and reuniting them with the Saints, and also used quick thinking and diplomacy to prevent Emmett's group from being killed by Native Americans).[488]

---

[483] Monson.
[484] Purported image of John Lowe Butler found in Tueller, Margaret. *Your Simmons Lybbert Family Tree*. FamilySearch, 2016. *FamilySearch*, https://www.familysearch.org/photos/artifacts/24310561?cid=mem_copy. Accessed 5 October 2020.
[485] Hartley, p. 96.
[486] "John Lowe Butler."
[487] Hartley, pp. 116–118.
[488] Hartley, pp. 135–208.

Caroline Farozine Skeen Butler

Caroline and her children accompanied John on his first **mission to the Sioux** in 1840.[489]

Caroline and her children also accompanied John on the mission to retrieve the Emmett Expedition.

Charity Skeen Butler

Charity, sister of Caroline and second wife of John, accompanied the family on the mission to retrieve the Emmett Expedition. Despite being deaf and mute, Charity was intelligent and able to communicate via a form of sign language, and she contributed to the wellbeing of the family and the group.

Figure 215: Caroline Farozine Skeen. Public domain via FamilySearch.

Royal Durfey & Lydia Abell Durfey

Called on a **colonization** mission, Royal and Lydia were called to help settle the area of Palmyra, Utah (near **Spanish Fork**). The family farmed in this area.[490]

Four Generations Back from Alan

Timothy Baldwin Clark

Timothy Baldwin Clark joined the Church in May of 1835, being converted by the efforts of his daughter Laura Clark Phelps and her husband Morris Phelps. Timothy did not serve a mission, but he did move his family to live with the body of Saints, and several of his children were baptized, including Ezra T. Clark, ancestor of Alan.

Figure 216: Royal Durfey and Lydia Abell. Public domain via FamilySearch.

Elizabeth Stevens Stevenson

Elizabeth Stevens joined the Church before 1833. She did not serve a mission, but she did raise her younger children in the gospel, including Mary Stevenson, who would be Alan's ancestor. She and four of her children went west over the Mormon Trail to Utah.

---

[489] Hartley, pp. 98–103.
[490] McQuivey, Dorene Davis. "Royal Durfey 1811 - 1879 Family records and Salem Springs Compiled by Dorene Davis McQuivey GG Granddaughter." *FamilySearch*, Intellectual Reserve, 4 April 2014, https://www.familysearch.org/photos/artifacts/6295317?cid=mem_copy. Accessed 6 November 2020.

Missions

Four Generations Back from Janet

Leven Simmons
A record wasn't available of Leven serving a mission.

Kenion Taylor Butler
Kenion Taylor (who went by "Taylor") served as assistant captain on a rescue mission to retrieve the Martin and Willie handcart companies.[491]

Taylor served a mission to the Southern States September 1882–October 1883 at the age of 51. He was set apart by Wm. W. Taylor.[492]

Figure 217: Kenion Taylor Butler. Public domain via FamilySearch.

Ebenezer Bryce
Ebenezer served what today may be considered work missions or service missions, as he was regularly called by the Church.

"He was constantly being called by the church to build sawmills. Some of these were to Mill Creek, then to Cottonwood in the Salt Lake Valley. The couple were also sent to help in the construction of the St. George Temple.

"When he was only twenty-nine, Ebenezer was called by the church Authorities to go to St. George to help build up that part of the country. Ebenezer had no family in the West and now Mary

Figure 218: Ebenezer Bryce. Public domain via FamilySearch.

---

[491] Hartley, pp. 293–296.
[492] The Church of Jesus Christ of Latter-day Saints. "Kenion Taylor Butler." *Church History*, Intellectual Reserve, https://history.churchofjesuschrist.org/chd/individual/kenion-taylor-butler-1831?lang=eng&timelineTabs=allTabs. Accessed 9 November 2020.

Figure 219: St. George Temple.
© *eric1513/Depositphotos*

Ann was away from her family. There were forty days of rain that winter while they lived in a covered wagon with five small children.

"Ebenezer was again called by Church Authorities to help construct a sawmill on the Graham mountains."[493]

In 1898, Ebenezer was called as a widower on a **genealogy mission to the Eastern States**.[494]

Apparently in his era a widowed man could serve on his own, as Ebenezer did not remarry after the death of Mary Ann.

---

[493] "Information on Mary Ann Park Bryce." *FamilySearch*, Intellectual Reserve, https://www.familysearch.org/photos/artifacts/1892384?cid=mem_copy. Accessed 6 November 2020.
[494] The Church of Jesus Christ of Latter-day Saints. "Ebenezer Bryce." *Church History*, Intellectual Reserve, https://history.churchofjesuschrist.org/chd/individual/ebenezer-bryce-1830?lang=eng&timelineTabs=allTabs. Accessed 9 November 2020.

Mary Ann Park Bryce

Mary Ann and the children of the family accompanied Ebenezer on his callings to help build settlements, sawmills, a church, and St. George.[495]

Mary Ann raised her children and ran the household while her husband Ebenezer attended to his mission service duties of carpentry.

Daniel Goulding

There is not a record available of Daniel serving a mission, though he was called to preside over his local Church units during at least three periods of his life.

*Figure 220: Mary Ann Park Bryce.
Public domain via FamilySearch.*

Three Generations Back from Alan

Ezra T. Clark

Ezra served many missions:

Public domain via FamilySearch.

- Colonization mission to **Iron County** in 1850. Sent grain twice and then was released.
- Mission to **Great Britain** September 1856–June 1858 (during which he converted future wife Susan Leggett).
- Colonization mission to **"Big Muddy"** in 1860. Ezra was allowed to delegate this instead to his nephew Ezra Doughetry, whom he financed to fill the call. The project was abandoned after a year.
- Assigned by Brigham Young to build a Weber County **flour mill**, which was run by his son Charles Rich Clark. Ezra sent seven yokes of oxen to the Missouri River to haul back necessary equipment and built the mill before the railroad came to Utah. The mill was kept in use until it was destroyed by fire in 1932. As of 2002, a feed store was located on the site.
- Mission to the **States** October 1869–March 1870.
- Colonization mission to **Bear Lake County**, Idaho, in 1870 in order to help establish a Latter-day Saint presence in the area in response to a perceived threat of settlement by "Gentiles." Multiple Clarks supported this settlement effort. Joseph Smith Clark went in Ezra's place and established a ranch. Ezra's son Wilford Woodruff Clark located in the area, as did his daughter-in-law Alice Randall Clark. The Clark Firm farmed and raised cattle in Bear Lake County, Idaho, and in Farmington, Utah. Other Saints supported the Bear Lake County settlement effort as well, including Apostle Charles C. Rich, who had married Ezra's niece Mary Ann Phelps as one of his plural wives (Laura Clark Phelps' daughter).

---

[495] "Information on Mary Ann Park Bryce." *FamilySearch*, Intellectual Reserve, https://www.familysearch.org/photos/artifacts/1892384?cid=mem_copy. Accessed 6 November 2020.

- Mission to **Eastern States** starting October 1871.
- Mission to **Canada** 1874–1875.
- Mission to **California** 17 January 1876–31 March 1876.
- Ezra supported a number of sons who served missions in various parts of the world. Two of his sons died in the mission field: Ezra James in New York on his way back from a mission to England, and John Alexander who died in Palestine. Ezra's life sketch records he is the only man known to have lost two sons in the missionary field as of the time of that writing.[496]

Alfred Randall

Alfred served a mission to the **White Mountains** in Beaver Valley, apparently to the Indians, starting April 6, 1855.

He also served a mission to the **Sandwich Islands (Hawaiian Islands)** with third wife Mildred Elizabeth Johnson Randall in 1865. Alfred was called to manage the Church Plantation on Laie.

Mildred Elizabeth Johnson Randall

President Brigham Young, Elder Heber C. Kimball, George A. Smith, and George Q. Cannon set apart Mildred and Alfred for missionary services in the **Sandwich Islands (Hawaiian Islands)**. Mildred was called on an **Education Mission** to teach school on Laie.

Mildred sold the home Alfred had given her in Salt Lake City to fund her missionary expenses, giving her furniture to her friends.

In Laie, she taught two schools, one for native children and one for foreign children. Under her care, the schools flourished, and the children made great progress. She served May 1865–1866.

In 1872, Mildred was called on a second **Education Mission** to the **Sandwich Islands (Hawaiian Islands)**, this time without her husband, serving May 1873–June 1876. This time she was set apart by George Q. Cannon. Mildred again taught school on her second mission. She borrowed money to fund her second mission.[497]

Mildred was the first woman[498] to serve a Latter-day Saint mission without her husband.[499]

The Story of the Beginnings of the Latter-day Saint Laie Plantation & Alfred and Mildred's Mission

The first Latter-day Saint branch in the Sandwich Islands (Hawaiian Islands) was established in Maui in August 1851. (The Church of Jesus Christ, "Hawaiian.") The Kingdom of Hawaii didn't allow its citizens to immigrate to the mainland, which prevented new converts from gathering to Utah.[500]

---

[496] "Ezra Thompson Clark."
[497] The Church of Jesus Christ of Latter-day Saints. "Mildred Elizabeth Johnson." *Church History*, Intellectual Reserve, https://history.churchofjesuschrist.org/chd/individual/mildred-elizabeth-johnson-1827?lang=eng&timelineTabs=allTabs. Accessed 9 November 2020.
[498] "Mildred Elizabeth Johnson." *Our Pioneer Heritage*, pp. 286–289. *FamilySearch*, https://www.familysearch.org/tree/person/memories/KWJB-JNM. Accessed 20 November 2020.
[499] "'I Am on a Foreign Mission' The First Woman to Serve a Mission without Her Husband." *Church History*, The Church of Jesus Christ of Latter-day Saints, 24 August 2018, https://history.churchofjesuschrist.org/content/i-am-on-a-foreign-mission?lang=eng. Accessed 6 November 2020.
[500] Hammond, John J. *Island Adventures: The Hawaiian Mission of Francis A. Hammond 1851–1865*. Salt Lake City, Signature Books, 2016. *Kindle*.

Joseph F. Smith, then serving as mission president in Hawaii, proposed to President Brigham Young that the Church purchase a plantation in the islands where convert natives could have their own gathering place.[501]

Francis A. Hammond, a leader of the Hawaiian mission, negotiated to purchase a 6,000-acre plantation from a Mr. Thomas Dougherty on Oahu, near the historic village of Laie, in January 1865.

A number of Latter-day Saint native people were active in Laie, making it a supportive location for a gathering place in the islands. The agreed upon price was $14,000 dollars. (Johnson.) In an unusual arrangement, Hammond and co-mission president George Nebeker were personally responsible for the mortgage payments, which would be made from the profits of the plantation, though the Church was the owner of the land. These two men bore the risk of the venture, which descendant John J. Hammond later described as a "financial and psychological burden."[502]

Alfred and Mildred were called to serve in Hawaii along with a number of other couples, including couples who brought young children, to help support the management of the newly purchased plantation. Alfred was called as manager of the plantation. (On other occasions, men were sometimes called to serve as both mission president and plantation manager simultaneously.)

Mildred kept a journal of her 1865 mission to Hawaii, which records some of their experiences. A copy of it was obtained by one of Alfred's two great-granddaughters from BYU–Hawaii and is now available on FamilySearch.

Mildred's impressions of the plantation and Church services in the weeks when the new missionaries first arrived in July of 1865 are happy:

"This is a very beautiful place. . . . There are three native houses, one lumber store-house, one rock house and the mansion or plantation house, which the President of the Mission will occupy."

Mildred noted that the meeting house was a large thatched building, in which the natives who attended sat cross-legged on mats, though the "new arrivals" (missionaries) carried chairs with them. "It was all new to them, as none of them had been in a meeting of this kind before."

Elder Hammond and two natives spoke, all in the Hawaiian language, and were listened to attentively.

"The new arrivals [missionaries] thought the meeting quite interesting," Mildred recorded, "for although they could not understand the language, they could feel the spirit of it, which was good."

That afternoon a meeting for whites alone was held in the mansion, where several brethren spoke.

The weekly format of a meeting for the natives followed by a meeting for the whites was consistent as recorded by Mildred.

Within a few weeks of the missionaries' arrival, a building committee, consisting of Francis Hammond, George Nebeker, and Alfred Randall, formed to locate a place for native Saints and missionaries to build their houses. Alfred obtained the building materials, the lots were laid out with a note by Mildred that there was a little disagreement, and construction got under way in August.

Then in autumn of 1865, with the building projects still under way, Alfred sailed for Utah with Elders Hammond and Pugsley on business regarding the Hawaiian Mission, arriving in Salt Lake on October 5.[503]

---

[501] The Church of Jesus Christ of Latter-day Saints. "Hawaiian." *Church History*, Intellectual Reserve, https://history.churchofjesuschrist.org/chd/organization/mission/hawaiian-1850?lang=eng. Accessed 20 November 2020.
[502] Hammond.
[503] Johnson.

Figure 222: Mildred and Alfred served a mission together to Hawaii. Public domain via FamilySearch.

Alfred gave a brief account of his trip to the Sandwich Islands in a conference.

He apparently expected to return to the islands in a short time, but instead he was released.[504]

Mildred, who had remained in Hawaii on the Laie plantation, continued to serve until the following year, teaching a small school of native children.

At the root of this unusual separation of a married missionary companionship may have been the unusual matter of a land and building dispute, which may have stemmed from Elder Nebeker's personal debt on the property, which apparently put him in a situation where he attempted to rent land to the missionaries to build their houses or else sell them land for gold.

Mildred wrote in her record:

"It might be stated here that when President Young called Elder Nebeker to this mission, it was with the understanding that he should assume all the responsibility of the mission, and what money he put into the plantation should be as if it were a personal investment and that he must assume the balance of the indebtedness on the place as though he was buying for himself in a private undertaking. This placed him in a very embarrassing position, as it related to the position he occupied with the brethren sent down to assist him, they assuming that they were sent there to help."[505]

The departure of Alfred and a few of the other missionaries was a challenging emotional blow to Elder Nebeker and the rest of the group.

---

[504] Kofoed, p. 18.
[505] Johnson.

In a letter Elder Nebeker wrote to Heber C. Kimball, a copy of which is included in the back of Mildred's Sandwich Islands Mission Journal, Elder Nebeker writes his perspective of Alfred's early departure:

"At the time the brethren left here last fall I was almost discouraged of doing anything. I was left in debt and without money. The brethren felt to condemn the land and everything that had been done. The brethren's feelings were almost as still and motionless as the land of Laie. However, in a short time the Lord seemed to breathe the breath of life within us, as he did man in the beginning. So we began to move and with a few exceptions have done remarkably well since then."[506]

Elder Nebeker and the others on the plantation rallied and plowed "60 or 70 acres" and hoped to put in nearly 100 acres of cotton by spring.

He then shared more information on the departure of Alfred and other missionaries:

Apparently, Alfred had told the brethren in Utah that he was not permitted to purchase land in Hawaii. There may have been a break-down in communication on this topic between Alfred and the mission leadership, as Elder Nebeker recounts that Alfred Randall became discouraged, and said he would do nothing until he heard from President Young, that he discouraged the other brethren, and that he eventually told Elder Nebeker that he had business with a Judge Smith and was obliged to return to Utah.

Elder Nebeker's account states:

"We told the brethren that we would sell to them any portion of our land at cost in gold, and if they had not the money, we would wait with them until our last payment became due. We offered to rent our lands; in fact we offered everything that was in justice or reason. The brethren write that Brother Young remarked, 'that the mission had gone in at the big end of the horn and would have to be squeezed out at the little end.' This remark was made no doubt. . . ."

Despite this somewhat rocky start, ultimately, the Laie property saw many successes.

Over the years following the Church's purchase of the plantation, the plantation's land was repurposed and developed for other uses.

In 1915, construction of the Hawaii Temple was begun on plantation acreage. In 1919 the plantation closed and the temple was dedicated. The land of the former plantation today also holds the campus of Brigham Young University–Hawaii, and the Polynesian Culture Center.[507]

Two presidents of the Church served as mission presidents of Hawaii before their tenures as prophets: Joseph F. Smith and Lorenzo Snow.[508]

---

[506] Johnson.
[507] Ensign Peak Foundation. "Laie Sugar Plantation, Laie, Hawaii, USA." *Ensign Peak Foundation*, Ensign Peak Foundation, https://ensignpeakfoundation.org/laie-sugar-plantation/. Accessed 20 November 2020.
[508] The Church of Jesus Christ, "Hawaiian."

Mads Christensen

Mads was called on a mission to serve as a Church teamster and help take pioneers across the plains.

Mads served a **proselytizing mission** to the **Scandinavian Mission** April 1875–October 1876, preaching the gospel to his native Denmark. He was set apart by Orson Pratt.[509]

From 1883 to 1885 Mads filled another mission: this time a **colonization mission to Arizona**.[510]

Jens Christensen Lamp

There isn't a record available of Jens serving a mission. He immigrated to Utah and raised his family in the Church.

Figure 223: Mads Christensen. Public domain via FamilySearch.

Two Generations Back from Alan

Edward Barrett Clark

Edward served a **proselytizing mission** to the **Northern United States, West Iowa** in 1908.[511]

Edward was called during a time when he already had two wives and several children. In those days, men could be called to serve a mission regardless of age or marital status.

Edward's oldest son, Walter, and Walter's son Alan would also be called to this same mission, years later.

Figure 224: Edward Barrett Clark. Public domain via FamilySearch.

---

[509] The Church of Jesus Christ of Latter-day Saints. "Mads Christensen." *Church History*, Intellectual Reserve, https://history.churchofjesuschrist.org/chd/individual/mads-christensen-1825?lang=eng&timelineTabs=allTabs. Accessed 9 November 2020.

[510] "Mads Christensen Life Sketch." *FamilySearch*, Intellectual Reserve, https://www.familysearch.org/tree/person/details/KWCT-YG1. Accessed 6 November 2020.

[511] Clark, Walter Edward. *Autobiography of Walter Edward Clark*.

Joseph Mads Christensen

As a young man, Joseph received a call to help with building a Washakie Indian schoolhouse. After coming home, he continued to do carpentry and it became his occupation.

Joseph was called on a **colonization mission** in 1884 to help build up the settlement of **St. Johns, Apache County, Arizona**. He built a house there and his wife and children then joined him.

Over the following years, he was in and out of St. Johns. At one point he came down with malaria, and was advised to go to a different climate until his health was restored. After he was well again, his family returned to St. John's, Arizona.[512]

On 24 January 1893, President Wilford Woodruff released Joseph from his mission, sending a letter of thanks for his service.[513]

Figure 225: Joseph Mads Christensen. Public domain via FamilySearch.

Two Generations Back from Janet

James Alma Simmons

There isn't a record of James serving a mission.

---

[512] Atkinson, Selma, and Pearl C. Card. "Life Sketch (part 1) by daughters Selma Atkinson and Pearl C. Card." *FamilySearch*, Intellectual Reserve, https://www.familysearch.org/photos/artifacts/38897918?cid=mem_copy. Accessed 6 November 2020.

[513] "Mission Release of Joseph Mads Christensen." *FamilySearch*, Intellectual Reserve, https://www.familysearch.org/photos/artifacts/8974187?cid=mem_copy. Accessed 6 November 2020.

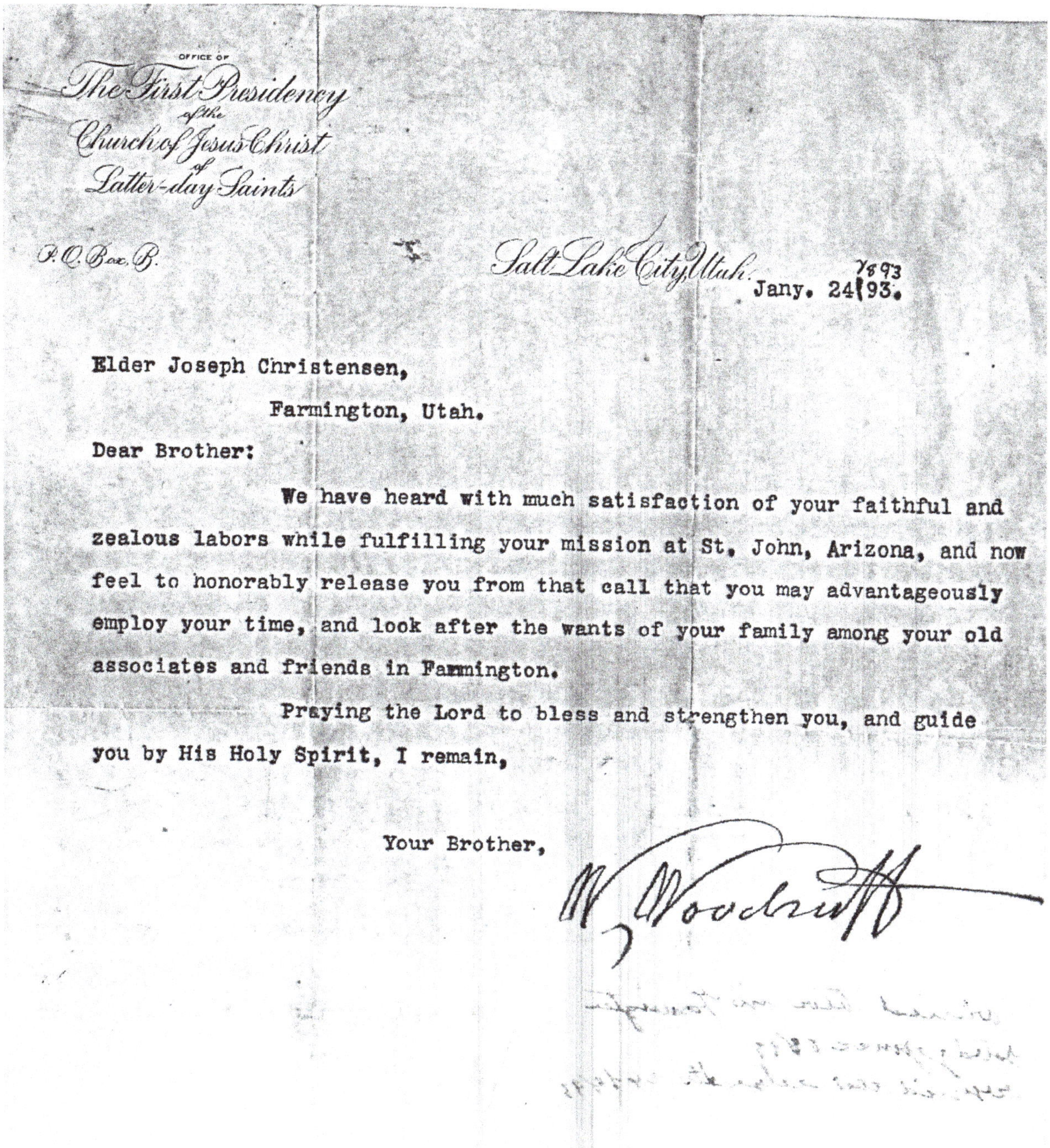

OFFICE OF
The First Presidency of the Church of Jesus Christ of Latter-day Saints

P.O. Box B.

Salt Lake City, Utah. Jany. 24 1893.

Elder Joseph Christensen,
    Farmington, Utah.

Dear Brother:

    We have heard with much satisfaction of your faithful and zealous labors while fulfilling your mission at St. John, Arizona, and now feel to honorably release you from that call that you may advantageously employ your time, and look after the wants of your family among your old associates and friends in Farmington.

    Praying the Lord to bless and strengthen you, and guide you by His Holy Spirit, I remain,

        Your Brother,

        W. Woodruff

Figure 226: Letter of release to Elder Joseph Christensen, signed by Wilford Woodruff. Public domain via FamilySearch.

One Generation Back from Alan

Figure 227: Walter Edward Clark.
Image used with permission.

Walter Edward Clark

Walter served a **proselytizing mission** to the **Northern States, Michigan and West Iowa** 1913–1916.

He later served two missions with wife Lela Willett Clark in the **Southwest Indian Mission.**

He first served in **Perea Branch, New Mexico,** as the president of the Perea Branch from 21 June 1969 to 20 December 1969. He next served in **Greasewood, Arizona,** from 6 January 1970 to 18 June 1970.[514]

Lela Willett Clark

Lela served with her husband, Walter Edward Clark, in the **Southwest Indian Mission** in 1969 and 1970.

One Generation Back from Janet

Cecil Putnam "Mike" Ruppe

Mike Ruppe served **stake missions**.[515]

Figure 228: Mike Ruppe and his horse, Blaze.
Public domain via FamilySearch.

---

[514] "90th Birthday Party to Honor Walter Clark." *The Herald* [Provo], 29 May 1979, p. 2, https://www.familysearch.org/photos/artifacts/73238978?cid=mem_copy. Accessed 6 November 2020.

[515] Bunn, Celeste. "Cecil Putnam Ruppe." *FamilySearch*, Intellectual Reserve, https://www.familysearch.org/photos/artifacts/1081584?cid=mem_copy. Accessed 6 November 2020.

Alan and Janet

Alan C Clark
Alan served three missions:
- **Proselytizing mission** to **New England**, serving in Nova Scotia June 1948–September 1950.
- **Senior mission** with Janet to **Solihull, England**, serving in the **Europe North Area office**, 1994–1996.
- **Temple mission** with Janet to **London, England Temple**, 2000–2002.

Janet Clark
Janet served two missions:
- **Senior mission** with Alan to **Solihull, England**, serving in the **Europe North Area office**, 1994–1996.
- **Temple mission** with Alan to **London, England Temple**, 2000–2002.

Figure 229: Alan and Janet Clark on a mission to England.
Image used with permission.

Brenda Clark Sederberg

Brenda served a mission as a Temple Square missionary part time while also working as an elementary school teacher in 1978.

Figure 230: Brenda Clark Sederberg.
Image used with permission.

Table of Missions Served

Name	Date	Mission
John Lowe Butler	1839	Illinois **(P)**
John L. & Caroline Butler	1840	Sioux Native American Tribes **(P)**
John Lowe Butler	1840–1841	Sioux Native American Tribes **(P)**
John Lowe Butler	1843	Southern States Mission **(P)**
John Lowe Butler	1843	Northern States Mission **(P)**
John L. & Caroline Butler	1844	Retrieve James Emmett Expedition **(L)**
Royal & Lydia Durfey	1850s–1870s	Palmyra, Utah (Spanish Fork) **(Col)**
Kenion Taylor Butler	1856	Rescue Martin and Willie Companies **(Res)**
Kenion Taylor Butler	1882–1883	Southern States **(P)**
Ebenezer & Mary Bryce	Many times	Utah, Arizona **(Col)**
Ebenezer Bryce	1898	Eastern States **(Gen)**
Ezra T. Clark	1856–1858	Great Britain **(P)**
Ezra T. Clark	1869–1870	States **(P)**
Ezra T. Clark	1871	Eastern States **(P)**
Ezra T. Clark	1874–1875	Canada **(P)**
Ezra T. Clark	1876	California **(P)**
Ezra T. Clark		Bear Lake County, Idaho **(Col)**
Ezra T. Clark		"Big Muddy" Nevada **(Col)**
Alfred Randall	1855	White Mountains in Beaver Valley **(P)**
Alfred Randall	1865	Sandwich Islands (Hawaii) **(S)**
Mildred Elizabeth Randall	1865–1866	Sandwich Islands (Hawaii) **(Ed)**
Mildred Elizabeth Randall	1873–1876	Sandwich Islands (Hawaii) **(Ed)**
Mads Christensen		Help pioneers cross the plains **(T)**
Mads Christensen	1875–1876	Scandinavia **(P)**
Edward Barrett Clark	1908	Eastern States **(P)**
Joseph Mads Christensen		Build Washakie Indian school **(W)**
Joseph & Emma Christensen	1884	St. Johns, Arizona **(Col)**
Walter E. Clark	1913–1916	Northern States **(P)**
Walter & Lela Clark	1969–70	Southwest Indian Mission **(P)**
Cecil "Mike" Ruppe		Stake missions, Vernal, Utah
Alan C Clark	1948–1950	New England (Nova Scotia) **(P)**
Alan & Janet Clark	1994–1996	Solihull, England (Europe North Area) **(Sen)**
Alan & Janet Clark	2000–2002	London, England Temple **(Sen)**
Brenda Clark	1978	Temple Square, Salt Lake City **(S)**

Key:
(Gen) = Genealogy
(Res) = Rescue
(T) = Teamster
(Col) = Colonization
(L) = Leadership
(Sen) = Senior Mission
(W) = Work Mission
(Ed) = Education
(P) = Proselytizing
(S) = Service

18. Conclusion

Book one of this series covered stories of ancestors who left their countries and came to America, often to pursue freedom of religion or belief.

Book two mostly covered the stories and journeys of ancestral families who gathered to Utah from the Eastern and Southern States and from overseas, in order to join the Latter-day Saint movement and gather Zion.[516]

The work of building this new society in the West was a monumental task, which spanned decades.

From the time that Elizabeth Stevens Stevenson was baptized in Michigan until the time that her great-grandson, Walter Edward Clark, was growing up as a contributing member of the Clark Firm in Georgetown, Idaho, spanned over fifty years and four generations.

From the era when the elder John Goulding was baptized until his descendant Brenda Clark was born spanned eight generations.

A few trends emerge as we look at the stories of this book as a whole:

Alan's ancestors from the time of baptism until Alan's generation covered fewer generations than Janet's ancestral spread. The generational gap on Janet's side of the family is on the whole shorter. Thus, there are more generations of stories on Janet's side.

Another trend points to overall talents and interests that span generations: There are definite trends toward leadership, craftsmanship, and civic engagement throughout the family lines.

The pattern that is perhaps most remarkable of all is that the wealth of stories available for many of the lineages once an ancestor joined the Latter-day Saint Church expanded significantly over what was preserved, and is today available for previous generations in most ancestral lines.

A value for telling family history and keeping records, journals, and stories seems to have uniformly become part of the tapestry of the family, largely due to the focus on the value of

---

[516] Plus, Mike Ruppe.

Conclusion

ancestors and family. In some cases, such as John Lowe Butler, these ancestors wrote their own life stories. In other cases, descendants such as grandchildren wrote the stories of their grandparents, whom they had known personally. It probably didn't hurt that many of these families had a lot of children—giving greater odds of raising at least a few family historians.

The resultant tapestry of stories is a rich web, offering much to the reader.

Here we can find insight into how some of the complex systems of our ancestral families were put together, such as the Clark Firm, which was a rare successful exercise of the United Order in practice. Or the practice of polygamy, which varied wildly in how it looked, based on the families that engaged in it.

We can also see the values of the ancestors displayed in their choices. They valued hard work, inspiration, and community. Many of them loved music and singing, and some, such as Alfred, are remembered by their posterity for having a great sense of humor and a wonderful laugh.

These remarkable men and women of Alan and Janet's lineages are more than just figures on a page, names with lines and dates beneath.

These people were family. They lived, and loved, and worked hard toward dreams, and raised their children and lifted them as best they could to walk through life as best they knew how.

Those children grew to have children of their own, carrying old traditions forward, inventing new ones, and passing along the torch of the stories as the years went by.

Gradually, over time, days turned to weeks, and then to years, and then to decades. Generations flew by so quickly that, in our time, looking backwards can seem as simple as turning the pages of a book.

The clues of their legacies are all around us, even now.

There you are, great-grandfather. I see you in the gardens of my family.

And there you are, great-grandmother. I see you in the quilts my sisters make.

But perhaps the true, deep legacy of the ancestors is the love of their hearts that they gave to their children, who passed that love on to children of their own, until the generations progressed to where we are today.

You are the legacy of your grandparents, great-grandparents, and beyond.

Your ancestors back in time may be a distant memory now, but their influence remains. Echoes of their choices and their love live with us still, like the stars beyond us in the sky, if we will only look up, and see.

19. Quilts through the Generations

The following pages feature a selection of quilts made by the Clark and Ruppe families through generations.

*Figure 231: Quilt made by Alice Randall Clark for her granddaughter Carol Clark Call.
Image used with permission.*

*Figure 232: Enlarged segment of log cabin quilt by Reva Marie Simmons Ruppe.
Quilt was owned for years by Brenda Clark Sederberg.
Photo by Tom Sederberg. Image used with permission.*

Figure 233: Full log cabin quilt by Reva Ruppe. Brenda said Reva used polyester fabrics in many of her quilt designs, making them extremely hardy and long-lasting.
Photo by Tom Sederberg.
Image used with permission.

Figure 234: Quilt by Leila Willet Clark, second wife of Walter Clark. Leila had poor eyesight and Walter used to thread multiple needles for her to work with before he went outside. This quilt took her 650 hours to make. Quilt currently in the possession of Sarah Farmer.
Image used with permission.

Figure 235: Yarn-tied quilt by Janet Ruppe Clark.
Janet joked that her mother did pieced quilts but she just did yarn-tied quilts. She explained that this one had one color on the top and a different one on the bottom so it could be reversible for two different looks. Brenda and Rebecca helped tie this quilt in the 1980s.
Photo by Tom Sederberg. Image used with permission.

Figure 236: Quilt by MaryLynn Olson, Alice's great-granddaughter and Brenda's cousin. Photo used with permission.

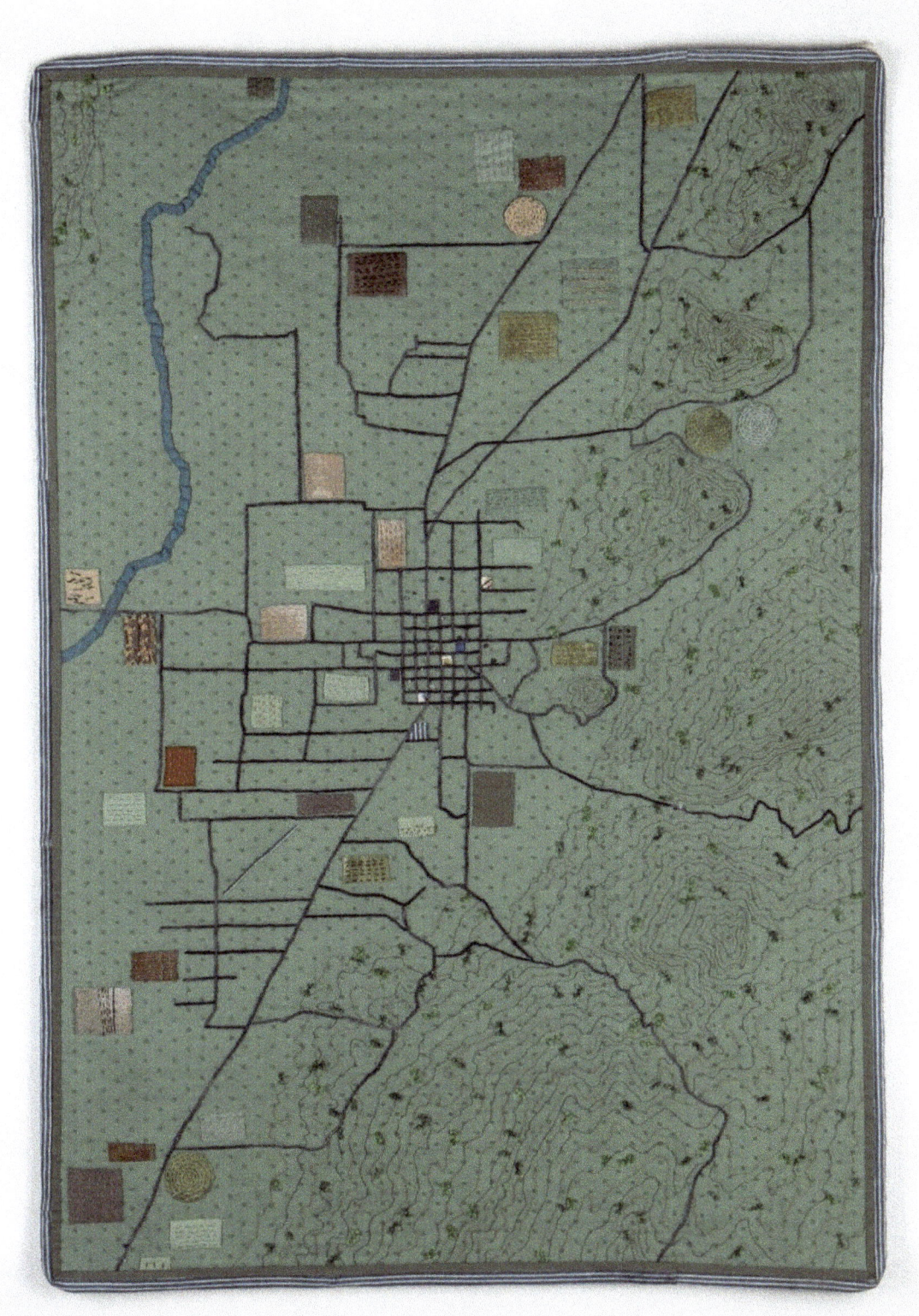

Figure 237: Art quilt by Rachel Farmer (Alice's great-grandchild).
Title: Generations of Springs (San Pitch Mountains & River, Wasatch Plateau, Ephraim, Utah)
Year: 2019. Photo by Kamilla Earlywine.
Image used with permission.

*Figure 238: Quilt by Maria Sederberg Longhurst, made for her daughter.
Photo by R.S. Kellogg.*

*Figure 239: Rag quilt lap blanket by the author.
Photo by R.S. Kellogg.*

*Figure 240: Quilt by Laura Sederberg Jaeger.
Image used with permission.*

*Figure 241: Quilt by Laura Sederberg Jaeger.
Image used with permission.*

*Figure 242: Quilt by Abby Sederberg.
Image used with permission.*

Works Cited

(Organized by ancestral line for ease of reference)

Clark

"A Brief History of Mary Elizabeth Robinson Porter." Biographies and autobiographies of the descendants of Ezra T. Clark, Box 4 Folder 41, L. Tom Perry Special Collections, Harold B. Lee Library, Brigham Young University, Provo, Utah.

Anderson, Clarice Stewart. "A sketch of the life of Elizabeth Stevens Stevenson, arrived in Salt Lake Valley October 1847," *FamilySearch*. https://www.familysearch.org/tree/person/memories/KWJT-JWW

"An Interview with Rhoda Clark Taylor," circa 1975. Biographies and autobiographies of the descendants of Ezra T. Clark, Box 4 Folder 54. L. Tom Perry Special Collections, Harold B. Lee Library, Brigham Young University, Provo, Utah.

Biography of Joseph Smith Clark, Sr. Biographies and autobiographies of the descendants of Ezra T. Clark, L. Tom Perry Special Collections, Harold B. Lee Library, Brigham Young University, Provo, Utah.

"Biography of Susan L. Clark." *FamilySearch*, Intellectual Reserve, https://www.familysearch.org/photos/artifacts/7929293?cid=mem_copy. Accessed 13 May 2021.

Charles Redd Center for Western Studies. *Bryant R. Clark Interviewed by Christ Nelson.* LDS Polygamy Oral History Project, 1981 January 11, Biographies and autobiographies of the descendants of Ezra T. Clark, Box 5 Folder 56, L. Tom Perry Special Collections, Harold B. Lee Library, Brigham Young University, Provo, Utah.

Charles Redd Center for Western Studies. *Walter Clark Oral History Transcript, Interviewed by Leonard R. Grover.* LDS Polygamy Oral History Project, 1979 October 12, File-folder: MSS OH 398, Identifier: MSS 7752 Series 1 Sub-series 2. L. Tom Perry Special Collections, Harold B. Lee Library, Brigham Young University, Provo, Utah.

Charles Rich Clark. Biographies and autobiographies of the descendants of Ezra T. Clark. L. Tom Perry Special Collections, Harold B. Lee Library, Box 1 Folder 7, Brigham Young University, Provo, Utah.

Clark, Alan C, *Line Upon Line*, Provo: 2006.

Clark, Alice Randall. *A Life Sketch of Alice Randall Clark.*

Clark, Annie Waldron (second wife of Charles R. Clark), "An Excerpt from a Diary and Life History of Mr. & Mrs. Charles R. Clark and Family While Living in or Near Farmington," Biographies and autobiographies of the descendants of Ezra T. Clark, L. Tom Perry Special Collections, Harold B. Lee Library, Brigham Young University, Provo, Utah.

Clark, Antone, *Noble Pioneer: A Biography of Ezra T. Clark*, Logan, Utah: 2017.

Clark, A. Charles. *Timothy Baldwin Clark: A Narrative of the Life and Times of a Connecticut Yankee Gone Westward*, 2004.

Clark, Bryant, *That You May Know Her Better: A Collection of Short Sketches and Tributes Written in Honor of Alice Randall Clark by Her Children, Some of Her Friends, and Admirers.* Chihuahua, Mexico: 1978.

Clark, Edward Barrett. "Incidents in the Life and Labors of Wealthy Richards Clark." *Autobiography of Edward B. Clark*, Ezra T. Clark Family Organization. *Ezra T. Clark: The Family Web Site of Ezra T. Clark*, Clark, http://ezratclark.org/familyfile_AEBC_IncidentsInLife.asp Accessed 21 November 2020.

Edward B. "Incidents in the Life and Labors of Alice Randall Clark," *Autobiography of Edward B. Clark*. Ezra T. Clark Family Foundation. http://ezratclark.org/familyfile_AEBC_IncidentsLifeLaborsAliceRandallClark.asp

Clark, Laura Blanche. "Autobiography of Laura Blanche Clark." *FamilySearch*, Intellectual Reserve, 7 December 2018, https://www.familysearch.org/tree/person/me☐mories/KWCZ-YQH. Accessed 28 September 2020.

Clark, Melvin J. Biographies and autobiographies of the descendants of Ezra T. Clark, Box 4 Folder 53, L. Tom Perry Special Collections, Harold B. Lee Library, Brigham Young University, Provo, Utah.

Clark, Melvin J. "Some Impressions and Lessons my Mother Left Me, Written by Melvin J Clark about his Mother Alice Randall Clark." Biographies and autobiographies of the descendants of Ezra T. Clark, Box 4 Folder 53, L. Tom Perry Special Collections, Harold B. Lee Library, Brigham Young University, Provo, Utah.

Clark, Mary Stevenson. "Autobiography of Mary Stevenson Clark." *FamilySearch*, Intellectual Reserve, 20 June 2013, https://www.familysearch.org/photos/artifacts/1542747?cid=mem_copy. Accessed 30 September 2020.

Clark, Nolan. "My Convert Ancestors."

Clark, Walter Edward. *Autobiography of Walter Edward Clark*.

Edward Franklin Clark. Biographies and autobiographies of the descendants of Ezra T. Clark, Box 4 Folder 51, L. Tom Perry Special Collections, Harold B. Lee Library, Brigham Young University, Provo, Utah.

Elmer Ruel Clark. Biographies and autobiographies of the descendants of Ezra T. Clark, L. Tom Perry Special Collections, Harold B. Lee Library, Brigham Young University, Provo, Utah.

"Elizabeth Stevenson Clark - Pioneer Woman of Faith." *FamilySearch*, Intellectual Reserve, https://www.familysearch.org/photos/artifacts/104801730?cid=mem_copy. Accessed 31 October 2020.

"Experiences in the Life of Joseph Smith Clark Jr. 1878-1963." Biographies and autobiographies of the descendants of Ezra T. Clark, Box 1 Folder 12, L. Tom Perry Special Collections, Harold B. Lee Library, Brigham Young University, Provo, Utah.

Hess, Margaret Steed. *My Farmington, a History of Farmington, 1847-1976*, Helen Mar Miller Camp: 1976.

Howard Nathan Clark. Biographies and autobiographies of the descendants of Ezra T. Clark, Box 5 Folder 61, L. Tom Perry Special Collections, Harold B. Lee Library, Brigham Young University, Provo, Utah.

Hyrum Don Carlos Clark Biography. Biographies and autobiographies of the descendants of Ezra T. Clark, Box 4 Folder 44, L. Tom Perry Special Collections, Harold B. Lee Library, Brigham Young University, Provo, Utah.

Knowlton, Clark S. and Ruth. Oral interview with Orson Clark. Biographies and autobiographies of the descendants of Ezra T. Clark, L. Tom Perry Special Collections, Harold B. Lee Library, Brigham Young University, Provo, Utah.

Larsen, Ora Steed. "A Brief Life History of John Alexander Clark," *Ezra T. Clark Family Organization Web Site.* http://ezratclark.org/index.asp

"Life Sketch of Bryant Randall Clark," Biographies and autobiographies of the descendants of Ezra T. Clark, Box 5 Folder 56, L. Tom Perry Special Collections, Harold B. Lee Library, Brigham Young University, Provo, Utah.

Mattice, Nancy Aretta Porter. "A Sketch of the Life of Nancy Aretta Porter Mattice." *Church History*, Intellectual Reserve, https://history.churchofjesuschrist.org/overlandtravel/sources/19152/a-sketch-of-the-life-of-nancy-aretta-porter-mattice-1-4 Accessed 18 May 2021.

Mary Elizabeth Clark. Biographies and autobiographies of the descendants of Ezra T. Clark, L. Tom Perry Special Collections, Harold B. Lee Library, Brigham Young University, Provo, Utah.

Parker Haddock, Edith, and Dorothy Hardy Matthews. "History of Bear Lake Pioneers." *Morris Charles Phelps*, Daughters of the Utah Pioneers, http://www.morrisphelps.org/history_of_bear_lake_pioneers.htm. Accessed 12 October 2020. (A. Charles Clark notes that Bruce Peterson, author of the Morris Phelps biography, has not been able to discover the origin of Morris having a middle name of Charles or any other name.)

Phelps, Morris Calvin. "Laura Clark Phelps History - by Morris Calvin Phelps." *FamilySearch*, Intellectual Reserve, https://www.familysearch.org/photos/artifacts/104250413?cid=mem_copy. Accessed 3 October 2020.

Rogers, Aurelia S. *Life Sketches of Orson Spencer and Others, and History of Primary Work*, Geo. Q. Cannon & Sons Company: 1898.

Stevenson, Edward. *Reminiscences of Joseph, The Prophet, and the Coming Forth of the Book of Mormon*. Project Gutenberg, 2017. *Project Gutenberg*, https://www.gutenberg.org/files/54337/54337-h/54337-h.htm Accessed 14 October 2020.

Tanner, Annie Clark. *A Biography of Ezra Thompson Clark*, Signature Books: 1975.

Tanner, Annie Clark. *A Mormon Mother*, Tanner Trust Fund: 2015.

Tanner, Obert Clark. *One Man's Journey in Search for Freedom*, University of Utah: 1994.

"The Forgotten Missionary," Ezra T. Clark Foundation, http://ezratclark.org/familyfile_forgottenMissionary.asp

Wiberg, Maurine Clark. "As I Remember." Biographies and autobiographies of the descendants of Ezra T. Clark, Box 5 Folder 55, Tom Perry Special Collections, Harold B. Lee Library, Brigham Young University, Provo, Utah.

Wiberg, Maurine. "Building My Faith." Biographies and autobiographies of the descendants of Ezra T. Clark. L. Tom Perry Special Collections, Harold B. Lee Library, Brigham Young University, Provo, Utah.

"90th Birthday Party to Honor Walter Clark." *The Herald* [Provo], 29 May 1979, p. 2, https://www.familysearch.org/photos/artifacts/73238978?cid=mem_copy. Accessed 6 November 2020.

Randall

"Alfred Randall." *FamilySearch*, Intellectual Reserve, https://www.familysearch.org/tree/person/memories/KWJB-JNS Accessed 26 October 2020.

Clark, Alice Randall. *A Life Sketch of Alice Randall Clark.*

"Emmerette Louisa Davis." *FamilySearch*, Intellectual Reserve, https://www.familysearch.org/tree/person/memories/KWJB-JNS. Accessed 26 October 2020.

Hammond, John J. *Island Adventures: The Hawaiian Mission of Francis A. Hammond 1851–1865*. Salt Lake City: Signature Books, 2016. *Kindle.*

"'I Am on a Foreign Mission' The First Woman to Serve a Mission without Her Husband." *Church History*, The Church of Jesus Christ of Latter-day Saints, 24 August 2018, https://history.churchofjesuschrist.org/content/i-am-on-a-foreign-mission?lang=eng. Accessed 6 November 2020.

Kofoed, Lucy Randall. *A Life Sketch of Hannah Severn Randall*. *FamilySearch*, https://www.familysearch.org/photos/artifacts/11461919?cid=mem_copy. Accessed 19 April 2021.

Kofoed, Lucy Randall. "My Grandfather Alfred Randall."

Kofoed, Lucy Randall. *The True Story of Alfred Randall, Pioneer*.

"Mildred Elizabeth Johnson." *Our Pioneer Heritage*, pp. 286–289. *FamilySearch*, https://www.familysearch.org/tree/person/memories/KWJB-JNM Accessed 29 November 2020.

Randall, Helen Torney. "Life History: Alfred Randall." *FamilySearch*, Intellectual Reserve, https://www.familysearch.org/photos/artifacts/6107656?cid=mem_copy. Accessed 2 October 2020.

Richards, Emily Randall. *Life Story of Emily Randall Richards*. *FamilySearch*, https://www.familysearch.org/tree/person/memories/KWCH-MFZ. Accessed 2 October 2020.

Richards, Emily Randall. "Margaret Harley Randall." *FamilySearch*, Intellectual Reserve, 1941, https://www.familysearch.org/photos/artifacts/24327746?cid=mem_copy. Accessed 2 October 2020.

Tingey. "Thurza Amelia Randall - Life Sketch." *FamilySearch*, Intellectual Reserve, 4 August 2013, https://www.familysearch.org/tree/person/memories/KWNN-H4X Accessed 28 September 2020.

The Church of Jesus Christ of Latter-day Saints. "Mildred Elizabeth Johnson." *Church History*, Intellectual Reserve, https://history.churchofjesuschrist.org/chd/individual/mildred-elizabeth-johnson-1827?lang=eng&timelineTabs=allTabs. Accessed 9 November 2020.

Christensen

Ashby, Ruth C. "Life Sketch of Mads Christensen." *Short Life Sketches of Our Ancestors*, 2002, p. 79. *FamilySearch*, https://www.familysearch.org/photos/artifacts/39845217?cid=mem_copy. Accessed 21 November 2020.

Atkinson, Selma, and Pearl C. Card. "Life Sketch (part 1) by daughters Selma Atkinson and Pearl C. Card." *FamilySearch*, Intellectual Reserve, https://www.familysearch.org/photos/artifacts/38897918?cid=mem_copy. Accessed 6 November 2020.

Bunn, Celeste. "Maren Johanne Jensen." *FamilySearch*, https://www.familysearch.org/photos/artifacts/1497291?cid=mem_copy

Bunn, Celeste. "Trein Bendtsen." *FamilySearch*, Intellectual Reserve, 27 June 2013, https://www.familysearch.org/photos/artifacts/1508929?cid=mem_copy. Accessed 5 October 2020.

Christensen, Phillis. "Life History of Hannah (Johanne) 2nd wife of Mads Christensen." *Short Life Sketches of Our Ancestors*, edited by Ruth Card Ashby, pp. 93–97. *FamilySearch*.

Christensen, Phillis. "Life Sketch of Mads Christensen." *Short Life Sketches of Our Ancestors*, Ruth C. Ashby, 2002, pp. 74–80. *FamilySearch*, https://www.familysearch.org/photos/artifacts/42728048?cid=mem_copy. Accessed 5 October 2020.

"Jens Christensen." *FamilySearch*, Intellectual Reserve, 9 July 2013, https://www.familysearch.org/photos/artifacts/1661839?cid=mem_copy. Accessed 5 October 2020.

jordananthonysmith1. "Mads Christensen and Family Story." *FamilySearch*, https://www.familysearch.org/photos/artifacts/118469412?cid=mem_copy

"Mads Christensen Life Sketch." *FamilySearch*, Intellectual Reserve, https://www.familysearch.org/tree/person/details/KWCT-YG1 Accessed 6 November 2020.

"Mads Christensen's Autograph Album." *FamilySearch*. https://www.familysearch.org/photos/artifacts/109606612?cid=mem_copy

Miller, Annie Christensen. "Sketch of Karen Marie Hansen." *FamilySearch*, Intellectual Reserve, https://www.familysearch.org/photos/artifacts/3335590?cid=mem_copy. Accessed 2 October 2020.

Miller, Annie C. "Sketch of My Mother, Maren Johanne Jensen Christensen," p. 92.

"Mission Release of Joseph Mads Christensen." *FamilySearch*, Intellectual Reserve, https://www.familysearch.org/photos/artifacts/8974187?cid=mem_copy. Accessed 6 November 2020.

Rogers, Aurelia S. *Life Sketches of Orson Spencer and Others, and History of Primary Work*, Geo. Q. Cannon & Sons Company: 1898.

Rogers, Tamara C. "Christian Lamp." *FamilySearch*, Intellectual Reserve, 2 March 2019, https://www.familysearch.org/photos/artifacts/78248864?cid=mem_copy. Accessed 19 October 2020.

Sederberg, Brenda Clark. "Emma Christensen Christensen." *Violet Catherine Clark*, p. 37.

The Church of Jesus Christ of Latter-day Saints. "Mads Christensen." *Church History*, Intellectual Reserve, https://history.churchofjesuschrist.org/chd/individual/mads-christensen-1825?lang=eng&timelineTabs=allTabs. Accessed 9 November 2020.

Ruppe

Bunn, Celeste. "Cecil Putnam Ruppe." *FamilySearch*, Intellectual Reserve, 20 May 2013, https://www.familysearch.org/photos/artifacts/1081584?cid=mem_copy. Accessed 12 October 2020.

Ruppe, Reva, Janet Clark, and Brenda Sederberg. *Side by Side: The Life Story of Cecil Putman "Mike" Ruppe and Reva Marie Simmons Ruppe*. Rexburg: Ricks College Press, 1994.

Simmons

Bunn, Celeste. "Harriette Bradford." *FamilySearch*, Intellectual Reserve, 17 June 2013, https://www.familysearch.org/photos/artifacts/1388056?cid=mem_copy. Accessed 4 December 2020.

Burch, Annie Fergusson. *Samuel Simmons and Elizabeth Scott: Their Ancestors and Descendants*. Salt Lake City: 1965.

Daughters of Utah Pioneers. "Biography of Leven Simmons." *FamilySearch*, Intellectual Reserve, https://www.familysearch.org/photos/artifacts/32269379?cid=mem_copy. Accessed 3 December 2020.

Daughters of Utah Pioneers. "Lydia Rebecca Fisher (from Daughters of Utah Pioneers)." *FamilySearch*, Intellectual Reserve, https://www.familysearch.org/photos/artifacts/32269519?cid=mem_copy. Accessed 28 December 2020.

Hertzel, Anna Lenz. "Vardis Fisher: Marriage, children and adult life." *FamilySearch*, Intellectual Reserve, 13 June 2014, https://www.familysearch.org/photos/artifacts/7811206?cid=mem_copy. Accessed 3 December 2020.

Huff, Elizabeth F. "Harriet Bradford (1821-1890)." *FamilySearch*, Intellectual Reserve, https://www.familysearch.org/photos/artifacts/35018993?cid=mem_copy. Accessed 4 December 2020.

Olsen, Gary Lamar. "Life History of Harriet Bradford Simmons." *FamilySearch*, Intellectual Reserve, 7 January 2018, https://www.familysearch.org/photos/artifacts/46276814?cid=mem_copy. Accessed 3 December 2020.

Ruppe, Reva, et al. *Side by Side*. Rexburg: Ricks College Press, 1994.

Simmons Jr., Benjamin Franklin. *Biography of Levan Simmons and Wives Harriet Bradford and Lydia Rebecca Fisher*, p. 1. *FamilySearch*, https://www.familysearch.org/photos/artifacts/32269379?cid=mem_copy. Accessed 5 October 2020.

Tueller, Margaret. *Your Simmons Lybbert Family Tree*. FamilySearch, 2016. *FamilySearch*, https://www.familysearch.org/photos/artifacts/24310561?cid=mem_copy. Accessed 5 October 2020.

Butler

"Biography of Kenion Taylor Butler." *FamilySearch*, https://www.familysearch.org/photos/artifacts/42968957?cid=mem_copy

Butler, Elder Ross E. "Charity Lowe Butler." *FamilySearch*, Intellectual Reserve, 24 September 2013, https://www.familysearch.org/photos/artifacts/2654806?cid=mem_copy. Accessed 5 October 2020.

Davis McQuivey, Dorene. "Royal Durfey 1811 - 1879 Family records and Salem Springs Compiled by Dorene Davis McQuivey GG Granddaughter." *FamilySearch*, Intellectual Reserve, 4 April 2014, https://www.familysearch.org/photos/artifacts/6295317?cid=mem_copy. Accessed 5 October 2020.

Hartley, William G. *My Best for the Kingdom*. C. L. Dalton Enterprises: 1993.

"Kenion Taylor Butler," *FamilySearch*. https://www.familysearch.org/tree/person/memories/KWJY-DQ8

Bryce

"Ann Brooks Park." *FamilySearch*. https://www.familysearch.org/photos/artifacts/8737851?cid=mem_copy

"Biography of William Henry Bryce." *FamilySearch*, https://www.familysearch.org/photos/artifacts/105577417?cid=mem_copy

Bryce, Betty Jane. "Ebenezer Bryce," p. 2, *FamilySearch*, https://www.familysearch.org/photos/artifacts/123680918?cid=mem_copy

"Bryce's Canyon," https://www.brycecanyoncountry.com/blog/post/bryces-canyon/

Bryce, Wendell A. "EBENEZER BRYCE." *FamilySearch*, Intellectual Reserve, 13 January 2015, https://www.familysearch.org/photos/artifacts/12688101?cid=mem_copy. Accessed 5 October 2020.

"Ebenezer Bryce." https://www.familysearch.org/tree/person/details/KWJ8-YBB

Egbert, Martin W. "PARKS, David and Ann Brooks (compiled by Martin W. Egbert, 3rd Great Grandson)." *FamilySearch*, Intellectual Reserve, 2013, https://www.familysearch.org/photos/artifacts/3522451?cid=mem_copy. Accessed 5 October 2020.

"Information on Mary Ann Park Bryce." *FamilySearch*, Intellectual Reserve, https://www.familysearch.org/photos/artifacts/1892384?cid=mem_copy. Accessed 6 November 2020.

Pace, James. "James Pace Papers." *Church History*, Intellectual Reserve, https://history.churchofjesuschrist.org/overlandtravel/sources/5788/james-pace-papers-1846-1861-autobiographical-sketch-circa-1861-9 Accessed 18 May 2021.

Goulding

"A Few Tidbits of Daniel's Life." *FamilySearch*, Intellectual Reserve, https://www.familysearch.org/photos/artifacts/47118511?cid=mem_copy. Accessed 24 October 2020.

Bunn, Celeste. "Elizabeth Merrifield Pratten." *FamilySearch*, Intellectual Reserve, 25 June 2013, https://www.familysearch.org/photos/artifacts/1487305?cid=mem_copy. Accessed 5 October 2020.

Bunn, Celeste. "Daniel Goulding." *FamilySearch*, Intellectual Reserve, https://www.familysearch.org/photos/artifacts/1487281?cid=mem_copy. Accessed 20 November 2020.

Farnsworth, Mint. "History of John Goulding Sr. & Daniel Goulding as Told to Mint Farnsworth by James A. Goulding." *FamilySearch*, Intellectual Reserve, https://www.familysearch.org/photos/artifacts/108653189?cid=mem_copy. Accessed 24 October 2020.

"GOULDING, Daniel and PRATTEN, Elizabeth Merrifield." *FamilySearch*, Intellectual Reserve, 30 December 2013, https://www.familysearch.org/photos/artifacts/4192428?cid=mem_copy. Accessed 5 October 2020.

"Goulding, John Sr by James A Goulding." *FamilySearch*, Intellectual Reserve, https://www.familysearch.org/photos/artifacts/87113575?cid=mem_copy. Accessed 24 October 2020.

Johnson, Sofe Wasden. "Physical traits as told by grand-daughter in-law, Sofe Wasden Johnson." *FamilySearch*, Intellectual Reserve, https://www.familysearch.org/photos/artifacts/41787505?cid=mem_copy. Accessed 5 October 2020.

Johnson, Zina E. Goulding. "Fanny Pratten Goulding (written by her daughter Zina E. Goulding Johnson when Fanny was 81 years old.)" *FamilySearch*, Intellectual Reserve, https://www.familysearch.org/photos/artifacts/72131151?cid=mem_copy. Accessed 19 October 2020.

Johnson, Zina E. Goulding. "History of the Life of Fanny Pratten Goulding." *FamilySearch*, Intellectual Reserve, https://www.familysearch.org/photos/artifacts/23104532?cid=mem_copy. Accessed 23 November 2020.

"Lye episode." *FamilySearch*, Intellectual Reserve, https://www.familysearch.org/photos/artifacts/43244780?cid=mem_copy. Accessed 22 November 2020.

Monson, Harold. "Daniel Goulding - Stalwart Mormon Pioneer." *FamilySearch*, Intellectual Reserve, 4 November 2014, https://www.familysearch.org/photos/artifacts/11352704?cid=mem_copy. Accessed 23 September 2020.

"The Meat Story." *FamilySearch*, Intellectual Reserve, https://www.familysearch.org/photos/artifacts/41535995?cid=mem_copy. Accessed 22 November 2020.

Workman, Phyllis. "Henrietta Goulding." *FamilySearch*, Intellectual Reserve, https://www.familysearch.org/photos/artifacts/33343081?cid=mem_copy. Accessed 22 November 2020.

www.ingramcontent.com/pod-product-compliance
Lightning Source LLC
Chambersburg PA
CBHW061355010526
44107CB00011B/936